Python

This Book Includes:

Learn How To Develop Programs And Apps In 7 Days With Python Programming And Start Deep Hands-on Learning For Beginners of Data Science And Machine Learning.

By

Oliver R. Simpson

Code Developer Academy

© Copyright 2020 - All rights reserved.

The content contained within this book may not be reproduced, duplicated or transmitted without direct written permission from the author or the publisher.

Under no circumstances will any blame or legal responsibility be held against the publisher, or author, for any damages, reparation, or monetary loss due to the information contained within this book. Either directly or indirectly.

Legal Notice:

This book is copyright protected. This book is only for personal use. You cannot amend, distribute, sell, use, quote or paraphrase any part, or the content within this book, without the consent of the author or publisher.

Disclaimer Notice:

Please note the information contained within this document is for educational and entertainment purposes only. All effort has been executed to present accurate, up to date, and reliable, complete information. No warranties of any kind are declared or implied. Readers acknowledge that the author is not engaging in the rendering of legal, financial, medical or professional advice. The content within this book has been derived from various sources. Please consult a licensed professional before attempting any techniques outlined in this book.

By reading this document, the reader agrees that under no circumstances is the author responsible for any losses, direct or indirect, which are incurred as a result of the use of information contained within this document, including, but not limited to, — errors, omissions, or inaccuracies.

Table of Contents

PYTHON MACHINE LEARNING

INTRODUCTION 6

CHAPTER 1: INTRODUCTION TO ARTIFICIAL INTELLIGENCE 8

CHAPTER 2: FUNDAMENTALS OF MACHINE LEARNING 20

CHAPTER 3: MACHINE LEARNING ALGORITHMS 33

CHAPTER 4: PYTHON AND MACHINE LEARNING LIBRARIES 60

CONCLUSION 73

PYTHON FOR DATA ANALYSIS

INTRODUCTION 76

CHAPTER 1: INTRODUCTION TO BIG DATA AND BIG DATA ANALYSIS 78

CHAPTER 2: FUNDAMENTALS OF PYTHON AND DATA ANALYSIS LIBRARIES ... 96

CHAPTER 3: PREDICTIVE MODELING, DATA VISUALIZATION AND CREATION OF TRAINING DATA SET 111

CHAPTER 4: APPLICATIONS OF BIG DATA ANALYSIS 132

CONCLUSION 142

PYTHON DATA SCIENCE FOR BEGINNERS

INTRODUCTION 145

CHAPTER 1: A SHORT INTRODUCTION TO PYTHON 146

CHAPTER 2: INTRODUCTION TO DATA SCIENCE 159

CHAPTER 3: RAW DATA 165

CHAPTER 4: INFERENTIAL STATISTICS 184

CHAPTER 5: PYTHON LIBRARIES-PYGAL 204

CHAPTER 6: DATA ANALYSIS 222

CHAPTER 7: EXPLORE MACHINE LEARNING 231

CHAPTER 8: DEEP DIVE- MACHINE LEARNING... 242

CHAPTER 9: PREDICTIONS USING LINEAR REGRESSION 260

CHAPTER 10: DATA ANALYSIS-DEEP DIVE 274

CONCLUSION 283

PYTHON PROGRAMMING LANGUAGE FOR BEGINNERS

INTRODUCTION 286

CHAPTER 1: HISTORY OF ARTIFICIAL INTELLIGENCE............................... 287

CHAPTER 2: INTRODUCTION TO PYTHON PROGRAMMING......................292

CHAPTER 3: VARIABLES AND DATA TYPES... 297

CHAPTER 4: CONDITIONAL EXECUTION 305

CHAPTER 5: PYTHON FUNCTIONS 317

CHAPTER 6: PYTHON OPERATORS 326

CHAPTER 7: FILE HANDLING... 328

CHAPTER 8: DICTIONARIES 331

CHAPTER 9: OBJECT-ORIENTED PROGRAMMING 339

CHAPTER 10: INHERITANCE 343

CHAPTER 11: INTRODUCTION TO DJANGO FRAMEWORK 346

CHAPTER 12: DJANGO INSTALLATION 352

CHAPTER 13: MVC PATTERN 357

CHAPTER 14: CREATE, INSTALL, DEPLOY FIRST DJANGO APP 362

CHAPTER 15: TIPS FOR DJANGO AND PYTHON BEGINNERS 376

CONCLUSION 380

Python Machine Learning

The Ultimate Basic Guide For Beginners To Learn How To Design Types Of Automatic Production With Classification Algorithms And Create A Data Pipelines With Unsupervised Learning

By

Oliver R. Simpson

Code Developer Academy

Table of Contents

INTRODUCTION 6
CHAPTER 1: INTRODUCTION TO ARTIFICIAL INTELLIGENCE 8
CHAPTER 2: FUNDAMENTALS OF MACHINE LEARNING 20
CHAPTER 3: MACHINE LEARNING ALGORITHMS 33
CHAPTER 4: PYTHON AND MACHINE LEARNING LIBRARIES 60
CONCLUSION 73

Introduction

Congratulations on downloading *Python Machine Learning: The Ultimate Basic Guide for Beginners to Learn How to Design Types of Automatic Production with Classification Algorithms and Create A Data Pipelines with Unsupervised Learning* and thank you for doing so.

The following chapters will discuss the fundamentals of machine learning technology to help you understand the process of creating a data pipeline for a machine learning model. You will start this book by developing a solid understanding of the basics of artificial intelligence technology and the fourth industrial revolution upon us. It is important to master the concepts of artificial intelligence technology and learn how researchers are breaking the boundaries of data science to mimic human intelligence in machines. The power of artificial intelligence has already started to manifest in our environment and our everyday objects. This chapter will also discuss how artificial intelligence technology is being applied in some of the most important industrial domains including finance and banking, journalism, travel, and the transportation industry.

The chapter 2 of this book titled "Fundamentals of Machine Learning" will introduce you to the basic concepts of machine learning, namely, "representation", "optimization" and "evaluation". You will learn how the definition of machine learning has been customized across the academic and business worlds. An overview of different types of machine learning algorithms along with the relationship between machine learning and Artificial Intelligence technology. A thorough understanding of the concept of "Statistical Learning" has been provided, which is a descriptive statistics-based machine learning framework that can be categorized as supervised or unsupervised.

In chapter 3 titled "Machine Learning Algorithms", a variety of supervised and unsupervised learning algorithms are explained in exquisite detail. Select algorithms such as "classification", "logistic regression" and a "Naïve Bayes classifier" algorithms have been explained with required mathematical equations for application in real life. You will learn the basics of some supervised algorithms including "regression", "Support Vector Machine", "Decision trees" and "k-nearest neighbors" as well as unsupervised algorithms including "K-Means clustering". You will also learn that the "Artificial Neural Networks" or (ANN) have been developed with inspiration from the structure of the human brain and utilize numerous processing units like human neurons or nodes working as a single unit. In this chapter, you will be given a stage by stage walkthrough of how you can create a data pipeline to build your own machine learning model. The 9 stages of this process are explained in detail with a focus on "offline" and "online" mode of execution of the solution.

The final chapter of this book, titled "Python and Machine Learning Libraries" will introduce you to the Python programming language and some of the key features that render it as the language of choice for coding beginners and advanced software programmers alike. A number of Python coding tips and tricks have also been provided that will help you sharpen up your Python programming skillset or get familiar with the coding if you are new to Python coding. This chapter also includes a brief overview of various renowned machine learning libraries such as "Scikit-Learn", "NumPy", "SciPy", "Matplotlib", "IPython", "SymPy" and "Pandas" among others. This book is filled with real-life examples to help you understand the nitty-gritty of the concepts and names and descriptions of multiple tools that you can further explore and selectively implement to make sound choices for the development of a desired machine learning model.

There are plenty of books on this subject on the market, thanks again for choosing this one! Every effort was made to ensure it is full of as much useful information as possible, please enjoy!

Chapter 1: Introduction to Artificial Intelligence

Humans or Homo Sapiens often claim to be the most superior species to have ever inhabited the planet Earth, mainly attributing to their "intelligence." Even the most complicated animal behavior is never regarded as smart, but intelligence is attributed to the simplest of human behavior. For example, when a female digger wasp returns with food to her burrow, she deposits the food on the threshold and checks for intruders prior to carrying her food inside. Sounds like wasps are quite smart, right? However, an experiment performed on these wasps, where the scientist moved the food a few inches away from the burrow's entrance while the wasp was inside the burrow, reported that the wasps continued to repeat the entire ordeal as often as the food was moved. This experiment revealed that the wasps fail to adapt to evolving conditions and therefore, "intelligence" in the wasps is noticeably absent. Then how do we define "human intelligence?" Psychologists characterize human intelligence as a composite of a variety of skills such as learning from experiences and adapting consequently, understanding abstract ideas, reasoning, problem-solving, linguistic use, and perception.

Artificial Intelligence (AI) can be defined as the science of developing human-controlled and operated machines, such as digital computers or robots, that are capable of imitating human intelligence, adapting to new inputs, and performing human-like activities. Thanks to Pop culture, upon hearing the words Artificial Intelligence, most people tend to think of robots coming to life to wreak havoc on human beings. But that is far from reality. The core principle of Artificial Intelligence is the capacity of Artificial Intelligence powered machines to rationalize (think like humans) and take action (mimic human actions) to achieve the targeted objective. To put it simply, Artificial Intelligence is designing a machine that will think and behave like human beings. Artificial Intelligence has three primary objectives, which are learning, reasoning, and perception.

Although the term Artificial Intelligence was coined in 1956, the British pioneer of Computer Sciences, Alan Mathison Turing, carried out extensive work in the field of Artificial Intelligence, in the mid-20th century. Turing created an abstract computing machine in the form of symbols, in 1935, with a scanner and unlimited memory. The scanner was able to move back and forth through the memory, read the available symbols and write additional memory symbols. A programming instruction dictated the activities of the scanner and was stored in the memory as well. Thus, Turing created a machine with implicit learning capacities that could alter its programming and enhance itself. This principle is commonly regarded as the universal "Turing Machine" and serves as a basis for all advanced computers. Turing asserted that computers are able to learn from their own experience and resolve problems using a guiding principle called "heuristic problem-solving."

The early Artificial Intelligence studies were concentrated on problem-solving and symbolic techniques, in the 1950s. By the 1960s, the AI research had a major leap of interest from the US Department of Defense, who started working towards training computers to mimic human reasoning. In the 1970s, the Defense Advanced Research Projects Agency (DARPA) has successfully performed its street mapping projects. It may come to you as a surprise that in 2003, long before the existence of the renowned Siri and Alexa, DARPA had effectively manufactured intelligent personal assistant machines. Long story short, this groundbreaking achievement in the field of Artificial Intelligence has set the stage for automation and reasoning observed in modern-day computers.

Here are the primary human characteristics that we strive to imitate in the machines:

1. **Knowledge** – Machines need an abundance of data and information related to the world around us, in order to be able to behave and respond like humans. In order to implement knowledge engineering, Artificial Intelligence powered machines are required to have undeterred access to data objects, data categories, and data properties as well as the relationship between them that can be managed and stored in the data storage.
2. **Learning** – Of all the various forms of learning that apply to AI, the "trial and error" technique is considered the easiest. For example, a computer chess learning program will try all possible moves until the mate-in-one move is found to win the game. The program then saves the winning move to be used the next time it encounters a similar scenario. This fairly easy to implement learning element is called "rote learning", which includes memorization of individual objects and processes in a straightforward way. The most difficult part of learning is called "generalization," which implies the application of prior experiences to the newly encountered similar situations.
3. **Problem Solving** – The systematic process of achieving a predefined objective or solution by looking through a range of viable actions can be

characterized as a problem solving the methods for problem-solving can be adjusted for a specific issue or used for a broad range of problems. A general-purpose problem-solving technique frequently used in AI is "means-end analysis," which includes an incremental decrease in the difference between the initial and final state of the goal. Think of some of the core functions of a robot, back and forth motion, or picking up factors that contribute to an objective being fulfilled.

4. **Reasoning** – The act of reasoning can be defined as the capacity to draw inferences suitable to the scenario in question. The two types of reasoning are called "deductive reasoning" and "inductive reasoning". In deductive reasoning, if the premise is true then the conclusion is presumed to be true. On the other hand, the conclusion may or may not be true in inductive reasoning, even if the premise is true. While significant success in programming computers to execute deductive reasoning has been attained, the application of "true reasoning" stays out of reach and one of the greatest challenges facing Artificial Intelligence.

5. **Perception** – The process of producing a multidimensional view of an object by means of multiple sensory organs can be defined as perception. A number of variables, such as the viewing angle, the direction, and intensity of the light, and the extent of contrast generated by the object with the surrounding area, can complicate this development of awareness of the environment. With the introduction of self-driving cars and robots that can collect empty soda cans while moving through the facilities, breakthrough developments have been rendered in the field of artificial perception and can be readily observed in our daily lives.

The Fourth Industrial Revolution

From the First Industrial Revolution of the 18th century that marked a transition of the world economy from an agriculture base to the one dominated by industries and machine manufacturing, today we find ourselves at the cusp of the Fourth Industrial Revolution. Remember the Second Industrial Revolution applied science to mass production and manufacturing, while the Third Industrial Revolution or Digital Revolution brought us digital technologies. The Fourth Industrial Revolution annunciates a series of social and economic upheavals, unfolding over the 21st century with technologies like Artificial Intelligence, 3-D printing, Augmented Reality and Genome Editing.

The Fourth Industrial Revolution will rapidly alter the way we produce, exchange, and distribute value. The CRISPR technology has revolutionized the gene-editing space by providing a low-cost gene sequencing and targeting mechanism. Automation continues to disrupt the transportation and manufacturing paradigms while blockchain technology is increasingly erasing the boundary between the physical and digital world. And of course, the applications of Artificial Intelligence in every industry imaginable can be deemed limitless. In line with the previous revolutions, the Fourth Industrial Revolution will profoundly transform our world for the next 50-100 years. The way we think about this revolution today and invest in it will eventually guide the near future transformation of the human race.

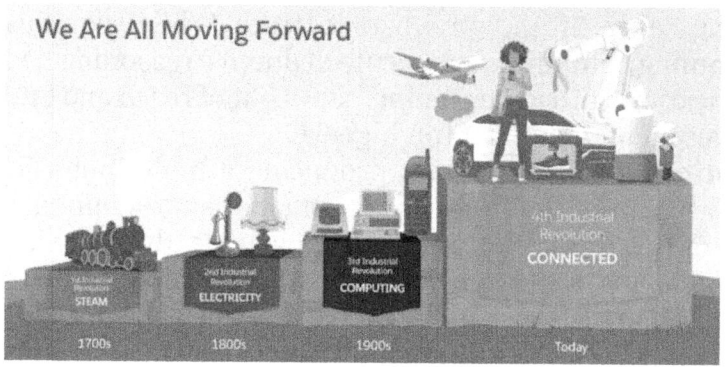

The global social transformation of the Fourth Industrial Revolution can be led by affecting the incentives, rules, and norms of the economy which in turn transforms how we communicate, learn, and entertain ourselves. Our understanding of human species and how we relate to one another is up for renewal with the adoption of cyber-physical systems such as the Internet of Things (IoT) and the Internet of Systems (IoS). The new technologies are being developed and implemented at lightning speed and poised to impact human identities, communities as well as the political structures. Therefore, our engagement with these revolutionizing technologies is intricately tied to our opportunities for self-realization and our ability to leave a lasting positive impact on the world. Some of the prominent technologies other than Artificial Intelligence, that is driving the Fourth Industrial Revolution include:

- **Blockchain** – The advent of digital currency like "Bitcoin", is attributed to the blockchain technology, which allows for secure and transparent recording and sharing of data using a decentralized server, instead of a

third-party intermediary. The blockchain technology can also be used to make supply chains traceable, secure sensitive medical data and even to combat voter fraud.
- **Smart computing** – Modern day computers are capable of processing a vast amount of data in minutes. The advent of "cloud" technology is allowing businesses to securely store and access information seamlessly from anywhere in the world with Internet access. Future computers are slated to become even more powerful with the use of Quantum computing technologies. These million times more powerful computers will potentially be capable of supercharging AI, create super complex data models within seconds and gear up the discovery of new materials.
- **Augmented and Virtual Reality** – The augmented reality as the name suggests will redefine and expand our realities by merging the physical and digital world into one. For example, the makeup application launched by L'Oréal which allows the users to digitally experiment with their products, without physically being in the store. On the other hand, virtual reality simulates the real world to create an immersive digital experience. For example, the virtual reality or VR headsets that you can buy at any electronics store to enhance your online gaming experience.
- **Biotechnology** – The vicious cycle of new diseases demanding new treatments will continue to haunt us for the foreseeable future. But the advances in biotechnology are propelling our usage of cellular and bio-molecular techniques to develop new pharmaceuticals and biomaterials. Our paramount need for clean and efficient energy sources, such as biofuels, to replace the depleting non-renewable fossil fuel sources is dependent on and driven by biotechnology. For example, some scientists are working to develop the strongest biomaterial ever produced.
- **Robotics** – The science of developing and using robots for personal as well as commercial use is called Robotics. Several headlines have been made by the Japanese robotics engineers working to develop increasingly sophisticated, "human-like" robots that can be used as human assistants in hotels and hospitals or stand to revolutionize the field of industrial manufacturing.
- **3D Printing** – The new hot gadget of today's modern technology is the 3D printer. We can print customized three-dimensional objects at a low cost and from the comforts of our home. Businesses now have the ability to print their own parts without needing significant tooling, at a much higher speed and low cost than the traditional process.

- **Internet of Things (IoT)** – If you think the idea of your car being able to track what's in your refrigerator is science fiction? Think again! The IoT technology constitutes the connection of our everyday items with the Internet allowing for their identification by all the other devices on the network. This technology is revolutionizing the marketing industry by collecting data from all of the connected devices of a customer and tailor marketing their products to better meet the customer's needs. The IoT sensors are also used in the field of agriculture, by allowing farmers to better monitor soil attributes and make informed decisions like the need for fertilization and irrigation of their farms.

Some economists like Erik Brynjolfsson and Andrew McAfee, argue that the Fourth Industrial Revolution could contribute to greater economic inequality, specifically in its potential to disrupt the labor markets around the world. With the increasing propensity of automation across the economy, the net displacement of labor by machines is likely to exacerbate the disparity between the returns to labor and return to capital. However, the other side of the coin signals the possibility that the displacement of workers by tech will result in a net gain of rewarding and less risky jobs. Not unlike the prior industrial revolutions that have resulted in positive as well as negative impacts on our world. Although nations across the globe have become wealthier, pulling entire societies out from the dearth of poverty, the universal disparity of economic distribution is getting increasing wider every day. To ensure that we as a humanity are foremost in receiving the benefits of the Fourth Industrial Revolution, we must align our core human values with technological progress. We must recognize the risk of technological advancements, such as cybersecurity threats, use of digital media in distribution of misleading or wrong information at a lightning speed on a massive scale as well as potential unemployment through automation, and take measures to mitigate these risks.

"The changes are so profound that, from the perspective of human history, there has never been a time of greater promise or potential peril. My concern, however, is that decision-makers are too often caught in traditional, linear (and non-disruptive) thinking or too absorbed by immediate concerns to think strategically about the forces of disruption and innovation shaping our future."

Professor Klaus Schwab

Industrial Applications of Artificial Intelligence

Artificial Intelligence technology is leading the Fourth Industrial Revolution with its growing influence on everyday consumer products. AI has revamped the manufacturing, retail and finance industries with new products, processes, and capabilities. Some of the most significant breakthroughs in physics and healthcare are also credited to AI. In this era of technological advancements as we move towards a future depicted in science fiction, AI has become an essential part of our world. Artificial Intelligence has exploded in recent years, thanks to the massive amount of online data we generate every day and the never seen before powerful computers. The business leaders and innovators are chasing the promise of AI to gain a competitive advantage while saving up on costs and time. From optimizing the delivery route to management of a global supply chain, AI is helping companies of all sizes across the industries to improve their bottom line with enhanced productivity. Companies are able to design, produce and deliver superior products and services while cutting back on their expenses. Isn't that every entrepreneur's dream come true?!?! In this chapter, we will explore the application of Artificial Intelligence in all the major industries and how the business processes are changing to adopt AI.

Here are some of the most significant applications of Artificial Intelligence in various industrial domains:

Finance or Banking Industry

Even though the technical advancements of the financial institutions have been overshadowed by the "Silicon Valley", some of the Applications of artificial intelligence based tools and technologies in this domain our groundbreaking. Considering the fact that the finance industry has a profound effect not only on the everyday consumer but also on other businesses across the industrial spectrum. Some of the traditional banking Industry problems such as fraud detection and prevention, catering to millions of customers across the globe, Data privacy and security concerns as well as flagging of false-positive transactions, among others are being addressed with the use of Machine learning algorithms and big data analytics. Some of the most popular Data science-driven trends in the finance industry are:

- Automation and personalization of customer service with the use of virtual personal assistance Chatbots.
- Real-time detection and prevention of fraudulent transactions by analyzing large volumes of customer transaction data and identifying patterns that can be easily missed by a human observer.
- Analyzing available customer transaction data, current market trends and remarks from other financial institutions that the prospective borrower might have approached, to assess potential risks in approving loans as well as to determine the eligibility of a potential credit card customer.
- Hedge funds are increasingly looking to utilize artificial intelligence based tools and technologies in their stock trading to gather inside from massive a mound of stock-related data in a fraction of time.

"We want to be there for customers in the moments that matter most. Incorporating artificial intelligence into our mobile banking offering will help customers manage their simple banking needs more efficiently and consistently, which then allows our specialists in our financial centers to spend more time with customers to understand their more complex needs and help them improve their financial lives."
- Thong Nguyen, Bank of America

Virtual Assistance Across Industrial Domains

From the healthcare industry to the finance industry, virtual assistance has become the new industry-standard for enhanced customer service. The leading online travel booking company, "Expedia" has launched there "Expedia Skill" application to provide customers information on their upcoming trips and flight details and even be able to book a rental car with a simple voice command. They have recently partnered with "Amazon" to allow their customers to check their upcoming travel plans and flight details with live updates using "Amazon Alexa" devices. Another travel company, "ATPI", deployed its artificial intelligence based tool called "Zeno by ATPI", which stores frequent traveler information such as seat preferences, preferred departure airport, preferred car rental service and favorite hotel to offer a personalized experience to every customer. The tool also supports "Zeno Chatbot" to resolve basic customer issues and route them to a customer service representative for more complex queries.

Virtual assistant in the hospitality industry such as "Hijiffy", which operates as an integration with the hotel's Facebook messenger application is revolutionizing the rigid monotonous Hotel booking websites. With the "Hijiffy" application prospective customers can get Hotel services information, resolve customer service issues, receive tips on destination cities, get access to real-time hotel rates and even make air Hotel room booking right from their Facebook messenger application.

Another groundbreaking virtual assistance platform in the hospitality industry called "Watson assistant for hospitality" was developed by IBM. This platform can store Hotel guest data and is highly customizable, allowing individual hotels to develop their own Hotel specific and uniquely named Chatbot. This powerful technology is designed to anticipate guess needs and generate product and service recommendations based on their prior stay at the same hotel and other pertinent information. "IBM Watson" is also capable of arranging transportation for guess prior to scheduled meetings as reflected in the guest's calendar and set up an alarm to remind them of Hotels breakfast start time.

Journalism Industry

The advancements in data science are resulting and the development of machines that could potentially process is highly subjective and emotionally driven content. Recently about one-third of the articles published by the "Bloomberg News" were generated by their artificial intelligence based system called "Cyborg". This system was designed to assist reporters and writing of News articles concerning the company's quarterly earnings reports. The moment applicable financial data is available in the system the underlying machine learning algorithms can dissect the report and create news articles containing the most relevant facts and figures.

"The Associated Press" also used robots to produce news articles on minor league baseball, "The Washington Post" used robots to produce news articles on high school football and "The Los Angeles Times" use robots to generate news articles on earthquakes. "The Guardians, Australia" successfully published robot-assisted news articles detailing annual contributions and donations made to the Australian political parties. Even "Forbes" is incorporating robots into their journalism and recently launched testing on a robot called "Bertie" that is designed to draft story templates and assist reporters. "Bloomberg", "The Associated Press" and "The Post" have designed their systems to receive an internal alert in case of date abnormalities beyond a threshold that requires human intervention and decision-making to make the final call on whether a bigger story on that topic is warranted or not. "The Post" put this alert system to test in the "2016 Summer Olympics", by triggering alerts to their designated reporters every time an outcome was 10% above or below an existing "Olympic World Record", via company's business messaging system called "Slack".

"The work of journalism is creative, it's about curiosity, it's about storytelling, it's about digging and holding governments accountable, it's critical thinking, it's judgment — and that is where we want our journalists spending their energy," – Lisa Gibbs, The Associated Press

"The Dow Jones" and "The Wall Street Journal" have also made their entrance in the realm of data science by experimenting with artificial intelligence technology on routine tasks like identification of fabricated images or "deep fakes" and the generation of interview transcripts. "The New York Times" is utilizing big data analytics and machine learning algorithms in digitizing its library archives as well as for personalization of newsletters.

Travel Industry

In a revolutionizing effort to coordinate airline bookings made by travel agents across the country, the travel industry adopted large-scale industrial computing and pioneered the computer-based airline booking systems in the 1960s. Travel companies are gathering customer data that can be analyzed by big data analytics and machine learning algorithms to provide customers relevant future travel programs based on their travel history and recent flight searches. One of the major applications of machine learning technology in the travel industry is Smart pricing tools that are capable of autonomously adjusting flight prices on the basis of market demand and the weather conditions to optimize the airline business.

All major airline companies are collecting Data on prospective travelers that have you browsed, shopped, booked, taken a flight or even changed their travel plans dad can be analyzed using artificial intelligence powered solutions degenerate actionable insights and provide personalized services to meet the customer needs and demands. The savvy air traveler has access to a variety of tools and sites to browse and compare slides, hotels, buses, rental cars, and trains to get the most out of their money by striking the best deal.

The fiercely competitive travel industry is adopting data science based technology to revolutionize the travel experience with highly customized and personalized services catering to specific customer preferences.

Transportation Industry

The two primary issues facing the day-to-day operations of the transportation industry are accidents and traffic, which can both be attributed to human error. Considering the inherently unpredictable nature of these problems they tend to be extremely difficult to model, but with the use of big data analytics and machine learning algorithms Machines can analyze a massive amount of data and generate forecasts and predictions that can be incorporated in the decision-making process. To tackle the growing challenges of high travel demands, safety concerns, increasing CO_2 emissions and catastrophically degrading the environment, the use of artificial intelligence based tools and technology has a promising solution. The transportation authorities are diving into the sea of data science to discover the treasure of powerful analytical tools that can be used to relieve traffic congestion and make travel time more reliable for the commuters.

Artificial intelligence technology has the potential to aid in the development of improved road infrastructure and provide assistance to drivers, generating an overall reliable transport system with little to no detrimental effect on the environment at an affordable price. Some of the real-world applications of artificial intelligence in the transportation industry are:

- Development of the first autonomous and completely electric vehicle called "Olli" which is powered by "IBM Watson".
- "Ford" has designed a "Smart City" driven by a "smart system" that allows "smart vehicles" to connect and coordinate with one another while cutting down on the risks of collisions and other accidents. The "Smart City" is designed to gather data from its residents and share it with multiple smart technologies working in tandem to create a digital utopia.
- "Rapid Flow Technologies" has developed an advanced traffic control system called "SURTRAC" which allows traffic lights to respond to the vehicular floor in real-time instead of being parsed by a centralized operating system.
- The company "Rolls-Royce" is expected to unveil its new cargo ships that can be controlled remotely by 2020.
The London underground train system tested their first autonomous train

in early 2019, that could carry passengers from one point to another without any human assistance.
- The "Google Flights" technology is capable of precisely predicting flight delays even before the airlines themselves, by leveraging Machine learning algorithms on available historical flight data to generate accurate predictions on the flight ETAs.
- For women who like to travel alone and are always concerned about their personal safety, the "JOZU" application is designed to help women identify the safest route and method of transportation to safely reach their destination.

Chapter 2: Fundamentals of Machine Learning

Machine Learning can be defined as a subsidiary of Artificial Intelligence technology driven by the hypothesis that machines are capable of learning from data by identifying patterns and making decisions with little to no human assistance. The science of machine learning was birthed as a theory that computers have the potential to self-learn specific tasks without needing to be programmed, using the pattern recognition technique. As the machines are exposed to new data the ability to adapt independently is the iterative aspect of machine learning. They can learn from and train themselves with prior computations, to generate credible and reproducible decisions and results. Machine learning algorithms have been in use for much longer than one would think, but their enhanced capability to analyze "big data" by automatically applying highly complex and sophisticated mathematical calculations rapidly and repeatedly, has been developed recently.

Now the topic of machine learning is so "hot" that the academia, business world and the scientific community have their own take on its definition. Here are some of the widely accepted definitions from select highly reputed sources:

- *"Machine learning is the science of getting computers to act without being explicitly programmed."* – Stanford University
- *"The field of Machine Learning seeks to answer the question, how can we build computer systems that automatically improve with experience, and what are the fundamental laws that govern all learning processes?"* – Carnegie Mellon University
- *"Machine learning algorithms can figure out how to perform important tasks by generalizing from examples."* – University of Washington
- *"Machine Learning at its most basic is the practice of using algorithms to parse data, learn from it, and then make a determination or prediction about something in the world."* – Nvidia
- *"Machine learning is based on algorithms that can learn from data without relying on rules-based programming."* – McKinsey.

Machine learning allows an analysis of large volumes of data and delivers faster and more accurate results. With proper training, this technology can allow organizations to identify profitable opportunities and business risks. Machine learning in combination with cognitive technologies and artificial intelligence tends to be even more effective and accurate in processing massive quantities of data. The machine learning algorithms can be categorized into four:

Supervised Machine Learning Algorithms

These algorithms are capable of applying the lessons from the previous runs to new data set using labeled examples to successfully make predictions for future events. For example, a machine can be programmed with data points labeled as "F" (failed) or "S" (success). The learning algorithm will receive inputs with corresponding correct outputs and run a comparison of its own actual output against the expected or correct, in an attempt to identify errors that can be fixed to make the model more efficient and accurate. With sufficient training, the algorithms are capable of providing 'targets' for any new data input through methods like regression, classification, prediction, and ingredient boosting. The analysis starts from a known training data set and the machine learning algorithm then produces an "inferred function" to make future predictions pertaining to the output values. For example, the supervised learning algorithm based systems are smart enough to anticipate and detect the likelihood of fraudulent credit card transactions being processed.

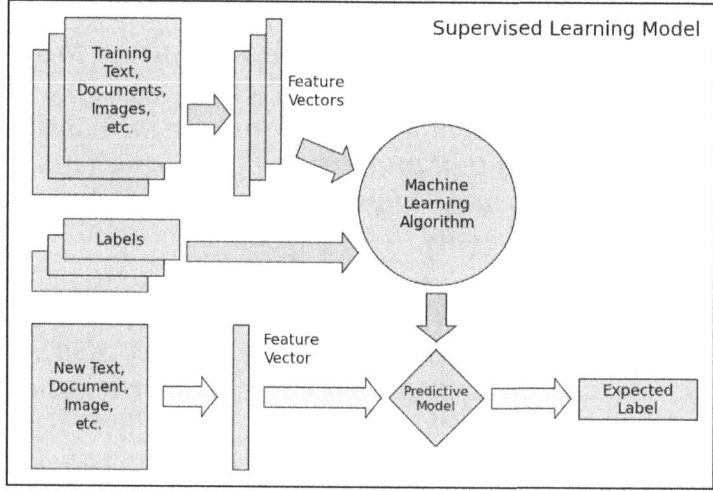

Unsupervised Machine Learning Algorithms

These algorithms are used in the absence of classified and labeled training data sources. According to SAS, "Unsupervised Learning algorithms are used to study ways in which the system can infer a function to describe a hidden structure from unlabeled data i.e. to explore the data and identify some structure within". Similar to the supervised learning algorithms, these algorithms are able to explore the data and draw inferences from data sets, but cannot figure out the right output. For example, identification of individuals with similar shopping attributes, who can be segmented together and targeted with similar marketing campaigns. These algorithms are widely used to identify data outliers, provide product recommendations, and segment text topics using techniques like "singular value decomposition", "self-organizing maps" and "k-means clustering".

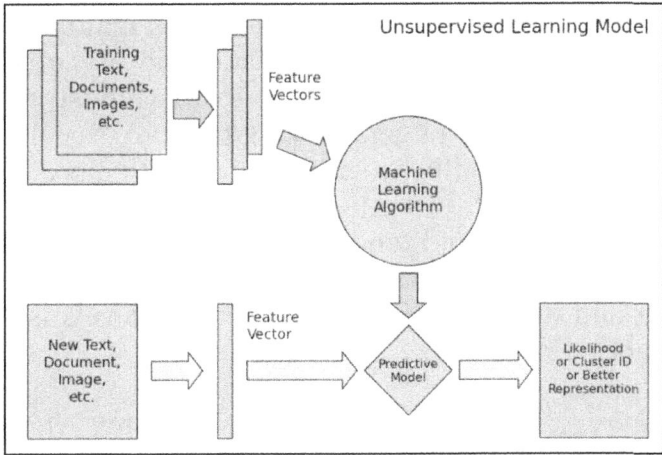

Semi-Supervised Machine Learning Algorithms

As the name indicates, these algorithms fall somewhere in between supervised and unsupervised learning and are capable of using labeled as well as unlabeled data as training sources. A typical training set would include a majority of the unlabeled data with a limited volume of the labeled data. The systems running on semi-supervised learning algorithms with methods such as prediction, regression, and classification are able to significantly improve their learning accuracy. In situations where the acquired labeled data requires relevant and skilled resources for the machine to be able to train or learn from it, the semi-supervised learning algorithms are best suited. For example, identification of individual faces on a web camera.

Reinforcement Machine Learning Algorithms

These algorithms are capable of interacting with their environment by producing actions and discovering errors or rewards. The primary characteristics of reinforcement learning are "trial and error research method and delayed reward". With the use of these algorithms, a machine can maximize its performance by automatically determining the ideal behavior within a specific context. The reinforcement signal is simple reward feedback that is required by the machine or software agents to learn which actions yield the fastest and accurate results. These algorithms are frequently used in robotics, gaming, and navigation.

Basic Concepts of Machine Learning

The biggest draw of machine learning is the engineered capacity of the system to learn programs from the data automatically instead of manually constructing the program for the machine. Over the last decade, the use of machine learning algorithms expanded from computer science to the industrial world. Machine learning algorithms are capable of generalizing tasks to execute them iteratively. The process of developing specific programs for specific tasks costs a lot of time and money, but occasionally it's just impossible to achieve. On the other hand, ML programming is often feasible and tends to be much more cost-effective. The use of machine learning in tackling ambitious issues of widespread importance such as global warming and depleting underground water levels is promising with a massive collection of relevant data.

"A breakthrough in machine learning would be worth ten Microsoft."
– Bill Gates

A number of types of machine learning exist today but the concept of machine learning largely boils down to three components "representation", "evaluation" and "optimization". Here are some of the standard concepts that are applicable to all of them:

Representation

Machine learning models are incapable of directly hearing, seeing, or sensing input examples. Therefore, data representation is required to supply the model with a useful vantage point into the key qualities of the data. To be able to successfully train a machine learning model selection of key features that best represent the data is very important. "Representation" simply refers to the act of "representing" data points to the computer in a language that it understands using a set of classifiers. A classifier can be defined as "a system that inputs a vector of discrete and or continuous feature values and outputs a single discrete value called the class". For a model to learn from the represented data the training data set or the "hypothesis space" must contain the desired classifier that you want the models to be trained on. Any classifiers that are external to the hypothesis space cannot be learned by the model.

The data features used to represent the input are very critical to the machine learning process. The data features are so important to the development of the desired machine learning model that can easily be the difference between successful and failed machine learning projects. A training data set containing multiple independent "features" that are well correlated with the "class" can make the machine learning much smoother. On the other hand, the class containing complex features may not be easy to learn from for the machine. This often requires the raw data to be processed so that desired features can be constructed from it, to be leveraged for the ML model. The process of deriving features from raw data tends to be the most time consuming and laborious part of the ML project. It is also considered the most creative and interesting part of the project where intuition and trial and error play just as important role as the technical requirements.

The process of ML is not a "one-shot process" of developing a training data set and executing it instead it is an iterative process that requires analysis of the post-run output, followed by modification of the training data set and then repeating the whole process all over again. Another reason for the extensive time and effort required to engineer the training data set is domain specificity. Training data set for an e-commerce platform to generate predictions based on consumer behavior analysis will be very different from the training data set required to develop a self-driving car. However, the actual machine learning process remains largely the same across industrial domains. No wonder, a lot of research is being done to automate the feature engineering process.

Evaluation

Essentially the process of judging multiple hypotheses or models to choose one model over another is referred to as an evaluation. To be able to differentiate between useful classifiers from the vague ones an "evaluation function" is required. The evaluation function is also called as "objective", "utility" or "scoring" function. The machine learning algorithm has its own internal evaluation function which tends to be different from the external evaluation function used by the researchers to optimize the classifier. Usually, the evaluation function is defined prior to the selection of the data representation tool, as the first step of the project. For example, the machine learning model for the self-driving car has the feature for identification of pedestrians in its vicinity at near-zero false negatives and a low false-positive as an evaluation function and the pre-existing condition that needs to be "represented" using applicable data features.

Optimization

The process of searching the space of presented models to achieve better evaluations or the highest scoring classifier is called as "optimization". For algorithms with more than one optimum classifier, the selection of optimization techniques is very critical in the determination of the classifier produced and to achieve a more efficient learning model. A variety of off-the-shelf optimizers are available in the market to kick start new machine learning models before eventually replacing them with custom-designed optimizers.

Table 1. The three components of learning algorithms.

Representation	Evaluation	Optimization
Instances	Accuracy/Error rate	Combinatorial optimization
K-nearest neighbor	Precision and recall	Greedy search
Support vector machines	Squared error	Beam search
Hyperplanes	Likelihood	Branch-and-bound
Naive Bayes	Posterior probability	Continuous optimization
Logistic regression	Information gain	Unconstrained
Decision trees	K-L divergence	Gradient descent
Sets of rules	Cost/Utility	Conjugate gradient
Propositional rules	Margin	Quasi-Newton methods
Logic programs		Constrained
Neural networks		Linear programming
Graphical models		Quadratic programming
Bayesian networks		
Conditional random fields		

Machine Learning in Practice

The complete process of machine learning is much more extensive than just the development and application of machine learning algorithms and can be divided into steps below:

1. Define the goals of the project taking into careful consideration all the prior knowledge and domain expertise available. Goals can easily become ambiguous since there are always additional things you want to achieve than practically possible to implement.
2. The data pre-processing and cleaning must result in a high-quality data set. This is the most critical and time-consuming step of the whole project. The larger the volume of data, the more noise it brings to the training data set which must be eradicated before feeding to the learner system.
3. Selection of appropriate learning model to meet the requirements of your project. This process tends to be rather simple given the various types of data models available in the market.
4. Depending on the domain the machine learning model is applied to, the results may or may not require a clear understanding of the model by human experts as long as the model can successfully deliver desired results.
5. The final step is to consolidate and deploy the knowledge or information gathered from the model to be used on an industrial level.
6. The whole cycle from step 1 to 5 listed above is iteratively repeated until a result that can be used in practice is achieved.

Machine Learning and Artificial Intelligence

The concept of Artificial Intelligence technology stems from the idea that machines are capable of human-like intelligence and can mimic human thought processing and learning capabilities, to adapt to new inputs and perform tasks without requiring human assistance. Machine learning is integral to the concept of artificial intelligence. Machine learning technology (ML) is referred to the concept of Artificial Intelligence technology that focuses primarily on the engineered capability of machines to explicitly learn and self-train, by identifying data patterns to improve upon the underlying algorithm and make independent decisions with no human intervention".

To get a sense of how significant machine learning is in our everyday lives, it is simpler to state what part of our cutting-edge way of life has not been touched by it. Each aspect of human life is being impacted by the "smart machines" intended to expand human capacities and improve efficiencies. Artificial Intelligence and machine learning technology is the focal precept of the "Fourth Industrial Revolution", that could possibly question our thoughts regarding being "human".

Here are a few reasons to help you understand the significance of machine learning in our daily lives and how machine learning and Artificial Intelligence are related to each other:

- Automation of repetitive learning and revelation from data. Not at all like hardware-driven robotic automation that simply automates manual assignments, machine learning allows the performance of high volume, high volume, computer-based tasks consistently and dependably.
- Machine learning algorithms are helping Artificial Intelligence to adapt to the evolving world by allowing the machine or system to learn, take note and improve upon its prior errors. The machine learning algorithm functions as a classifier or a predictor to acquire new skills and identify data patterns and structure. For example, the machine learning algorithm has generated a system that can teach itself how to play chess and even how to generate product recommendations based on customer activity and behavior data. The beauty of this model is that it adapts with every new set of data.
- Machine learning has made the analysis of deeper and larger data set feasible with the use of neural networks containing multiple hidden layers. Think about it, a fraud detection system with numerous concealed layers would be deemed a work of fantasy just a couple of years ago. With the advent of big data and unlikely to envision computer powers, a whole new world is on the horizon. Data to the machines resemble the gas to the vehicle, the more data you can add to them, the faster and more accurate results will get. Deep learning models flourish with an abundance of data because they gain straightforwardly from the data.
- The "deep neural networks" of the machine learning algorithms have resulted in unbelievable accuracy. For example, frequent and repeated use of smart tech like "Amazon Alexa" and "Google Search", results in increased accuracy derived from deep learning. These "deep neural networks" are also empowering our medical field. Image classification and object recognition are now capable of finding cancer on MRIs with similar accuracy as that of a highly trained radiologist.

- Artificial Intelligence is allowing for enhanced and improved use of big data analytics in conjunction with machine learning algorithms. Data has evolved as its own currency and when algorithms are self-learning it can easily become "intellectual property". The raw data is similar to a gold mine in that the more and deeper you dig, the more "gold" or valuable insight you can dig out or extract. Application of machine learning algorithms to the data can enable you to find the correct solutions quicker and makes for an upper hand. Keep in mind the best information will consistently win, despite the fact that everyone is utilizing comparative techniques.

Statistical Learning Framework

"Statistical learning" is a descriptive statistics-based learning framework that can be categorized as supervised or unsupervised. "Supervised statistical learning" includes constructing a statistical model to predict or estimate output based on single or multiple inputs, on the other hand, "unsupervised statistical learning" involves inputs but no supervisory output, but helps in learning data relationships and structure. One way of understanding statistical learning is to identify the connection between the "predictor" (autonomous variables, attributes) and the "response" (autonomous variable), in order to produce a specific model which is capable of predicting the "response variable (Y)" on the basis of "predictor factors (X)".

"$X = f(X) + \varepsilon$ where $X = (X_1, X_2, \ldots, X_p)$", where "f" is an "*unknown function*" & "ε" is "*random error (reducible & irreducible)*".

Here are some fundamental concepts of Statistical Learning:

Prediction and Inference

If there are a number of inputs "X" easily accessible, but the output "B" production is unknown, "f" is often treated as a black box, provided that it generates accurate predictions for "Y". This is called "prediction". There are circumstances in which we need to understand how "Y" is influenced as "X" changes. We want to estimate "f" in this scenario, but our objective is not simply to generate predictions for "Y". In this situation, we want to establish and better understand the connection between "Y" and "X". Now "f" is not regarded as a black box since we have to understand the underlying process of the system. This is called "inference". In everyday life, various issues can be categorized into the setting of "predictions", the setting of "inferences", or a "hybrid" of the two.

Parametric and Non-Parametric Techniques

The "parametric technique" can be defined as an evaluation of "f" by calculating the set parameters (finite summary of the data) while establishing an assumption about the functional form of "f". The mathematical equation of this technique is "$f(X) = \beta_0 + \beta_1 X_1 + \beta_2 X_2 + \ldots + \beta_p X_p$". The "parametric models" tend to have a finite number of parameters which is independent of the size of the data set. This is also known as "model-based learning". For example, "k-Gaussian models" are driven by parametric techniques.

On the other hand, the "non-parametric technique" generates an estimation of "f" on the basis of its closeness to the data points, without making any assumptions on the functional form of "f". The "non-parametric models" tend to have a varying number of parameters which grows proportionally with the size of the data set. This is also known as "memory-based learning". For example, "kernel density models" are driven by a non-parametric technique.

Predictions Accuracy and Model Interpretability

Some of the many methods used to learn from statistical data are less adaptable and extremely restrictive. When "inference" is the target, the use of easy and comparatively inflexible techniques of statistical learning has significant benefits. On the other hand, if the target is the generation of forecasts and predictions flexible models are preferred.

The performance of the model can be estimated on the basis of its accuracy to predict the occurrence of an event on new input data. A more accurate model is deemed as a more valuable model. The interpretability of the model offers insight into the input-output relationship. An interpreted model can provide insight into the capability of independent features to generate predictions for the dependent attribute. The problem occurs because, at the expense of interpretability, as model accuracy improves so does the complexity of the model.

A more accurate model can offer a business more possibilities, advantages, time, or money. But the model accuracy needs to be optimized for such prediction. The optimization of accuracy extends the complexity of the model even further by introducing additional model parameters (and resources needed to adjust those parameters). It is much easier and quicker to interpret a model with a relatively small number of parameters. An input coefficient and an intercept term are part of a linear regression model. For instance, every single term can be explored to assess how it contributes to the production of the output. Switching to a logistic regression model provides greater authority in the context of the relationships underlying the potential transformation of a function to output, that too should be explored along with the coefficients.

It is relatively easy to understand a decision tree of small size, but a heavily loaded decision tree needs a distinct perspective to understand why the event is predicted to occur. Furthermore, the optimized combination of several models into one prediction tends to have no significant or timely interpretation. Interpretation is deemed ancillary to model accuracy. For example, models designed to separate and classify "spam" emails from "non-spam" emails as well as models designed to evaluate the price of a real estate.

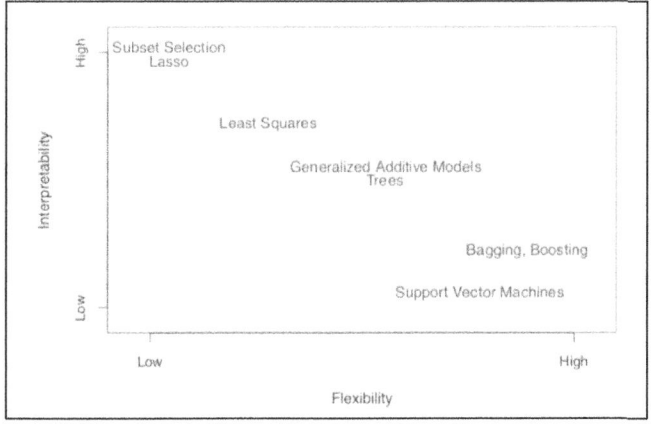

Assessing Model Accuracy

There is no-one-size-fits-all or jack-of-all-trades technique in the field of statistics, it is impossible for a single technique to dominate across the vast variety of data sets. The most frequently used metric in the "regression" environment is the "mean squared error (MSE)", which can be used for quantification of the extent to which the "predicted answer value" is near to the true answer value for the target observation. For the predicted responses that are extremely close to the true responses, the MSE is computed as small but if the predicted and true responses vary considerably with respect to some of the observations then the MSE is computed as large. For example, assume we have clinical data for a number of patients such as their weight, blood pressure, gender, age, history of family illnesses along with information stating if they are diabetic or not. This patient-related data set can be used to train a statistical technique for predicting diabetes risk on the basis of clinical measures.

$$MSE = \frac{1}{n}\sum_{i=1}^{n}(y_i - \hat{f}(x_i))^2,$$

The most frequently used metric in the "classification" environment is the "confusion matrix". The core characteristic of statistical learning is that with continuous learning the model becomes more flexible and the training errors are reduced, although the test error may not be decreased.

Bias and Variance

In the context of machine learning, bias is defined as "the simplified assumptions made by a model to further simplify the learning of the target task". Parametric models are designed with an inherent strong bias, which makes learning much faster and simpler but significantly reduces the overall flexibility of the model for a wider variety of applications. "Decision trees", "k-nearest neighbors", and "support vector machines" are categorized as low-bias algorithms for machine learning models. The "high-bias" ML algorithms are "linear regression", "linear discriminant analysis", and "logistic regression".

In the context of machine learning, a variance can be defined "as the amount by which the estimation of the target function will be altered with the use of a different training data set". Non-parametric models" with high flexibility tend to have a high variance score. "Linear regression", "linear discriminant analysis", and "logistic regression" are low-variance ML algorithms. "Decision Trees", "k-Nearest neighbors", and "Support Vector Machines" are high variance ML algorithms.

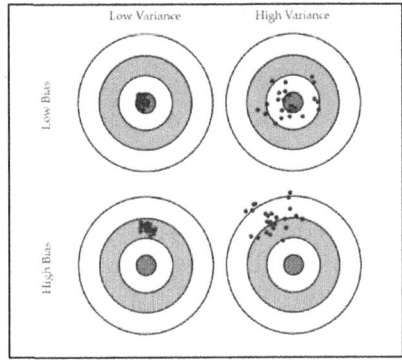

The Trade-Off between Bias and Variance

In the context of statistical learning, "bias" and "variance" are inversely related. For a model exhibiting high bias, the variance score will be reduced significantly and vice versa. There is a compromise that needs to be made between these two factors, which drives the selection of the model and its configuration to resolve the targeted issue by achieving a fine balance between the two. The right level of flexibility is critical to the efficiency and performance of any statistical learning technique in both the "regression" and "classification" environments. The trade-off between "bias" and "variance" of the model and the subsequent "U-shape" in the test error poses a major challenge.

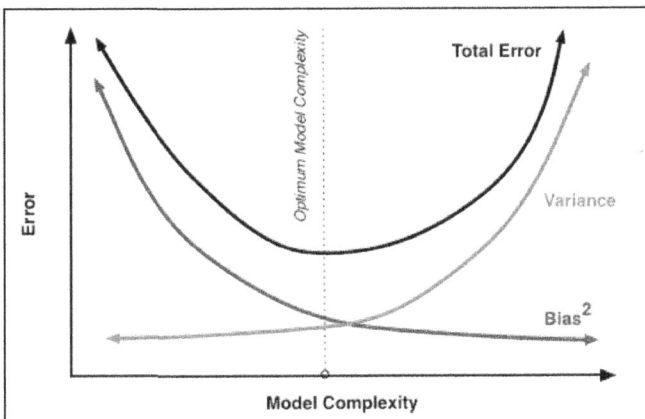

Chapter 3: Machine Learning Algorithms

Machines are now able to learn from and train on their own by using previous computations and underlying algorithms to produce high-quality, easily reproducible decisions and results. Machine learning has been around for a long time now, but the recent developments in machine learning algorithms have made it possible for machines to process and analyze large volumes of data efficiently. This is accomplished by using high speed and frequency automation to apply advanced and complex mathematical calculations to the machines. The sophisticated computing machines of today are able to rapidly evaluate the ginormous volumes of data and produce faster and more accurate results. Companies that use machine learning algorithms have improved flexibility to adapt the training data set to meet their business requirements and train the machines accordingly. These tailor-made machine learning algorithms allow businesses to identify potential hazards and growth opportunities. Typically, in collaboration with artificial intelligence technology and cognitive technologies, machine learning algorithms are used to produce computers that are highly effective and extremely efficient in processing huge amounts of information or big data and to produce highly accurate results.

Hundreds and thousands of machine learning algorithms have already been generated as this research field continues to proliferate. Here are some of the most commonly used algorithms categorized on the basis of its type of machine learning:

SUPERVISED Learning Algorithms

To refresh your memory, "Supervised learning" is driven by the data scientists who provide guidance for teaching the algorithm of what conclusions it must make, using predefined training data set. "Supervised learning" requires information on all possible outputs of the algorithm and the training data set that has already been labeled with expected or correct results.

Let's look at some of these supervised learning algorithms used to develop machine learning models.

1. Classification

The method of "classification" is another class of "supervised machine learning", which can generate predictions or explanations for a "class value". For example, this method can be used to predict if an online customer will actually purchase a particular product. The result generated will be reported as a yes or no response i.e. "buyer" or "not a buyer". But techniques of classification are not restricted to two classes. A classification technique, for instance, could assist to evaluate whether a specified picture includes a sedan or an SUV. The output will be three different values in this case: 1) the picture contains a sedan, 2) the picture contains an SUV, or 3) the picture does not contain either a sedan or an SUV.

"Logistic regression" is considered the easiest classification algorithm, though the term comes across as a "regression" technique, but that is far from reality. "Logistic regression" generates estimations for the likelihood of an event taking place based on single or multiple input values. For example, to generate estimation for the likelihood of a student being accepted to a specific university, a "logistic regression" will use the standardized testing scores and university testing scores for a student as inputs. The generated prediction is a probability, ranging between '0' and '1', where '1' is complete assurance. For the student, if the estimated likelihood is greater than 0.5, then the prediction would be that they will be accepted. If the projected probability is less than 0.5, the prediction would be that they will be denied admission. Logistic regression enables the creation of a line graph that can represent the "decision boundary".

The "Logistic regression" technique is "borrowed" by ML technology from the world of statistical analysis. It is widely used for binary classification tasks that involve two different class values. Logistic regression is so named owing to the fundamental statistical function at the root of this technique called the "logistic function". Statisticians created the "logistic function", also called the "sigmoid function", to define the attributes of population growth in ecosystems which continues to grow rapidly and nearing the maximum carrying capacity of the environment. The logistic function is "an S-shaped curve capable of taking any real-valued integer and mapping it to a value between '0' and '1', but never precisely at those boundaries, where 'e' is the base of the natural log (Euler's number or the EXP)" and 'value' is the actual numerical value that you are looking to transform".

"1 / (1 + e^-value)"

Here is a graph of figures ranging from "-5 and 5" which has been transformed by the logistic function into a range between 0 and 1.

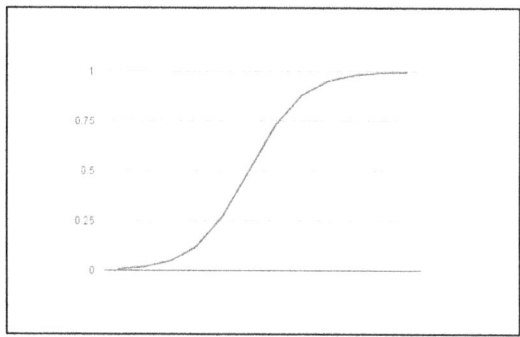

Similar to the "linear regression" technique, "logistic regression" utilizes an equation for data representation.

Input values (X) are grouped linearly to forecast an output value (Y), with the use of weights or coefficient values (presented as the symbol "Beta"). The primary difference from "linear regression" is that the modeled output value tends to be binary (0 or 1) instead of a range of values.

Below is an example of the "logistic regression" equation, where 'Y' is "the expected result", 'b0' is the "bias or intercept term" and 'b1' is "the single input value coefficient (X)". Every column in the input data set has a connected coefficient "b" with it, which is required to be learned from the training data set. The actual model representation, which is stored in the system memory or a file would be "the coefficients in the equation (the beta values)".

"y=e^(b0 + b1*x)/(1 +e^(b0 + b1*x))"

The "logistic regression" algorithm's coefficients (the beta values) must be estimated on the basis of the training data. This can be accomplished using another statistical technique called "maximum-likelihood estimation", which is a popular ML algorithm utilized by a multitude of other ML algorithms. "Maximum-likelihood estimation" works by making certain assumptions about the distribution of the input data set.

A machine learning model that can predict a value nearer to "1" for the "default class" and a value nearer to "0" for the "other class" can be obtained by employing the best coefficients of the model. The underlying assumption for maximum likelihood of the "logistic regression" technique is that "a search procedure attempts to find values for the coefficients that will reduce the error in the probabilities estimated by the model pertaining to the input data set (e.g. probability of '0' if the input data is not the default class)".

Without going into mathematical details, it is sufficient to state that you will be using "a minimization algorithm to optimize the values of the best coefficients from your training data set". In practice, this can be achieved with the use of an effective "numerical optimization algorithm", for example, the "Quasi-newton" technique).

Generating predictions using logistic regression

It is as straightforward as plugging in measurements into the "logistic regression" equation and calculating the outcome to generate predictions with the "logistic regression" model. Let's take a look at an example to solidify this concept. Let's assume there is a model that is capable of generating predictions if an individual is masculine or woman depending on with fictitious values of their height. If the value of the height for an individual is set as 150 cm, would the individual be predicted as a male or female? Assuming we have already discovered the values of coefficients "b0= -100" and "b1= 0.6". By leveraging the above equation, the probability of male with a height of 150 cm or "P(male|height=150)" can be easily calculated. The function EXP() will be used for "e" because if you log this instance into your spreadsheet, this is what you can use:

"$y = e^{(b0 + b1*X)} / (1 + e^{(b0 + b1*X)})$"

"$y = exp(-100 + 0.6*150) / (1 + EXP(-100 + 0.6*X))$"

"$y = 0.0000453978687$"

Or a near "0" probability that the individual is a male.

In theory, we can simply use probabilities. But since this is a "classification" algorithm and we want a sharp outcome; the probabilities can be tagged on to a binary class value. For instance, the model can predict "0" if "p (male) < 0.51" and predict "1" if "p (male) >= 0.5". Now that you understand how to generate predictions using "logistic regression", you can easily pre-process the training data set to get the most out of this technique.

The assumptions made pertaining to the distribution and relations within the data set by the "logistic regression" technique are nearly identical to the assumptions made in the "linear regression" technique.

A lot of research has been done to define these hypotheses and to use accurate probabilistic and statistical language. It is recommended to use these as directives or thumb rules and experiment with various processes for data preparation.

The ultimate goal of the "predictive modeling" machine learning initiative is the generation of highly accurate predictions rather than an analysis of the outcomes. Considering everything some assumptions could be broken if the designed model is stable and has high performance.

- **"Binary Output Variable":** This may be evident as we have already discussed it earlier, but "logistic regression" is designed specifically for issues with "binary (two-class) classification". This will generate predictions for the probability of a default class instance that can be tagged into a classification of "0" or "1".
- **"Remove Noise":** Logistic regression does not assume errors in the "output variable ('y')", therefore, the "outliers and potentially misclassified" cases should be removed from the training data set.
- **"Gaussian Distribution":** Logistic regression can be considered as a type of "linear algorithm but with a non-linear transform on the output". It assumes a linear connection with the output between the input variables. Data transforms of the input variables may lead to a more accurate model with a higher capability of revealing the linear relationships of the data set. For instance, to better reveal these relationships, we could utilize "log", "root", "Box-Cox" and other single variable transformations.
- **"Remove Correlated Inputs":** If you have various highly correlated inputs, the model could potentially be "over-fit" similar to the "linear regression" technique. To address this issue, you can "calculate the pairwise correlations between all input data points and remove the highly correlated inputs".
- **"Failure to converge":** It is likely for the "expected likelihood estimation" method that is trained on the coefficients to fail to converge. It

could occur if the data set contains several highly correlated inputs or the data is very limited (e.g. loads of "0" in the input data).

"Naïve Bayes classifier algorithm" is another "classification" learning algorithm with a wide variety of applications. It is a method of classification derived from the "Bayes theorem", which assumes predictors are independent of one another. Simply put, a "Naïve Bayes classifier" assumes that "all the features in a class are unrelated to the existence of any other feature in that class". For instance, if input data has an image of a fruit that is green, round, and about 10 inches in diameter, the model can consider the input to be a watermelon. Although these attributes rely on one another or the presence of a specific feature, all of the characteristics contribute independently to the probability that the image of the fruit is that of a watermelon, hence it is referred to as "Naive". "Naïve Bayes model" for large volumes of data sets is relatively simple to construct and extremely effective.

"Naïve Bayes" has reportedly outperformed even the most advanced techniques of classification, along with its simplicity of development. "Bayes theorem" can also provide the means to calculate the posterior probability "P(c|x)" using "P(c), P(x) and P(x)". On the basis of the equation shown in the picture below, where the probability of "c" can be calculated if "x" has already occurred.

"P(c|x)" is the posterior probability of "class (c, target)" provided by the "predictor (x, attributes)". "P(c)" is the class's previous probability. "P(x|c)" is the probability of the class provided by the predictor. "P(x)" is the predictor's prior probability.

$$P(c|x) = \frac{P(x|c)P(c)}{P(x)}$$

Likelihood — $P(x|c)$; Class Prior Probability — $P(c)$; Posterior Probability — $P(c|x)$; Predictor Prior Probability — $P(x)$

$$P(c|X) = P(x_1|c) \times P(x_2|c) \times \cdots \times P(x_n|c) \times P(c)$$

Here is an example to better explain the application of the "Bayes Theorem". The picture below represents the data set pertaining to the problem of identifying suitable weather days to play golf. The columns depict the weather features of the day and the rows contain individual entries. Considering the first row of the data set, it can be concluded that the weather will be too hot and humid with rain so the day is not suitable to play golf. Now the primary assumption here is that all these features or predictors are independent of one another. The other assumption being made here is that all the predictors have the potentially same effect on the end result. Meaning, if the day was windy it would have the same relevance to the decision of playing golf as the rain. In this example, the variable (c) is the class (playing golf) representing the decision if the weather is suitable for golf and variable (x) represents the features or predictors.

	OUTLOOK	TEMPERATURE	HUMIDITY	WINDY	PLAY GOLF
0	Rainy	Hot	High	False	No
1	Rainy	Hot	High	True	No
2	Overcast	Hot	High	False	Yes
3	Sunny	Mild	High	False	Yes
4	Sunny	Cool	Normal	False	Yes
5	Sunny	Cool	Normal	True	No
6	Overcast	Cool	Normal	True	Yes
7	Rainy	Mild	High	False	No
8	Rainy	Cool	Normal	False	Yes
9	Sunny	Mild	Normal	False	Yes
10	Rainy	Mild	Normal	True	Yes
11	Overcast	Mild	High	True	Yes
12	Overcast	Hot	Normal	False	Yes
13	Sunny	Mild	High	True	No

2. Regression

The "regression" techniques fall under the category of supervised machine learning. They help predict or describe a particular numerical value based on the set of prior information, such as anticipating the cost of a property based on previous cost information for similar characteristics. Regression techniques vary from simple (such as "linear regression") to complex (such as "regular linear regression", "polynomial regression", "decision trees", "random forest regression" and "neural networks", among others).

The simplest method of all is **"linear regression"**, where the line's "mathematical equation (y= m*x+b) is used to model the data collection". Multiple "data pairs (x, y)" can train a "linear regression" model by calculating the position and slope of a line that can decrease the total distance between the data points and the line. In other words, the calculation of the "slope (m)" and "y-intercept (b)" is used for a line that produces the highest approximation for data observations.

For example, using the "linear regression" technique to generate predictions for the energy consumption (in kWh) of houses by collecting the age of the house, no. of bedrooms, square footage area and a number of installed electronic equipment. Now, we have more than one input (year built, square footage) it is possible to use "linear multi-variable regression". The underlying process is the same as "one-to-one linear regression", however, the line created was based on the number of variables in multi-dimensional space.

3. Support Vector Machines

"Support Vector Machine" or (SVM) is another form of "supervised ML algorithm", used for "classification" and/or "regression", where the data set trains SVM on "classes" in order to be able to classify new inputs. This algorithm operates by classifying the data into various "classes" by discovering a line (hyperplane) that divides the collection of training data into "classes". Due to the availability of various linear hyper-planes, this algorithm attempts to maximize the distance between the different "classes" involved, which is called as "margin maximization". By identifying the line that maximizes the class distance, the likelihood of generalizing apparent to unseen data can be improved.

SVM's can be categorized into two as follows:

- "Linear SVM's" – The training data or classifiers can be divided by a hyper-plane.
- "Non-Linear SVM's" – Unlike linear SVMs, in "non-linear SVM's" the possibility to separate the training data with a hyper-plane is non-existent. For example, the Face Detection training data consists of a group of facial images and another group of non-facial images. The training data is so complicated under such circumstances, that it is difficult to obtain a feature

representation of every single vector. It is extremely complex to separate the facial data set linearly from the non-facial data set.

SVM is widely used by different economic organizations for stock market forecasting. For example, SVM is leveraged to compare relative stock performances of various stocks in the same industrial sector. The classifications generated by SVM, aids in the investment-related decision-making process.

4. Decision Trees

A machine learning decision tree can be defined as "a tree-like graphical representation of the decision-making process, by taking into consideration all the conditions or factors that can influence the decision and the consequences of those decisions". Decision trees are considered one of the simplest "supervised machine learning algorithms", with three main elements: "branch nodes" representing conditions of the data set, "edges" representing the ongoing decision process and "leaf nodes" representing the end of the decision.

The two types of decision trees are: "Classification tree" that is used to classify data based on the current data available in the system; "Regression tree" which is used to make a forecast for predictions for future events based on the current data in the system. Both of these trees are heavily used in machine learning algorithms. A widely used terminology for decision trees is "Classification and Regression trees" or "CART".

Let's look at how you can build a simple decision tree based on a real-life example.

Step 1: Identify what decision needs to be made, which will serve as a "root node" for the decision tree. For this example, a decision needs to be made on "What would you like to do over the weekend?". Unlike real trees, the decision tree has its roots on top instead of the bottom.

Step 2: Identify conditions or influencing factors for your decision which will serve as "branch nodes" for the decision tree. For this example, conditions could include "would you like to spend the weekend alone or with your friends?" and "how is the weather going to be?".

Step 3: As you answer the conditional questions, you may run into additional conditions that you might have ignored. You will now continue to your final decision by processing all the conditional questions individually, these bifurcations will serve as "edges" of your decision tree.

Step 4: Once you have processed all of the permutations and combinations and eventually made your final decision, that final decision will serve as the "leaf node" of your decision tree. Unlike "branch nodes", there are no further bifurcations possible from a "leaf node".

Here is the graphical representation of your decision for the example above:

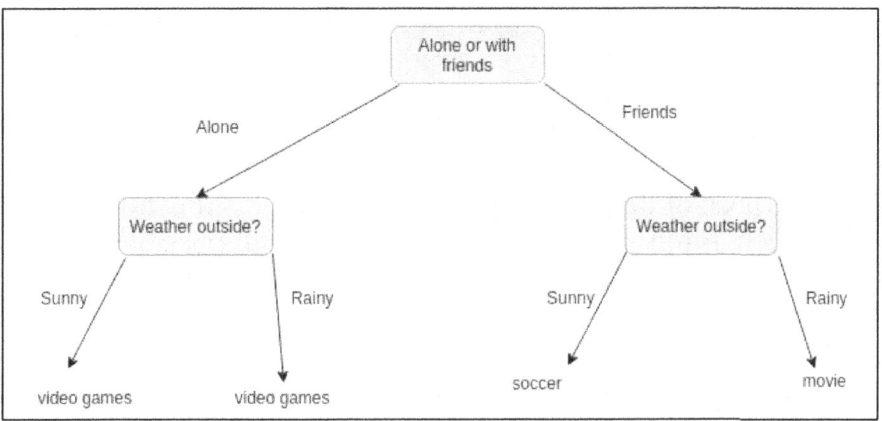

As you would expect from a decision tree, you have obtained a "model representing a set of sequential and hierarchical decisions that ultimately lead to some final decision". This example is at a very high-level to help you develop an understanding of the concept of decision trees. The data science and machine learning decision trees are much more complicated and bigger with hundreds and thousands of branch nodes and edges.

The best tool on the market to visualize and understand decision trees is "Scikit-Learn". Machine learning decisions tree models can be developed using two steps: "Induction" and "Pruning".

Induction
In this step, the decision trees are actually developed by selecting and modeling all of the sequential and hierarchical decision boundaries on the basis of the existing data set. For your ease of understanding, here are 4 high-level steps required to develop the tree:

1. Gather, classify, and label the training data set with "feature variables" and "classification or regression output".
2. Identify the best and most cost-effective feature within the training data set that will be used as the point for bifurcating the data.
3. Based on the possible values of the selected "best feature", create subsets of data by bifurcating the data set. These bifurcations will define the "branch nodes" of the decision tree, wherein each node serves as a point of bifurcation based on specific features from the data set.
4. Iteratively develop new tree nodes with the use of data subsets gathered from step 3. These bifurcations will continue until an optimal point is reached, where maximum accuracy is achieved while minimizing the number of bifurcations or nodes.

Pruning

The inherent purpose of decision trees is to support training and self-learning of the system, which often requires overloading of all possible conditions and influencing factors that might affect the final result. To overcome the challenge of setting the correct output for the least number of instances per node, developers make a "safe bet" by settling for that "least number" as rather small. This results in a high number of bifurcations on necessary, making for a very complex and large decision tree. This is where "tree pruning" comes into the picture. The verb "prune" literally means "to reduce especially by eliminating superfluous matter". This is the same kind of concept taken from real-life tree pruning and applied to the machine learning decision tree pruning process.

The process of pruning effectively reduces the overall complexity of the decision tree by "transforming and compressing strict and rigid decision boundaries into generalized and smooth boundaries". The number of bifurcations in the decision trees determines the overall complexity of the tree. The easiest and widely used pruning method is reviewing individual branch nodes and evaluating the effect of its removal on the cost function of the decision tree. If the cost function has little to no effect of the removal, then the branch node under review can be easily removed or "pruned".

5. Ensemble Method

Think that you have chosen to construct a car because you are not pleased with the variety of cars available in the market and online. You may start by discovering the best option for every component that you need. The resulting car will outshine all the other alternatives with the assembly of all these excellent components.

"Ensemble methods" use the same concept of mixing several predictive models (controlled machine learning) to obtain results of greater quality than any of the models can generate on their own. The "Random Forest" algorithms, for instance, is an "ensemble method" that collates various trained "Decision Trees" with different data set samples. Consequently, the quality of predictions generated by the "Random Forest" method is better than the quality of the estimated predictions generated by only one "Decision Tree".

Think of "ensemble methods" as an approach for reducing a single machine learning model's variance and bias. This is essential because, under certain circumstances, any specified model may be accurate but completely incorrect under other circumstances. The relative accuracy could be overturned with another model. The quality of the predictions is balanced by merging the two models. In the context of machine learning, the concept of random forest pertains to "an ensemble approach for finding the decision tree that best fits the training data by developing multiple decision trees with a random selection of features".

6. K-nearest Neighbors Classifier

The "k-nearest neighbors (k-NN)" algorithm is referred to as "a non-parametric method used for classification and regression in pattern recognition". In cases of classification and regression, "the input consists of the nearest k closest training examples in the feature space". K-NN is a form of "instance-based learning", or "lazy learning", in which the function is only locally estimated and all calculations are delayed until classification. The output is driven by the fact, whether the classification or regression method is used for "k-NN":

- "k-nearest neighbors classification" - The "output" is a member of the class. An "object" is classified by its neighbors' plurality vote, assigning the object to the most prevalent class among its nearest "k-neighbors", where "k" denotes a small positive integer. If k= 1, the "object" is simply allocated to the closest neighbor's class.
- "k-nearest neighbors regression" - The output is the object's property value, which is computed as an average of the "k-nearest neighbors" values.

A helpful method for both "classification" and "regression" can be assigning of weights to the neighbors' contributions, to allow closer neighbors to make more contributions in the average, compared to the neighbors located far apart. For instance, a known "weighting scheme" is to assign individual neighbor a weight of "$1/d$", where "d" denotes the distance from the neighbor. The neighbors are selected from a set of objects for which the "class" (for "k-NN classification") or the feature value of the "object" (for "k-NN regression") has already been identified.

UNSUPERVISED Learning Algorithms

To refresh your memory, "Unsupervised learning" is widely used to define how the machine can generate "inferred features" to elucidate a concealed construct from the stack of unlabeled and unclassified data collection. These algorithms can explore the data in order to define a structure within the data mass.

Clustering

We enter the category of unsupervised machine learning, with "clustering methods" because its objective is to "group or cluster observations with comparable features". Clustering methods do not use output data to train but allow the output to be defined by the algorithm. Only data visualizations can be used in clustering techniques to check the solution's quality.

"K-Means clustering", where 'K' is used to represent the number of "clusters" that the customer elects to generate and is the most common clustering method. (Note that different methods for selecting K value, such as the "elbow technique", are available.)

Steps used by K-Means clustering to process the data points:

1. The data centers are selected randomly by 'K'.
2. Assigns each data point to the nearest centers that have been randomly generated.
3. Re-calculates each cluster's center.
4. If centers do not change (or have minor change), the process will be completed.

Otherwise, we'll go back to step 2. (Set a maximum amount of iterations in advance to avoid getting stuck in an infinite loop, if the center of the cluster continues to alter.)

The following plot applies "K-Means" to a building data set. Each column in the plot shows each building's efficiency. The four measurements relate to air conditioning, heating, installed electronic appliances (refrigerators, TV) and cooking gas. For simplicity of interpretation of the results, 'K' can be set to value '2' for clustering, wherein one cluster will be selected as an efficient building group and the other cluster as an inefficient building group. You see the place of the structures on the left as well as a couple of the building characteristics used as inputs on the right: installed electronic appliances and heating.

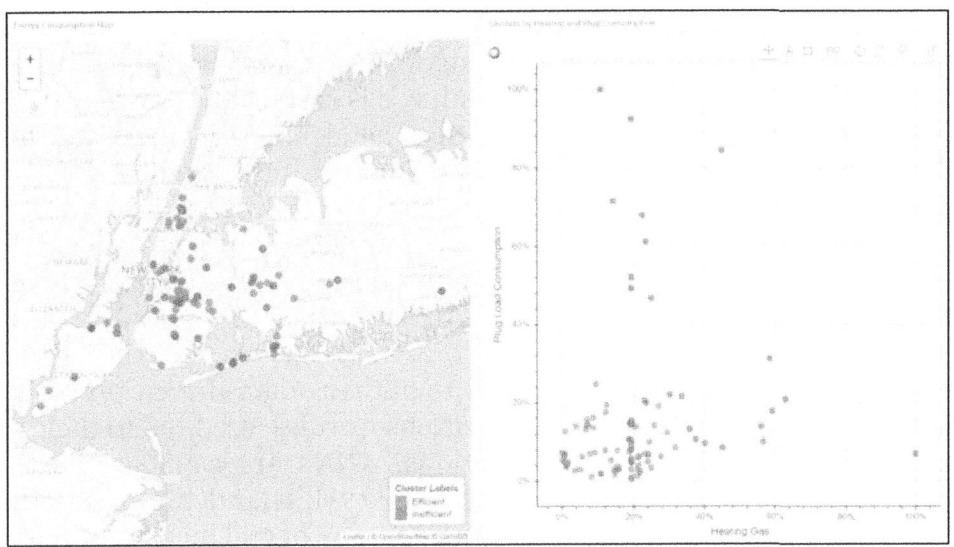

Artificial Neural Networks

"Artificial Neural Networks" or (ANN) have been developed with inspiration from the structure of the human brain and utilizes numerous processing units like human neurons or nodes working as one. Each ANN has numerous concealed layers including an input and an output layer. These neurons are connected in a complex with one another by weighted links. A solitary neuron is capable of accepting input from various neurons. When a neuron gets activated, it casts a "weighted vote" to control the activation of the subsequent neuron that is collecting that input. An algorithm modifies these weights in accordance with the training data to optimize learning. A simple algorithm called "fire together, wire together" increases the weight between two connected neurons when the activation of either neuron leads to subsequent activation of the other neuron. "Concepts" are formed and distributed through the sub-network of shared neurons.

The most widely recognized ANN deal with the unidirectional progression of information and are called "Feedforward ANN". However, ANN can also be used for bidirectional and cyclic progression of information to gain state equilibrium. ANNs are less dependent on prior assumptions and able to learn from prior cases by modifying the connected weights. They can be utilized with either supervised or unsupervised learning. The use of supervised learning will generate correct ANN output for every input pattern. By varying the weights, the error between the target output and the output produced by ANN can be effectively minimized. For example, a type of "supervised learning algorithm" called "reinforced learning", informs the ANN whether the output it produced is correct or not in lieu of directly supplying the correct output. On the other hand, an "unsupervised learning algorithm" is capable of providing a variety of input patterns to the ANN which are then processed by the ANN to self-explore the relationship between the provided input patterns and learn to categorize them accordingly. Artificial Neural Networks utilizing a combination of "supervised" and "unsupervised" learning is also available.

ANN is the choice of the learning model to address data-driven problems with unknown or difficult to comprehend algorithms or rules, credited to their defined data structure and non-linear computations. ANNs are capable of efficiently processing complex information and can easily withstand multi-variable data errors. Problems requiring a complete understanding of and insight into the actual process are not suitable for the ANN model, given its black box nature providing no view into the underlying process.

ANNs are widely used to resolve problems that require:

- **"Pattern classification"** by assigning input pattern to one of the pre-determined classes. For example, classification of land-based on satellite images.

- **"Clustering"**, which is simply an unsupervised pattern classification model. For example, the prediction of the ecological status of water streams using defined input patterns.
- **"Function approximation or regression"**, which is capable of creating a function out of the provided set of training patterns. For example, prediction of ozone concentration in the atmosphere, estimation of the amount of nitrate in groundwater and modeling water supply.
- **"Prediction"**, which utilized prior data samples in a time series to estimate the output. For example, prediction of air and water quality.
- **"Optimization"**, which is used to maximize or minimize a "cost function" subject to predefined constraints. For example, calibration of infiltration equations.
- **"Retrieval by content"**, which is capable of recalling memory even if the input is incomplete or distorted. For example, using satellite images to produce water quality proxies.
- **"Process control"**, which seeks to keep the velocity under changing data load close to constant by changing the throttle angle. For example, engine speed control.

Building a Data Pipeline for Machine Learning

Computer programmers will typically "define a pipeline for data as it flows through their machine learning model". Every stage of the pipeline utilizes the data generated from the previous stage once it has processed the data as needed. The word "pipeline" can be a little misleading as it indicates a unidirectional flow of data, when in reality the machine learning pipelines are "cyclical and iterative", as each stage would be repeated in order to eventually produce an effective algorithm.

While looking to develop a machine learning model, programmers work in select development environments geared for "Statistics" and 'Machine Learning" such as Python and R among others. These environments enable training and testing of the models, using a single "sandboxed" environment while writing reasonably fewer lines of code. This is excellent for the development of interactive prototypes that can be quickly launched in the market, instead of developing production systems with low latency.

The primary goal of developing a machine learning pipeline is to construct a model with features listed below:

- Should allow for a reduction of system latency.
- Integration but loose coupling with other components of the model, such as data storage systems, reporting functionalities and "Graphical User Interface (GUI)".
- It should allow for horizontal as well as vertical scalability.
- It should be driven by messages, meaning the model should be able to communicate through the transfer of "asynchronous, non-blocking messages".
- Ability to generate effective calculations for management of the data set.
- It should be resilient to system errors and be able to recover with minimal to no supervision, known as breakdown management.
- It should be able to support "batch processing" as well as "real-time" processing of the input data.

Conventionally, data pipelines require "overnight batch processing", which means gathering the data, transmitting it with an "enterprise message bus" and then processing it to generate pre-calculated outcomes and guidelines for future transactions. While this model has proven to work in certain industrial sectors, in others, and particularly when it comes to machine learning models, "batch processing" doesn't meet the challenge.

The picture below demonstrates a machine learning data pipeline as applied to a real-time business problem in which attributes and projections are dependent on the time taken to generate the results. For instance, product recommendation systems used by Amazon, the system to estimate time of arrival used by Lyft, the system to recommend potential new links used by LinkedIn, search engines used by Airbnb, among others.

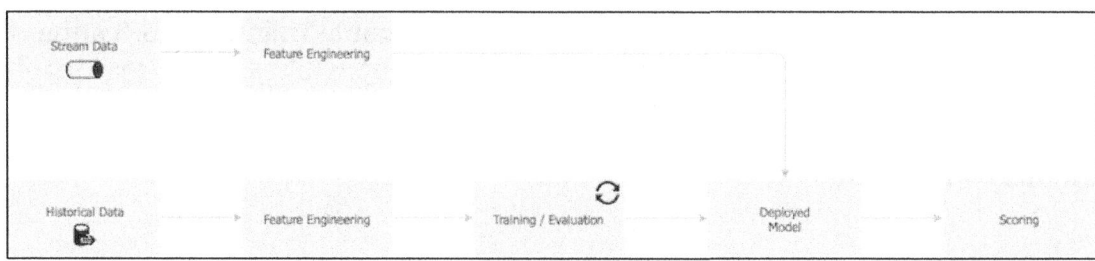

The swim lane diagram above consists of two explicitly specified components:

1. "Online Model Analytics": In the top swim lane of the picture, the elements of the application required for operation are depicted. It shows where the model is used to make decisions in real-time.

2. "Offline Data Discovery": The bottom swim lane shows the learning element of the model, which is used to analyze historical data and generate the machine learning model using the "batch processing" method.

There are 8 fundamental stages in the creation of a data pipeline, which are shown in the picture below and explained in detail here:

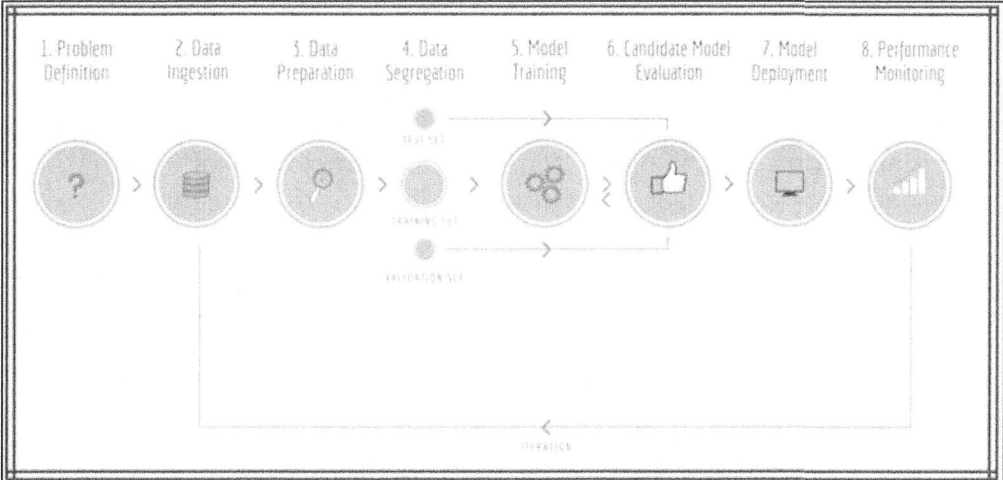

1. Problem Definition
In this stage, the business problem that needs to be resolved using a machine learning model will be identified and documented with all pertinent details.

2. Data Ingestion
The first stage of any machine learning workflow is to channel input data into a database server. The most important thing to remember is that the data is ingested raw and with no modification to enable us to have an invariable record of the original dataset. Data may be supplied from a variety of sources which can be acquired either through request or transmitted from other systems.

"NoSQL document databases" are best suited to store huge amount of defined and labeled as well as unorganized raw data, that is quickly evolving as they do not need to adhere to a predefined scheme. It even provides a "distributed, scalable and replicated data storage".

"Offline"
Data will flow in the "offline" layer to the raw data storage through an "Ingestion Service", which is a "composite orchestration service that is capable of encapsulating the data sourcing and persistence". A repository model is used internally to communicate with a data service that will interact with the data storage in exchange. When you save the data in the database, a unique batch Id will be given to the dataset, which allows for an effective query of the data as well as end-to-end tracking and monitoring of the data.

To be computationally efficient, the ingestion of the data is distributed into two folds.

- The first one is a specific pipeline for every dataset so that each of the datasets can be processed individually and simultaneously.
- The second aspect is that within each pipeline data can be divided to make the best of a variety of server cores, processors and perhaps even the entire server.

Distributing the prepping of data across several vertical and horizontal pipelines will reduce the total time required to perform the tasks.

The "ingestion service" would run at regular intervals on the basis of a predefined schedule (one or more times a day) or upon encountering a trigger. A subject will decouple producers (data source) from processors, which would be the data pipeline for this example, so when the source data is collected, the "producer system" will send a notification to the "broker" and subsequently the "embedded notification service" will respond by inducing ingestion of the data. The "notification service" would also inform the "broker" that the processing of the original dataset was completed with success and now the dataset is being stored in the database.

"Online"
The "Online Ingestion Service" makes up the entrance to the "streaming architecture" of the online layer, as it would decouple and manage the data flow

from the source to the processing and storage components by offering consistent, high performance, low latency functionalities. It also works as an enterprise-level "Data Bus". Data would be stored on a long-term "Raw Data Storage", which also serves as a mediating layer to the subsequent online streaming service for further processing in real-time. For instance, such techniques that are utilized in this case may be "Apache Kafka (pub/sub messaging system)" and "Apache Flume (data collection to the long-term database)". A variety of other similar techniques are available and can be selectively applied based on the technology stack of the business.

3. Data Preparation

After the information has been ingested, a centralized pipeline would be produced that can evaluate the condition of the data, meaning it would search for format variations, outliers, patterns, inaccurate, incomplete, or distorted information and correct any abnormalities through the process. The "feature engineering process" is also included in this stage. The 3 primary characters of a feature pipeline as depicted in the picture below are: "extraction, transformation, and selection".

Phase	Input	Output
Extract	Raw data	Feature
Transform	Feature	Feature
Select	List<Feature>	List<Feature>

Since this tends to be the most complicated component of any machine learning project, it is essential to introduce appropriate design patterns. In the context of coding, it implies the use of a factory technique to produce features on the basis of certain shared abstract function behavior and a strategy pattern for selecting the correct features at the time of execution can be considered a logical approach. It is important to take into consideration the composition and re-usability of the pipeline while structuring the "feature extractors" and the "transformers".

The selection of functionalities could be attributed to the caller or could be automated. For instance, a "chi-square statistical test" can be applied to classify the impact of each functionality on the concept label, while discarding the low impact features before starting to train the model. To accomplish this, a number of "selector APIs" can be identified. In any case, a unique Id must be allocated to each feature set so as to make sure that the features used as model inputs and for impact scoring are consistent. Overall, it is necessary to assemble a data preparation pipeline into a set of unalterable transformations, which could be readily combined. Now the importance of "testing and high code coverage" will become a critical factor in the success of the model.

4. Data Segregation

The primary goal of the machine learning model is the development of a high accuracy model on the basis of the quality of its forecasts and predictions for information derived from the new input data, which was not part of the training dataset. Therefore, the available labeled dataset will be utilized as a "proxy" for future unknown input data by dividing the data into training and testing datasets. Many approaches are available to split the dataset and some of the most widely used techniques are:

- Using either the default or customized ratio to sequentially divide the dataset into two subsets in order to ensure that there is no overlap in the sequence in which the data appears from the source. For example, you could select the first 75% of data to train the model and the consequent 25% of data to test the accuracy of the model.
- Splitting the dataset into training and testing subset using a default or custom ratio with a random seed. For example, you could choose a random 75% of the dataset to train the model and the remaining 25% of the random dataset to test the model.
- Using either of these techniques ("sequential vs. random") and then also mixing the data within each data subset.
- Using a customized injected approach for splitting the data when extensive control over the segregation of the data is required.

Technically the data segregation stage is not considered as an independent machine learning pipeline, however, an "API" or tool has to be provided to support this stage. In order to return the required datasets, the next 2 stages ("model training" and "model assessment") must be able to call this "API". As far as the organization of the code is concerned, a "strategy pattern" is required so that the "caller service" can select the appropriate algorithm during execution and the capability to inject the percentage or random seed is obviously required. The "API" must also be prepared to return the information with or without labels, to train and test the model respectively. A warning can be created and passed along with the dataset to secure the "caller service" from defining parameters that could trigger the uneven distribution of the data.

5. Model Training

The model pipelines are always "offline", and its schedule will vary from a matter of few hours to just one run per day, based entirely on the complexity of the application. The training can also be initiated by time and event, and not just by the system schedulers.

It includes a number of libraries of machine learning algorithms such as "linear regression, ARIMA, k-means, decision trees" and many more, which are designed to make provisions for the rapid production of new model types as well as making the models interchangeable. Containment is also important for the integration of "third-Party APIs" using the "facade pattern" (at this stage the "Python Jupyter notebook" can also be called).

You have several choices for "parallelization":

- A specialized pipeline for individual models tends to be the easiest method, which means all the models can be operated at the same time.
- Another approach would be to duplicate the training dataset, i.e. the dataset can be divided and each data set will contain a replica of the model. This approach is favored for the models that require all fields of an instance for performing the computations, for example, "LDA", 'MF".
- Another approach can be to parallelize the entire model, meaning the model can be separated and every partition can be responsible for the maintenance of a fraction of the variables. This approach is best suited for linear machine learning models like "Linear Regression", "Support Vector Machine".
- Lastly, a hybrid strategy could also be utilized by leveraging a combination of one or more of the approaches mentioned above.

It is important to implement train the model while taking error tolerance into consideration. The data checkpoints and failures on training partitions must also be taken into account, for example, if every partition fails due to some transient problem like timeout, then every partition could be trained again.

6. Candidate Model Evaluation

The model evaluation stage is also always "offline". By drawing a comparison of the predictions generated with the testing dataset with the actual data values using several key performance indicators and metrics, the "predictive performance" of a model can be measured. To generate a prediction on future input data, the "best" model from the testing subset will be preferred. An evaluator library consisting of a number of evaluators can be designed to generate accuracy metrics such as "ROC curve" or "PR curve", which can also be stored in a data storage against the model. Once more, the same techniques are applied to make it possible to flexibly combine and switch between evaluators.

The "Model Evaluation Service" will request the testing dataset from the "Data Segregation API" to orchestrate the training and testing of the model. Moreover, the corresponding evaluators will be applied for the model originating from the "Model Candidate repository". The findings of the test will be returned to and saved in the repository. In order to develop the final machine learning model, an incremental procedure, hyper-parameter optimization, as well as regularization methods, would be used. The best model would be deemed as deployable to the production environment and eventually released in the market. The deployment information will be published by the "notification service".

7. Model Deployment

The machine learning model with the highest performance will be marked for deployment for "offline (asynchronous)" and "online (synchronous)" prediction generation. It is recommended to deploy multiple models at the same time to ensure the transfer from obsolete to the current model is made smoothly, this implies that the services must continue to respond to forecast requirements without any lapse, while the new model is being deployed.

Historically, the biggest issue concerning deployment has been pertaining to the coding language required to operate the models that have not been the same as the coding language used to build them. It is difficult to operationalize a "Python or R" based model in production using languages such as "C++, C #or Java". This also leads to a major reduction in the performance in terms of speed and accuracy, of the model being deployed.

This problem can be dealt with in a few respects as listed below:

- Implementing new language for rewriting the code, for example, "Python to C# translate".
- Creating customized "DSL (Domain Specific Language)" to define the model.
- Creating a "micro-service" that is accessible through "RESTful APIs".
- Implementing an "API first" approach through the course of the deployment.
- Creating containers to store the code independently.
- Adding serial numbers to the model and loading them to "in-memory key-value storage".

In practice, the deployment activities required to implement an actual model are automated through the use of "continuous delivery implementation", which ensures the packaging of the necessary files, validation of the model via a robust test suite as well as the final deployment into a running container. An automated building pipeline can be used to execute the tests, which makes sure that the short, self-containing and stateless unit tests are conducted first. When the model has passed these tests, its quality will be evaluated in larger integrations and by executing regression tests. If both the test phases have been cleared, the model is deemed ready for deployment in the production environment.

8. Model Scoring

The terms "Model Scoring" and "Model Serving" are being used synonymously throughout the industry. Model Scoring" can be defined as "the process of generating new values with a given model and new input data". Instead of the term "prediction", a generic term "score" is being used to account for the distinct values it may lead to, as listed below:

- List of product recommendations.
- Numerical values, for the "time series models" as well as "regression models".
- A "probability value" indicates the probability that a new input can be added to a category that already exists in the model.
- An alphabetical value indicating the name of a category that most closely resembles the new input data.

- A "predicted class or outcome" can also be listed as a model score particularly for "classification models".

After the models have been deployed, they can be utilized to score on the basis of the feature data supplied by the prior pipelines or provided directly by a "client service". It is critical that the models generate predictions with the same accuracy and high performance, in both the online and the offline mode.

"Offline"
The "scoring service" would be optimized in the offline layer for a big volume of data to achieve high performance and generate "fire and forget" predictions. A model is able to send an "asynchronous request" to initiate its scoring, however, it must wait for the batch scoring process to be completed and gain access to the batch scoring results before the scoring can be started. The "scoring service" will prepare the data, produce the features as well as retrieve additional features from the "Feature Data Store". The results of the scoring will be stored in the "Score Data Store", once the scoring has been completed. The "broker" will be informed of the completion of the scoring by receiving a notification from the service. This event is detected by the model, which will then proceed to collect the scoring results.

"Online"
In the "online" mode, a "client" will send a request to the "Online Scoring Service". The client can potentially request to invoke a specific version of the model, to allow the "Model Router" to inspect the request and subsequently transfer the request to the corresponding model.
According to request and in the same way as the offline layer, the "client service" will also prepare the data, produces the features and if needed, fetch additional functions from the "Feature Data Store". When the scoring has been done, the scores will be stored in the "Score Data Store" and then returned via the network to the "client service".

Totally dependent on the use case, results may be supplied asynchronously to the "client", which means the scored will be reported independent of the request using one of the two methods below:

- Push: After the scores have been obtained, they will be pushed to the "client" in the form of a "notification".

- Poll: After the scores have been produced, they will be saved in a "low read-latency database" and the client will poll the database at a regular interval to fetch any existing predictions.

There are a couple of techniques listed below, that can be used to reduce the time taken by the system to deliver the scores, once the request has been received:

- The input features can be saved in a "low-read latency in-memory data store".
- The predictions that have already been computed through an "offline batch-scoring" task can be cached for convenient access as dictated by the use-case, since "offline predictions" may lose their relevance.

9. Performance Monitoring

A very well-defined "performance monitoring solution" is necessary for every machine learning model. For the "model serving clients", some of the data points that you may want to observe include:

- "Model Identifier"
- "Deployment date and time"
- The "number of times" the model was served.
- The "average, min and max" of the time it took to serve the model.
- The "distribution of the features" that were utilized.
- The difference between the "predicted or expected results" and the "actual or observed results".

Throughout the model scoring process, this metadata can be computed and subsequently used to monitor the model performance.

Another "offline pipeline" is the "Performance Monitoring Service", which will be notified whenever a new prediction has been served and then proceed to evaluate the performance while persisting the scoring result and raising any pertinent notifications. The assessment will be carried out by drawing a comparison between the scoring results to the output created by the training set of the data pipeline. To implement fundamental performance monitoring of the model, a variety of methods can be used. Some of the widely used methods include "logging analytics" such as "Kibana", "Grafana" and "Splunk".

A low performing model that is not able to generate predictions at high speed will trigger the scoring results to be produced by the preceding model, to maintain the resiliency of the machine learning solution. A strategy of being incorrect rather than being late is applied, which implies that if the model requires an extended period to time for computing a specific feature then it will be replaced by a preceding model in lieu of blocking the prediction. Furthermore, the scoring results will be connected to the actual results as they are accessible. This implies continuously measuring the precision of the model and at the same time, any sign of deterioration in the speed of the execution can be handled by returning to the preceding model. In order to connect the distinct versions together, a "chain of responsibility pattern" could be utilized. The monitoring of the performance of the models is an on-going method, considering that a simple prediction modification can cause a model structure to be reorganized. Remember the advantages of the machine learning model are defined by its ability to generate predictions and forecasts with high accuracy and speed to contribute to the success of the company.

Chapter 4: Python and Machine Learning Libraries

Python

Python is a high-level programming language, commonly used for general purposes. It was originally developed by Guido van Rossum at the "Center Wiskunde & Informatica (CWI), Netherlands", in the 1980s and introduced by the "Python Software Foundation" in 1991. It was designed primarily to emphasize the readability of programming code, and its syntax enables programmers to convey ideas using fewer lines of code. Python programming language increases the speed of operation while allowing for higher efficiency in creating system integrations. Developers are using Python for "web development (server-side), software development, mathematics, system scripting".

Here are some of the key features of Python that render it as the language of choice for coding beginners and advanced software programmers alike:

1. **Readability**: Python reads a lot like the English language which contributes to its ease of readability.

2. **Learnability**: Python is a high-level programming language and considered easy to learn due to the ability to code using the English language like expressions, which implies it is simple to comprehend and thereby learn the language.

3. **Operating Systems**: Python is easily accessible and can be operated across different Operating systems including Windows, Macintosh, Unix, Linux, among others. This renders Python as a versatile and cross-platform language.

4. **Open Source**: Python is an "open source" programming language, which means that the developer community can seamlessly make updates to the code which are always available to anyone using Python for their software programming needs.

5. **Standardized Data Libraries**: Python features a big standard data library with a variety of useful codes and functionalities that can be

used when writing Python code for data analysis and development of machine learning models. (Details on machine learning libraries will be provided later in this chapter)

6. **Free**: Considering the wide applicability and usage of Python, it is hard to believe that it continues to be freely available for easy download and use. This implies that anyone looking to learn or use Python can simply download and use it for their applications completely free of charge. Python is indeed a perfect example of a "FLOSS (Free/Libre Open Source Software)", meaning one could "freely distribute copies of this software, read its source code and modify it".

7. **Supports managing of exceptions**: An "exception" can be defined as "an event that can occur during program exception and can disrupt the normal flow of program". Python is capable of supporting handling of these "exceptions", implying that you could write fewer error-prone codes and test your code with a variety of cases, which could potentially lead to an "exception" in the future.

8. **Advanced Features**: Python can also support "generators and list comprehensions".

9. **Storage governance**: Python is also able to support "automatic memory management", which implies that the storage memory will be cleared and made available automatically. You are not required to clear and free up the system memory.

Applications:
1. Web designing – Some of the widely used web frameworks such as "Django" and "Flask" have been developed using Python. These frameworks assist the developer in writing server-side codes that enable management of the database, generation of backend programming logic, mapping of URL, among others. Machine learning –A variety of machine learning models have been written exclusively in Python. Machine learning is a way for a machine to write the logic in order to learn and fix a specific issue on its own. For instance, Python-based machine learning algorithms used in the development of "product recommendation systems" for eCommerce businesses such as Amazon, Netflix, YouTube and many more. Other instances of Python-based machine learning models are facial

recognition and the voice recognition technologies available on our mobile devices.

2. Data Analysis – Python can also be used in the development of data visualization and data analysis tools and techniques such as scatter plots and other graphical representations of data.

3. "Scripting" – It can be defined as the process of generating simple programs for automation of straightforward tasks like those required to send automated email responses and text messages. You could develop these types of software using the Python programming language.

4. Gaming Industry – A wide variety of gaming programs have been developed with the use of Python.

5. Python also supports the development of "embedded applications".

6. Desktop apps – You could use data libraries such as "TKinter" or "QT" to create desktop apps based on Python.

Python Tips and Tricks for Developers

Python was first implemented in 1989 and is regarded as highly user-friendly and simple to learn programming language for entry-level coders and amateurs. It is regarded as ideal for individuals newly interested in programming or coding and needs to comprehend programming fundamentals. This stems from the fact that Python reads almost the same as the English language. Therefore, it requires less time to understand how the language works and focus can be directed in learning the basics of programming.

Python is an interpreted language that supports automatic memory management and object-oriented programming. This extremely intuitive and flexible programming language can be used for coding projects such as machine learning algorithms, web applications, data mining and visualization, game development.

Some of the tips and tricks you can leverage to sharpen up your Python programming skill set are:

In-place swapping of two numbers:
"x, y = 10, 20
print(x, y)
x, y = y, x
print(x, y)"

Resulting Output =
10 20
20 10

Reversing a string:
"a ="computer""
"print("Reverse is", a[::-1])"

Resulting Output =
Reverse is retupmoc.

Creating a single string from multiple list elements:
"a = ["machine", "learning", "algorithms"]
print(" ".join(a))"

Resulting Output =
machine learning algorithms

Stacking of comparison operators:
"n = 100
result = 1 < n < 200
print(result)
result = 1 > n <= 90
print(result)"

Resulting Output =
True
False

Print the file path of the imported modules:
"import os;
import socket;

print(os)
print(socket"

Resulting Output =
"<module 'os' from '/usr/lib/python3.5/os.py'>
<module 'socket' from '/usr/lib/python3.5/socket.py'>"

Use of enums in Python:
"class MyName:
　Chic, For, Chic = range(3)

print(MyName.Chic)
print(MyName.For)
print(MyName.Chic)"

Resulting Output =
2
1
2

Return multiple values from functions:
"def x():
　return 10, 20, 30, 40
a, b, c, d = x()

print(a, b, c, d)"

Resulting Output =
"10 20 30 40"

Identify the value with highest frequency:
"test = [10, 20, 30, 40, 20, 20, 30, 10, 40, 40, 40]
print(max(set(test), key = test.count))"

Resulting Output =
40

Check the memory usage of an object:
"import sys
x = 1
print(sys.getsizeof(x))"

Resulting Output =
28

Printing a string N times:
"n = 2;
a ="ArtificialIntelligence";
*print(a * n);"*

Resulting Output =
ArtificialIntelligenceArtificialIntelligenceArtificialIntelligence

Identify anagrams:
"from collections import Counter
def is_anagram(str1, str2):
*   return Counter(str1) == Counter(str2)*
print(is_anagram('geek', 'eegk'))

print(is_anagram('geek', 'reek'))"

Resulting Output =
True
False

Transposing a matrix:
"mat = [[10, 20, 30], [40, 50, 60]]
*zip(*mat)"*

Resulting Output =
[(10, 40), (20, 50), (30, 60)]

Print a repeated string without using loops:
*"print "machine"*3+' '+"learning"*4"*

Resulting Output =

Machinemachinemachine learninglearninglearninglearning

Measure the code execution time:
"import time"
"startTime = time.time()"
" write your code or functions calls"
" write your code or functions calls"

"endTime = time.time()"
"totalTime = endTime – startTime"
"print('Total time required to execute code is=' , totalTime)"

Resulting Output =
Total time

Obtain the difference between two lists:
"list1 = ['Brian', 'Pepper', 'Kyle', 'Leo', 'Sam']
list2 = ['Sam', 'Leo', 'Kyle']
set1 = set(list1)
set2 = set(list2)
list3 = list(set1.symmetric_difference(set2))
print(list3)"

Resulting Output =
list3 = ['Brian', 'Pepper']

Calculate the memory being used by an object in Python:
"import sys"
"list1 = ['Brian', 'Pepper', 'Kyle', 'Leo', 'Sam']"
"print("size of list = ",sys.getsizeof(list1))"
"name = 'pynative.com'"
"print('size of name =', sys.getsizeof(name))"

Resulting Output =
('size of list = ', 112)
('size of name = ', 49)

Removing duplicate items from the list:
"listNumbers = [20, 22, 24, 26, 28, 28, 20, 30, 24]"
"print ('Original=' , listNumbers)"
"listNumbers = list(set(listNumbers))"
"print ('After removing duplicate= ' , listNumbers)"

Resulting Output =
"'Original= ', [20, 22, 24, 26, 28, 28, 20, 30, 24]"
"'After removing duplicate= ', [20, 22, 24, 26, 28, 30]"

Find if a list contains identical elements:
"listOne = [20, 20, 20, 20]
print('All element are duplicate in listOne', listOne.count(listOne[0]) == len(listOne))

listTwo = [20, 20, 20, 50]
print('All element are duplicate in listTwo', listTwo.count(listTwo[0]) == len(listTwo))"

Resulting Output =
"'All elements are duplicate in listOne', True"
"'All elements are duplicate in listTwo', False"

Efficiently compare two unordered lists:
"from collections import Counter
one = [33, 22, 11, 44, 55]
two = [22, 11, 44, 55, 33]
print('the two lists are b equal', Counter(one) == Counter(two))"

Resulting Output =
"'the two lists are b equal', True"

Check if list contains all unique elements:
"def isUnique(item):
tempSet = set()
return not any(i in tempSet or tempSet.add(i) for i in item)
listOne = [123, 345, 456, 23, 567]
print('All List elements are Unique' , isUnique(listOne))

listTwo = [123, 345, 567, 23, 567]
print('All List elements are Unique' , isUnique(listTwo))"

Resulting Output =
"All List elements are Unique True"
"All List elements are Unique False"

Convert Byte into String:
"byteVar = b"pynative""
"str = str(byteVar.decode('utf-8'))"
"print('Byte to string is' , str)"

Resulting Output =
"Byte to string is pynative"

Merge two dictionaries into a single expression:
"currentEmployee = {1: 'Scott', 2: 'Eric', 3:'Kelly'}
formerEmployee = {2: 'Eric', 4: 'Emma'}
def merge_dicts(dictOne, dictTwo):
dictThree = dictOne.copy()
dictThree.update(dictTwo)
return dictThree
print(merge_dicts(currentEmployee, formerEmployee))"

Machine Learning Libraries

Machine learning libraries are sensitive routines and functions that can be written in a variety of programming languages. Software developers need a robust set of libraries to perform complex tasks so as to avoid rewriting multiple lines of code to develop desired machine learning models. Machine learning is largely based on mathematical optimization, probability, and statistics. (These concepts were discussed in detail earlier in this book.)

Python has widely become the language of choice in the field of machine learning primarily due to its consistent development time and flexibility. It is well suited to develop sophisticated models and production engines that can be directly plugged into production systems. One of its greatest assets being an extensive set of libraries that can help researchers who are less equipped with developer knowledge to easily execute machine learning.

Scikit-Learn

"Scikit-Learn" has evolved as the gold standard for machine learning using Python, offering a wide variety of "supervised" and "unsupervised" ML algorithms. It is touted as one of the most user-friendly and cleanest machine learning libraries to date. For example, decision trees, clustering, linear and logistics regressions, and K-means. Scikit-learn uses a couple of basic Python libraries: NumPy and SciPy and adds a set of algorithms for data mining tasks including classification, regression, and clustering. It is also capable of implementing tasks like feature selection, transforming data and ensemble methods in only a few lines.

In 2007, David Cournapeau developed the foundational code of "Scikit-Learn" as part of a "Summer of Code" project for "Google". Scikit-learn has become one of Python's most famous open-source machine learning libraries since its launch in 2007. But it wasn't until 2010 that Scikit-Learn was released for public use. Scikit-Learn is an open-sourced and BSD licensed, data mining and data analysis tool used to develop supervise and unsupervised machine learning algorithms build on Python. Scikit-learn offers various ML algorithms such as "classification", "regression", "dimensionality reduction", and "clustering". It also offers modules for feature extraction, data processing, and model evaluation.

Designed as an extension to the "SciPy" library, Scikit-Learn is based on "NumPy" and "matplotlib", the most popular Python libraries. NumPy expands Python to support efficient operations on big arrays and multidimensional matrices. Matplotlib offers visualization tools and science computing modules are provided by SciPy. For scholarly studies, Scikit-Learn is popular because it has a well-documented, easy-to-use, and flexible API. Developers are able to utilize Scikit-Learn for their experiments with various algorithms by only altering a few lines of the code. Scikit-Learn also provides a variety of training datasets, enabling developers to focus on algorithms instead of data collection and cleaning. Many of the algorithms of Scikit-Learn are quick and scalable to all but huge datasets. Scikit-learn is known for its reliability and automated tests are available for much of the library. Scikit-learn is extremely popular with beginners in machine learning to start implementing simple algorithms.

Prerequisites for Application of Scikit-Learn Library

The "Scikit-Learn" library is based on the "SciPy (Scientific Python)", which needs to be installed before using "Scikit-Learn". This stack involves the following:

NumPy (Base N-Dimensional Array Package)

"NumPy" is the basic package with Python to perform scientific computations. It includes among other things: "a powerful N-dimensional array object; sophisticated (broadcasting) functions; tools for integrating C/C++ and Fortran code; useful linear algebra, Fourier transform, and random number capabilities". NumPy is widely reckoned as an effective multi-dimensional container of generic data in addition to its apparent scientific uses. It is possible to define arbitrary data types. This enables NumPy to integrate with a broad variety of databases seamlessly and quickly. The primary objective of NumPy is the homogeneity of the multidimensional array. It consists of an element table (generally numbers), all of which are of the same sort and are indicated by tuples of non-negative integers. The dimensions of NumPy are called "axes" and array class is called "ndarray".

Pandas (Data Structures and Analysis)

Pandas provide highly intuitive and user-friendly high-level data structures. Pandas has achieved popularity in the machine learning algorithm developer community, with built-in techniques for data aggregation, grouping, and filtering as well as results of time series analysis. The Pandas library has two primary structures: one-dimensional "Series" and two-dimensional "Data Frames".

IPython (Enhanced Interactive Console)

"IPython (Interactive Python)" is an interface or command shell for interactive computing using a variety of programming languages. "IPython" was initially created exclusively for Python, which supports introspection, rich media, shell syntax, tab completion, and history. Some of the functionalities provided by IPython include: "interactive shells (terminal and Qt-based); browser-based notebook interface with code, text, math, inline plots and other media support; support for interactive data visualization and use of GUI tool kits; flexible interpreters that can be embedded to load into your own projects; tools for parallel computing".

SciPy (Fundamental Library for Scientific Computing)

SciPy is a "collection of mathematical algorithms and convenience functions built on the NumPy extension of Python", capable of adding more impact to interactive Python sessions, by offering high-level data manipulation and visualization commands and courses for the user. An interactive Python session with SciPy becomes an environment that rival's data processing and system prototyping technologies including "MATLAB, IDL, Octave, R-Lab, and Scilab".

Another advantage of developing "SciPy" on Python, is the accessibility of a strong programming language in the development of advanced programs and specific apps. Scientific apps using SciPy benefit from developers around the globe developing extra modules in countless software landscape niches. Everything produced has been made accessible to the Python programmer, from database subroutines and classes as well as "parallel programming to the web". These powerful tools are provided along with the "SciPy" mathematical libraries.

Matplotlib (Comprehensive 2D/3D Plotting)

"Matplotlib" is a 2-dimensional graphic generation library from Python that produces high-quality numbers across a range of hardcopy formats and interactive environments. The "Python script", the "Python", "IPython shells", the "Jupyter notebook", the web app servers, and select user interface toolkits can be used with matplotlib. Matplotlib attempts to further simplify easy tasks and make difficult tasks feasible. With only a few lines of code, you can produce tracks, histograms, scatter plots, bar graphs, error graphs, etc.

A MATLAB-like interface is provided for easy plotting of the Pyplot Module, especially when coupled with IPython. As a power user, you can regulate the entire line styles, fonts properties, and axis properties, through an object-oriented interface or through a collection of features similar to the one provided to MATLAB users.

SymPy (Symbolic Mathematics)

Developed by Ondřej Čertík and Aaron Meurer, SymPy is "an open-source Python library for symbolic computation". It offers algebra computing abilities to other apps, as a stand-alone app and/or as a library as well as live on the internet applications with "SymPy Live" or "SymPy Gamma". "SymPy" is easy to install and test, owing to the fact that it is completely developed in Python boasting limited dependencies. SymPy involves characteristics ranging from calculus, algebra, discrete mathematics, and quantum physics to fundamental symbolic arithmetic. The outcome of the computations can be formatted as the "LaTeX" code. In combination with a straightforward, expandable code base in a widespread programming language, the ease of access provided by SymPy makes it a computer algebra system with a comparatively low entry barrier.

Conclusion

Thank you for making it through to the end of *Python Machine Learning: The Ultimate Basic Guide for Beginners to Learn How to Design Types of Automatic Production with Classification Algorithms and Create A Data Pipelines with Unsupervised Learning*, let's hope it was informative and able to provide you with all of the tools you need to achieve your goals whatever they may be.

The next step is to make the best use of your new-found wisdom on the modern-day technologies of machine learning and artificial intelligence that have generated the powerhouse, which is the "Silicon Valley". The day machines will be able to operate independently with no human assistance whatsoever may not be as far as you think. Today machine learning and artificial intelligence have given rise to sophisticated machines that can study human behavior and activity to identify underlying human behavioral patterns and precisely predict what products and services consumers are interested in. businesses with an eye on the future are gradually turning into Technology companies under the façade of their intended business model. With an understanding of how much is at stake for the corporate businesses. You can position yourself to use your deep knowledge and understanding of artificial intelligence and machine learning technologies obtained from this book to contribute to the growth of any company and land yourself a new high paying and rewarding job!

Finally, if you found this book useful in any way, a review on Amazon is always appreciated!

Python for Data Analysis

A Basic Guide For Beginners To Learn The Language Of Python Programming Codes Applied To Data Analysis With Libraries Software Pandas, Numpy, And Ipython

By

Oliver R. Simpson

Code Developer Academy

Table of Contents

INTRODUCTION 76

CHAPTER 1: INTRODUCTION TO BIG DATA AND BIG DATA ANALYSIS 78

CHAPTER 2: FUNDAMENTALS OF PYTHON AND DATA ANALYSIS LIBRARIES 96

CHAPTER 3: PREDICTIVE MODELING, DATA VISUALIZATION AND CREATION OF TRAINING DATA SET 111

CHAPTER 4: APPLICATIONS OF BIG DATA ANALYSIS 132

CONCLUSION 142

Introduction

Congratulations on purchasing *Python for Data Analysis: A Basic Guide for Beginners to Learn the Language of Python Programming Codes Applied to Data Analysis with Libraries Software Pandas, Numpy, and IPython* and thank you for doing so.

The following chapters will discuss the fundamental concepts of Data Analysis in light of the Python-based data libraries. You will start with a deep dive into the definition of "Big Data," along with its history and importance in the contemporary world. To further your understanding of this term, you will learn about different types of data. In the same chapter, you will learn all about Big Data Analytics and the steps involved in analyzing such large volumes of data. The topic of Data Analysis is incomplete without an understanding of the process of data mining, which can be defined as "the process of exploring and analyzing large volumes of data to gather meaningful patterns and rules." You will not only learn the end-to-end process of data mining but also be informed about its advantages and challenges. The first chapter of the book will conclude with an overview of select Data Analysis strategies.

In the chapter 2 of this book titled, "Fundamentals of Python and Data Analysis Libraries", you will be introduced to the concept of the "Python" programming language followed by a variety of Data Analysis libraries including "Django", "Scikit-Learn", "NumPy", "Matplotlib", "Pandas", "IPython", and "TensorFlow" among others. The majority of the Data Analysis and machine learning models are developed in Python, as it is well suited to develop sophisticated models and production engines that can be directly plugged into production systems. One of the greatest assets of Python is its extensive set of libraries that can help researchers who are less equipped with developer knowledge to easily execute data analysis and machine learning activities.

In chapter 3 of this book titled, "Predictive Modeling, Data Visualization, and Creation of Training Data Set," you will start by getting a brief overview of machine learning and various machine learning algorithms to help you understand the difference between "Big Data Analytics" and machine learning. We will then explore the concept of predictive analysis of data in the context of real-world customer behavior analysis, as practiced by most eCommerce business including

"Amazon" and "Netflix." Machine learning models are used to generate predictions and forecasts for the growth of the business. A variety of data libraries that you will learn about in chapter 2 of this book will be used with the "Scikit-Learn" platform to give you a step-by-step walkthrough of how you can create your own predictive data analysis model starting with data exploration and data visualization. Once you have a good understanding of the raw data available for your analysis, you will be able to learn how to process raw data set and generating high-quality training and test data set for your model. This chapter will conclude a brief overview of scatter plots that can be used to visualize the data.

In the final chapter of the book titled "Applications of Big Data Analysis," you will learn how big data and big data analytics are being leveraged by businesses across the industrial spectrum, with a focus on eCommerce, healthcare, and entertainment industry.

There are plenty of books on this subject on the market, thanks again for choosing this one! Every effort was made to ensure it is full of as much useful information as possible; please enjoy!

Chapter 1: Introduction to Big Data and Big Data Analysis

Big Data

In 2001, Gartner defined Big data as "Data that contains greater variety arriving in increasing volumes and with ever-higher velocity." This led to the formulation of the "three V's." Big data refers to an avalanche of structured and unstructured data that is endlessly flooding and from a variety of endless data sources. These data sets are too large to be analyzed with traditional analytical tools and technologies but have a plethora of valuable insights hiding underneath.

The "Vs" of Big data

Volume – To be classified as big data, the volume of the given data set must be substantially larger than traditional data sets. These data sets are primarily composed of unstructured data with limited structured and semi-structured data. The unstructured data or the data with unknown value can be collected from input sources such as webpages, search history, mobile applications, and social media platforms. The size and customer base of the company is usually proportional to the volume of the data acquired by the company.

Velocity – The speed at which data can be gathered and acted upon the first to the velocity of big data. Companies are increasingly using a combination of on-premise and cloud-based servers to increase the speed of their data collection. The modern-day "Smart Products and Devices" require real-time access to consumer data in order to be able to provide them a more engaging and enhanced user experience.

Variety – Traditionally, a data set would contain majority of structured data with low volume of unstructured and semi-structured data, but the advent of big data has given rise to new unstructured data types such as video, text, and audio that require sophisticated tools and technologies to clean and process these data types to extract meaningful insights from them.

Veracity – Another "V" that must be considered for big data analysis is veracity. This refers to the "trustworthiness or the quality" of the data. For example, social media platforms like "Facebook" and "Twitter" with blogs and posts containing a hashtag, acronyms, and all kinds of typing errors can significantly reduce the reliability and accuracy of the data sets.

Value – Data has evolved as a currency of its own with intrinsic value. Just like traditional monetary currencies, the ultimate value of the big data is directly proportional to the insight gathered from it.

History of Big Data

The origin of large volumes of data can be traced back to the 1960s and 1970s when the Third Industrial Revolution had just started to kick in, and the development of relational databases had begun along with the construction of data centers. But the concept of big data has recently taken center stage primarily since the availability of free search engines like Google and Yahoo, free online entertainment services like YouTube, and social media platforms like Facebook. In 2005, businesses started to recognize the incredible amount of user data being generated through these platforms and services, and in the same year, an open-source framework called "Hadoop" was developed to gather and analyze these large data dumps available to the companies. During the same period, a non-relational or distributed database called "NoSQL" started to gain popularity due to its ability to store and extract unstructured data. "Hadoop" made it possible for the companies to work with big data with high ease and at a relatively low cost.

Today, with the rise of cutting edge technology, not only humans but machines also generate data. The smart device technologies like "Internet of things" (IoT) and "Internet of systems" (IoS) have skyrocketed the volume of big data. Our everyday household objects and smart devices are connected to the Internet and able to track and record our usage patterns as well as our interactions with these products and feeds all this data directly into the big data. The advent of machine learning technology has further increased the volume of data generated on a daily basis. It is estimated that by 2020, "1.7 MB of data will be generated per second per person." As the big data will continue to grow, its usability still has many horizons to cross.

Importance of Big Data
To gain reliable and trustworthy information from a data set, it is very important to have a complete data set that has been made possible with the use of big data technology. The more data we have, the more information and details can be

extracted out of it. To gain a 360 view of a problem, and its underlying solutions, the future of big data is very promising. Here are some examples of the use of big data:

Product development – Large and small e-commerce businesses are increasingly relying upon big data to understand customer demands and expectations. Companies can develop predictive models to launch new products and services by using primary characteristics of their past and existing products and services and generating a model describing the relationship of those characteristics with the commercial success of those products and services. For example, a leading fast manufacturing commercial goods company, "Procter & Gamble" extensively uses big data gathered from the social media websites, test markets, and focus groups in preparation for their new product launch.

Predictive maintenance – In order to leave project potential mechanical and equipment failures, a large volume of unstructured data such as error messages, log entries, and normal temperature of the machine must be analyzed along with available structured data such as make and model of the equipment and year of manufacturing. By analyzing this big data set using the required analytical tools, companies can extend the shelf life of their equipment by preparing for scheduled maintenance ahead of time and predicting future occurrences of potential mechanical failures.

Customer experience – The smart customer is aware of all of the technological advancements and is loyal only to the most engaging and enhanced user experience available. This has triggered a race among the companies to provide unique customer experiences analyzing the data gathered from customers' interactions with the company's products and services. Providing personalized recommendations and offers to reduce customer churn rate and effectively kind words prospective leads into paying customers.

Fraud and compliance – Big data helps in identifying the data patterns and assessing historical trends from previous fraudulent transactions to effectively detect and prevent potentially fraudulent transactions. Banks, financial institutions, and online payment services like "PayPal" are constantly monitoring and gathering customer transaction data in an effort to prevent fraud.

Operational efficiency – With the help of big data predictive analysis. Companies can learn and anticipate future demand and product trends by analyzing production capacity, customer feedback, and data pertaining to top-selling items and product returns to improve decision-making and produce products that are in line with the current market trends.

Machine learning – For a machine to be able to learn and train on its own, it requires a humongous volume of data, i.e. big data. A solid training set containing structured, semi-structured, and unstructured data will help the machine to develop a multidimensional view of the real world and the problem it is engineered to resolve.

Drive innovation – By studying and understanding the relationships between humans and their electronic devices as well as the manufacturers of these devices, companies can develop improved and innovative products by examining current product trends and meeting customer expectations.

"The importance of big data doesn't revolve around how much data you have, but what you do with it. You can take data from any source and analyze it to find answers that enable 1) cost reductions, 2) time reductions, 3) new product development and optimized offerings, and 4) smart decision making."
- SAS

The Functioning of Big Data

There are three important actions required to gain insights from big data:

Integration – The traditional data integration methods such as ETL (Extract, Transform, Load) are incapable of collating data from a wide variety of unrelated sources and applications that are at the heart of big data. Advanced tools and technologies are required to analyze big data sets that are exponentially larger than traditional data sets. By integrating big data from these disparate sources, companies are able to analyze and extract valuable insight to grow and maintain their businesses.

Management – Big data management can be defined as "the organization, administration, and governance of large volumes of both structured and unstructured data." Big data requires efficient and cheap storage, which can be accomplished using servers that are on-premises, cloud-based, or a combination of both. Companies are able to seamlessly access required data from anywhere across the world and then processing this is a data using required processing engines on an as-needed basis. The goal is to make sure the quality of the data is high-level and can be accessed easily by the required tools and applications. Big data are gathered from all kinds of Dale sources including social media platforms, search engines, history and call logs. The big data usually contain large sets of unstructured data and the semi-structured data which are stored in a variety of formats. To be able to process and store this complicated data, companies require more powerful and advanced data management software beyond the traditional relational databases and data warehouse platforms.

New platforms are available in the market that is capable of combining big data with the traditional data warehouse systems in a "logical data warehousing architecture." As part of this effort, companies are required to make decisions on what data must be secured for regulatory purposes and compliance, what data must be kept for future analytical purposes, and what data has no future use and can be disposed of. This process is called "data classification," which allows a rapid and efficient analysis of a subset of data to be included in the immediate decision-making process of the company.

Analysis – Once the big data has been collected and is easily accessible, it can be analyzed using advanced analytical tools and technologies. This analysis will provide valuable insight and actionable information. Big data can be explored to make discoveries and develop data models using artificial intelligence and machine learning algorithms.

Types of Data

Now that you understand the concept of big data let us look at different types of data so you can choose the most appropriate analytical tools and algorithms based on the type of data that needs to be processed. Data types can be divided into two at a very high level: qualitative and quantitative.

Qualitative data – Any data that cannot be measured and only observed subjectively by adding a qualitative feature to the object it's called as "qualitative data." Classification of an object using unmeasurable features results in the creation of qualitative data. For example, attributes like color, smell, texture, and taste. There are three types of qualitative data:

- **"Binary or binomial data"** – Data values that signal mutually exclusive events where only one of the two categories or options is correct and applicable. For example, true or false, yes or no, positive or negative. Consider a box of assorted tea bags. You try all the different flavors and group the ones that you like as "good" and the ones you don't as "bad." In this case, "good or bad" would be categorized as the binomial data type. This type of data is widely used in the development of statistical models for predictive analysis.

- **"Nominal or unordered data"** – Data characteristics that lack an "implicit or natural value" can be referred to as nominal data. Consider a box of M&Ms. You can record the color of each M&M in the box in a worksheet, and that would serve as nominal data. This kind of data is widely used to assess statistical differences in the data set, using techniques like "Chi-Square analysis," which could tell you "statistically significant differences" in the amount of each color of M&M in a box.

- **"Ordered or ordinal data"** – The characteristics of this Data type do have certain "implicit or natural of value" such as small, medium, or large. For example, online reviews on sites like "Yelp," "Amazon," and "Trip Advisor" have a rating scale from 1 to 5, implying a 5-star rating is better than 4, which is better than 3 and so on.

Quantitative data – Any characteristics of the data that can be measured objectively are called as "quantitative data." Classification of an object in using measurable features and giving it a numerical value results and creation of quantitative data. For example, product prices, temperature, dimensions like length, etc. There are two types of quantitative data:

- **"Continuous Data"** – Data values that can be defined to a further lower level, such as units of measurement like kilometers, meters, centimeters, and on and on, are called the continuous data type. For example, you can purchase a bag of almonds by weight like 500g or 8 ounces. This accounts for the continuous data type, which is primarily used to test and verify different kinds of hypotheses such as assessing the accuracy of the weight printed on the bag of almonds.

- **"Discrete Data"** – numerical data value that cannot be divided and reduced to a higher level of precision, such as the number of cars owned by a person which can only be accounted for as indivisible numbers (you cannot have 1.5 or 2.3 cars), is called as discrete data types. For example, you can purchase another bag of ice cream bars by the number of ice cream bars inside the package, like four or six. This accounts for the discrete data type, which can be used in combination with a continuous data type to perform a regression analysis to verify if the total weight of the ice cream box (continuous data) is correlated with the number of ice cream bars (discrete data) inside.

Big Data Analytics

The terms of big data and big data analytics are often used interchangeably owing to the fact that the inherent purpose of big data is to be analyzed. "Big data analytics" can be defined as a set of qualitative and quantitative methods that can be employed to examine a large amount of unstructured, structured, and semi-structured data to discover data patterns and valuable hidden insights. Big data analytics is the science of analyzing big data to collect metrics, key performance indicators, and Data trends that can be easily lost in the flood of raw data, by using machine learning algorithms and automated analytical techniques. The different steps involved in "big data analysis" are:

Gathering Data Requirements – It is important to understand what information or data needs to be gathered to meet the business objective and goals. Data organization is also very critical for efficient and accurate data analysis. Some of the categories in which the data can be organized are gender, age, demographics, location, ethnicity, and income. A decision must also be made on the required data types (qualitative and quantitative) and data values (can be numerical or alphanumerical) to be used for the analysis.

Gathering Data – Raw data can be collected from disparate sources such as social media platforms, computers, cameras, other software applications, company websites, and even third-party data providers. The big data analysis inherently requires large volumes of data, the majority of which is unstructured with a limited amount of structured and semi-structured data.

Data organization and categorization – Depending on the company's infrastructure, Data organization could be done on a simple Excel spreadsheet or using many tools and applications that are capable of processing statistical data. Data must be organized and categorized based on data requirements collected in step one of the big data analysis process.

Cleaning the data – to perform the big data analysis sufficiently and rapidly, it is very important to make sure the data set is void of any redundancy and errors. Only a complete data set fulfilling the Data requirements must have proceeded to the final analysis step. Preprocessing of data is required to make sure the only high-quality data is being analyzed, and company resources are being put to good use.

"Big data is high-volume, high-velocity, and/or high-variety information assets that demand cost-effective, innovative forms of information processing that enable enhanced insight, decision-making, and process automation."
- Gartner

Analyzing the data – Depending on the insight that is expected to be achieved by the completion of the analysis, any of the following four different types of big data analytics approach can be adopted:

- **Predictive analysis** – This type of analysis is done to generate forecasts and predictions for future plans of the company. By the completion of a predictive analysis of the company's big data, the future state of the company can be more precisely predicted and derived from the current state of the company. The business executives are keenly interested in this analysis to make sure the company day-to-day operations are in line with the future vision of the company.

  For example, to deploy advanced analytical tools and applications in the sales division of a company, the first step is to analyze the leading source of data. Once it believes source analysis has been completed, the type and number of communication channels for the sales team must be analyzed. This is followed by the use of machine learning algorithms on customer data to gain insight into how the existing customer base is interacting with the company's products or services. This predictive analysis will conclude with the deployment of artificial intelligence-based tools to skyrocket the company's sales.

- **Prescriptive analysis** – Analysis that is carried out by primarily focusing on the business rules and recommendations to generate a selective analytical path as prescribed by the industry standards to boost company performance. The goal of this analysis is to understand the intricacies of various departments of the organization and what measures should be taken by the company to be able to gain insights from its customer data by using a prescribed analytical pathway. This allows the company to embrace domain specificity and conciseness by providing a sharp focus on its existing and future big data analytics process.

- **Descriptive analysis** – All the incoming data received and stored by the company can be analyzed to produce insightful descriptions on the basis of the results obtained. The goal of this analysis is to identify data patterns and current market trends that can be adopted by the company to grow its business. For example, credit card companies often require risk assessment results on all prospective customers to be able to make predictions on the likelihood of the customer failing to make their credit payments and make a decision whether the customer should be approved for the credit or not. This risk assessment is primarily based on the customer's credit history but also takes into account other influencing factors, including remarks from other financial institutions that the customer had approached for credit, customer income, and financial performance as well as their digital footprint and social media profile.

- **Diagnostic analysis** – As the name suggests, this type of analysis is done to "diagnose" or understand why a certain event unfolded and how that event can be prevented from occurring in the future or replicated if needed. For example, web marketing strategies and campaigns often employ social media platforms to get publicity and increase their goodwill. Not all campaigns are as successful as expected; therefore, learning from failed campaigns is just as important, if not more. Companies can run diagnostic analysis on their campaign by collecting data pertaining to the "social media mentions" of the campaign, number of campaign page views, the average amount of time spent on the campaign page by an individual, number of social media fans and followers of the campaign, online reviews and other related metrics to understand why the campaign failed, and how future campaigns can be made more effective.

The big data analysis can be conducted using one or more of the tools listed below:

- Hadoop – Open source data framework.
- Python – Programming language widely used for machine learning.

- SAS – Advanced analytical tool used primarily for big data analysis.
- Tableau – Artificial intelligence-based tool used primarily for data visualization.
- SQL – the Programming language used to extract data from relational databases.
- Splunk – Analytical tool used to categorize machine-generated data
- R-programming – the Programming language used primarily for statistical computing.

Big Data Analysis vs. Data Visualization

In the wider data community, data analysis and data visualization are increasingly being used synonymously. Professional data analysts are expected to be able to skillfully represent data using visual tools and formats. On the other hand, new professional job positions called "Data visualization expert" and "data artist" have hit the market. But companies stool need professionals to analyze their data and extract valuable insights from it. As you have learned by now, Data analysis or big data analysis is an "exploratory process" with defined goals and specific questions that need to be answered from a given set of big data. Data visualization pertains to the visual representation of data, using tools as simple as an Excel spreadsheet or as advanced as dashboards created using Tableau. Business executives are always short on time and need to capture a whole lot of details; therefore, the data analyst is required to use effective visualizations that can significantly lower the amount of time needed to understand the presented data and gather valuable insights from the data.

By developing a variety of visual presentations from the data, an analyst can view the data from different perspectives and identify potential data trends, outliers, gaps, and anything that stands out and warrants further analysis. This process is referred to as "visual analytics." Some of the widely used visual representations of the data are "dashboard reports," "infographics," and "data story." These visual representations are considered as the final deliverable from the big data analysis process, but in reality, they frequently serve as a starting point for future political activities. The two completely different activities of data visualization and big data analysis are inherently related and loop into each other by serving as a starting point as well as the endpoint of the other activity. (The concept of data visualization will be explained in detail in chapter 3 of this book.)

Data Mining

Data mining can be defined as "the process of exploring and analyzing large volumes of data to gather meaningful patterns and rules." Data mining falls under the umbrella of data science and is heavily used to build artificial intelligence-based machine learning models, for example, search engine algorithms. Although the process of "digging through data" to uncover hidden patterns and predict future events has been around for a long time and referred to as "knowledge discovery in databases," the term "Data mining" was coined as recently as the 1990s.

Data mining consists of three foundational and highly intertwined disciplines of science, namely, "statistics" (the mathematical study of data relationships), "machine learning algorithms" (algorithms that can be trained with an inherent capability to learn), and "artificial intelligence" (machines that can display human-like intelligence). With the advent of big data, Data mining technology has been evolved to keep up with the "limitless potential of big data" and affordable computing power. The once considered tedious, labor-intensive, and time-consuming activities have been automated using advance processing speed and power of the modern computing systems.

"Data mining is the process of finding anomalies, patterns, and correlations within large data sets to predict outcomes. Using a broad range of techniques, you can use this information to increase revenues, cut costs, improve customer relationships, reduce risks, and more."
– SAS

According to SAS, "unstructured data alone makes up 90% of the digital universe". This avalanche of big data does not necessarily guarantee more knowledge. The application of data mining technology allows the filtering of all the redundant and unnecessary data noise to garner the understanding of relevant information that can be used in the immediate decision-making process.

The Data Mining Process

Most widely used data mining processes can be broken down into six steps as listed below:

1. Business understanding
It is very critical to understand the project goals and what is it that you're trying to achieve through the data mining process. Companies always start with the establishment of a defined goal and a project plan that includes details such as individual team member roles and responsibility, project milestones, project timelines, and key performance indicators and metrics.

2. Data understanding
Data is available from a wide variety of input sources and in different formats. With the use of data visualization tools, the data properties, and features can be assessed to ensure the existing data set is able to meet the established business requirements and project goals.

3. Data preparation
The preprocessing of data collected in multiple formats is very important. The data set must be scrubbed to remove data redundancies and identify gaps before it is deemed appropriate for mining. Considering the amount of data to be analyzed, the data pre-processing and processing steps can take a long time. To enhance the speed of the data mining process, instead of using a single system company, prefer using distributed systems as part of their "database management systems." The distributed systems also provide enhanced security measures by segregating the data into multiple devices rather than a single data warehouse. At this stage, it is also very crucial to account for backup options and failsafe measures in the event of data loss during the data manipulation stage.

4. Data modeling
Applicable mathematical models and analytical tools are applied to the data set to identify patterns.

5. Evaluation
The modeling results and data patterns are evaluated against the project goal and objectives to determine if the data findings can be released for use across the organization.

6. Deployment
Once the insights gathered from the data have been evaluated as applicable to the functioning and operations of the organization, these insights can be shared across the company to be included in its day-to-day operations. With the use of a Business Intelligence tool, the data findings can be stored at a centralized location

and accessed using the BI tool as needed.

Pros of Data Mining

Automated decision-making
With the use of data mining technology, businesses can seamlessly automate tedious manual tasks and analyze large volumes of data to gather insights for the routine and critical decision-making process. For example, financial lending institutions, banks, and online payment services use data mining technology to detect potentially fraudulent transactions, verify user identity, and ensure data privacy to protect their customers against identity theft. When the company's operational algorithms are working in coordination with the data mining models, the company can independently gather, analyze, and take actions on data to improve and streamline their operational decision-making process.

Accurate prediction and forecasting
Project planning is fundamental to the success of any company. Managers and executives can leverage data mining technology to gather reliable forecasts and predictions on future market trends and include in their future planning process. For example, one of the leading retail company "Macy's" has implemented demand forecasting models to generate reliable demand forecasts for Mary is clothing categories at individual stores in order to increase the efficiency of their supply chain by routing the forecasted inventory to each store and cater to the needs of the market more efficiently.

Cost reduction
With the help of data mining, technology companies can maximize the use of their resources by smarty allocating them across the business model. The use of data mining technology in planning, as well as an automated decision-making process, results in accurate forecasts leading to significant cost reductions. For example, a major airline company "Delta" implemented RFID chips inside their passengers checked-in baggage and gathered baggage handling data that was analyzed using data mining techniques to identify improvement opportunities in their process and minimizing the number of mishandled baggage. This not only resulted in a cost-saving on the search and rerouting process of the lost baggage but also translated into higher customer satisfaction.

Customer insights
Companies across different industrial sectors have deployed Data mining models

to gather valuable insights from existing customer data, which can be used to segment and target customers with similar shopping attributes using similar marketing strategies and campaigns. Customer personas can be created using data mining techniques to provide a more engaging and personalized user experience to the customer. For example, "Disney" has recently invested over a billion dollars in developing and deploying "Magic bands," offering the convenience and enhanced the experience of Disney resorts. At the same time, these bands can be used to collect data on patron activities and interactions with different "Disney" products and services at the park to further enhance the "Disney experience."

"When [data mining and] predictive analytics are done right, the analyses aren't a means to a predictive end; rather, the desired predictions become a means to analytical insight and discovery. We do a better job of analyzing what we need to analyze and predicting what we want to predict."
– Harvard Business Review Insight Center Report

Challenges of data mining

1. Big data

Our digital life has inundated companies with large volumes of data, which is estimated to reach 1.7 MB per second per person by 2020. This exponential increase in volume and complexity of big data has presented challenges for the data mining technology. Companies are looking to expedite their decision-making process by swiftly and efficiently extracting and analyzing data to gain valuable insights from their data treasure trove. The ultimate goal of data mining technology is to overcome these challenges and unlock the true potential of data value. The "4Vs" of big data namely velocity, variety, volume, and veracity, represent the four major challenges facing the data mining technology.

The skyrocketing "velocity" or speed at which new data is being generated poses a challenge of increasing storage requirements. The "variety" or different data types collected and stored require advance data mining capabilities to be able to simultaneously process a multitude of data formats. Data mining tools that are not equipped to process such highly variable big data provide low value due to their inefficiency and analyzing unstructured and structured data together.

The large volume of big data is not only challenging for storage, but it's even more challenging to identify correct data in a timely manner, owing to a massive reduction in the speed of the data mining tools and algorithms. To add on to this challenge, the data "veracity" denoting that all of the collected data is not accurate and can be incomplete or even biased. The data mining tools are struggling to deliver high-quality results in a timely manner by analyzing high quantity or big data.

2. Overloading models

Data models that describe the natural errors of the data set instead of the underlying patterns are often "over-fitted" or overloaded. These models tend to be highly complex and require a large number of independent media values to precisely predict a future event. Data volume and variety further increase the risk of overloading. A high number of variables tend to restrict the data model within the confines of the known sample data. On the other hand, an insufficient number of variables can compromise the relevance of the model. To obtain the required number of variables for the data mining models, to be able to strike a balance between the accuracy of the results and the prediction capabilities is one of the major challenges facing the data mining technology today.

3. Data privacy and security

To cater to the large volume of big data generated on a daily basis, companies are investing in cloud-based storage servers along with their on-premise servers. The cloud computing technology is relatively new in the market, and the inherent nature of this service poses multiple security and privacy concerns. Data privacy and security is one of the biggest concerns of Smart consumers who are willing to take their business to the company that can promise them the security of their personal information and data. This requires organizations to evaluate their customer relationships and prioritize customer privacy over the development of policies that can potentially compromise customer data security.

4. Scaling costs

With the increasing speed of data generation leading to a high volume of complex data, organizations are required to expand their data mining models and deploy them across the organization. To unlock the full potential of data mining tools, companies are required to heavily invest in computing infrastructure and processing power to efficiently run the data mining models. Big-ticket item purchase-including data servers, software, and advanced computers must be made to scale the analytical capabilities of the organization.

Data Mining Trends

Increased Computing Speed
With the increasing volume and complexity of big data, Data mining tools need more powerful and faster computers to efficiently analyze data. The existing statistical techniques like "clustering" art equipment to process only thousands of input data with a limited number of variables. However, companies are gathering over millions of new data observations with hundreds of variables making the analysis too complicated for the computing system to process. The big data is going to continue to explode, demanding supercomputers that are powerful enough to rapidly and efficiently analyze the growing big data.

Language Standardization
The data science community is actively looking to standardize a language for the data mining process. This ongoing effort will allow the analyst to conveniently work with a variety of data mining platforms by mastering one standard Data mining language.

Scientific Mining
The success of data mining technology in the industrial world has caught the eye of the scientific and academic research community. For example, psychologists are using "association analysis" to capture her and identify human behavioral patterns for research purposes. Economists are using protective analysis algorithms to forecast future market trends by analyzing current market variables.

Web mining
Web mining can be defined as "the process of discovering hidden data patterns and chains using similar techniques of data mining and applying them directly on the Internet." The three main types of web mining are: "content mining," "usage mining," and "structure mining." For example, "Amazon" uses web mining to gain an understanding of customer interactions with their website and mobile application, to provide more engaging and enhanced user experience to their customers.

Data mining tools

Some of the most widely used data mining tools are:

Orange
Orange is "open-source component-based software written in Python." It is most frequently used for basic data mining analysis and offers top-of-the-line data pre-processing features.

RapidMiner
RapidMiner is an "open-source component-based software written in Java." It is most frequently used for "predictive analysis" and offers integrated environments for "machine learning," "deep learning," and "text mining."

Mahout
Mahout is an open-source platform primarily used for unsupervised learning process" and developed by "Apache." It is most frequently used to develop "machine learning algorithms for clustering, classification, and collaborative filtering." This software requires advanced knowledge and expertise to be able to leverage the full capabilities of the platform.

MicroStrategy
MicroStrategy is a "business intelligence and data analytics software that can complement all data mining models." This platform offers a variety of drivers and gateways to seamlessly connect with any enterprise resource and analyze complex big data by transforming it into accessible visualizations that can be easily shared across the organization.

Data Analysis Strategies

Data science is mainly used in decision-making by making precise predictions with the use of "predictive causal analytics," "prescriptive analytics," and machine learning.

Predictive causal analytics – It can be applied to develop a model that can accurately predict and forecast the likelihood of a particular event occurring in the future. For example, financial institutions use predictive causal analytics-based tools to assess the likelihood of a customer defaulting on their credit card payments by generating a model that can analyze the payment history of the customer with all of their borrowing institutions.

Prescriptive analytics - The "prescriptive analytics" are widely used in the development of "intelligent tools and applications" that are capable of modifying and learning with dynamic parameters and make their own "decisions." The tool not only predicts the occurrence of a future event but is also capable of providing recommendations on a variety of actions and its resulting outcomes. For example, the self-driving cars gather driving-related data with every driving experience and use it to train themselves to make better driving and maneuvering decisions.

Machine learning to make predictions – To develop models that can determine future trends based on the transactional data acquired by the company, machine learning algorithms are a necessity. This is considered "supervised machine learning," which we will elaborate on later in this book. For example, fraud detection systems use machine learning algorithms on the historical data pertaining to fraudulent purchases to detect if a transaction is fraudulent.

Machine learning for pattern discovery – To be able to develop models that are capable of identifying hidden data patterns but lack required parameters to make future predictions, the "unsupervised machine learning algorithms," such as "Clustering," need to be employed. For example, telecom companies often use the "clustering" technology to expand their network by identifying network tower locations with optimal signal strength in the targeted region.

Chapter 2: Fundamentals of Python and Data Analysis Libraries

Python

Python is a highly useful software programming language, which is rapidly becoming a standard in big data analysis. It is free with open source code and fully standardized across multiple operating systems, including "Windows," "MacOS," and "Linux."
Python is touted as an extremely versatile, simple to use and learn the programming language, and ideal for software programming beginners. In the 1980s, Python was developed, by Guido van Rossum at the "Center Wiskunde & Informatica (CWI), Netherlands," as a successor to the "ABC language" and with the capability of managing and interacting with the "Amoeba operating system."
It was launched at the end of the year 1989. In late 2000, Python v2.0 was introduced with a variety of enhancements such as "cycle-detecting garbage collector" and support for "Unicode." In December 2008, Python v3.0 was released. I, which resulted in a complete revision of Python making it more backward-compatible. Several of the main characteristics of Python v3.0 have been reverted to versions "2.6.x" and "2.7.x".

Python-based software programs are extremely readable and tend to be more succinct than similar programs written in other programming languages such as "C" or "Fortran." In addition, Python integrates seamlessly with conventional modules that provide a wide range of features and algorithms for tasks such as "parsing text data, manipulating and finding disk files, reading and writing compressed files, and downloading data from web servers." Python is equipped with capabilities of all the sophisticated methods including object-orientation that are prerequisites for advanced programmers.

Python is rather distinct from "C," "C++," or "Fortran," which require that the source code is first compiled into an executable format prior to the execution. On the other hand, there is no compilation phase in Python, and the source code is processed on a line-by-line basis. This means Python will execute the source code as though it is written as a script. The significant benefit of an interpreted language is that it tends to be extremely versatile; the variables are not required to be indicated in advance, and the program can easily adapt on the fly. However, there is also a drawback, in that statistically-rich programs based on Python report higher execution time in comparison to similar programs based on compiled languages. To address this issue and make Python a preferable option for data analysis, time-consuming subroutines could be compiled in "C" and "Fortran" and imported into Python in a way that resembles Python features.

Data Analysis or Machine Learning Libraries

Data Analysis libraries are sensitive routines and functions that are written in any given language. Software developers require a robust set of libraries to perform complex tasks without needing to rewrite multiple lines of code. Machine learning is largely based on mathematical optimization, probability, and statistics.

Python is the language of choice in the field of data analysis and machine learning credited to consistent development time and flexibility. It is well-suited to develop sophisticated models and production engines that can be directly plugged into production systems. One of its greatest assets being an extensive set of libraries that can help researchers who are less equipped with developer knowledge to easily execute data analysis and machine learning.

Django

According to the Django Software Foundation, "Django is a free and open-source, high-level Python Web framework that encourages rapid development and clean, pragmatic design. Built by experienced developers, it takes care of much of the hassle of Web development, so you can focus on writing your app without needing to reinvent the wheel". The main objective of Django is to facilitate the development of sophisticated websites that are driven by databases. Its name is credited to the famous guitarist "Django Reinhardt" and was developed in late 2003 by computer scientists at the "Lawrence Journal World" newspaper, Adrian Holovaty and Simon Willison. In July 2005, "Django" was launched under a "BSD license" and was rolled up to the management of the "Django Software Foundation" in June 2008.

This framework promotes reusability and easy plugging in of the component, fewer codes, limited connection, faster development, and the no repetition principle. "Django" extensively uses Python for the development of configuration documents and data models. "Django" can be equipped with an optional administrative interface, which is dynamically developed by introspection and administrative model configurations to allow creating, reading, updating, and deleting files as needed. Several of the widely renowned websites are based on "Django," such as "Public Broadcasting Service," "Instagram," "Mozilla," "Washington Times," "Disqus," "Bitbucket," and "Nextdoor."

Although the fundamental framework of "Django" has its naming conventions, like naming the objects that can be called and used to generate "views" of the "HTTP responses," it could still be considered a "model-template-view (MTV)" architectural pattern. It comprises of an "object-relational mapper (ORM)" that acts as a mediator between data models ("Python classes") and a relational database ("Model"), a system to process "HTTP requests" using a "web template system" or "View", and a standard expression driven "URL dispatcher" or "Controller".

The underlying framework also contains the features listed below:

- A "standalone and lightweight webserver" to develop and test the websites.
- A system to serialize and validate HTML forms, which is capable of translating between appropriate database storage values and these forms.
- A template system using the principle of inheritance as found in the "object-oriented programming."
- A "caching framework," which is capable of using a variety of caching techniques.
- Support for middleware classes, which are capable of intervening and performing custom tasks at different phases of request processing.
- An "internal dispatcher system" allowing application components to relay occurrences to one another, through pre-defined signals.
- An internationalization system, which includes translations of various components of "Django" into a multitude of languages.
- A serialization system, which is capable of producing and reading "XML and/or JSON representations" of the "Django" model instances
- A system that allows extension of the template engine functionality.
- An interface to the integrated unit test framework of "Python."
- "Django REST Framework" constitutes a strong and adaptable "Web API construction" toolkit.

Scikit-Learn

"Scikit-Learn" has evolved as the gold standard for machine learning using Python, offering a wide variety of "supervised and unsupervised machine learning algorithms." It is touted as one of the most user-friendly and cleanest machine learning libraries to date. For example, decision trees, clustering, linear and logistics regressions, and K-means. Scikit-learn uses a couple of basic Python libraries: NumPy and SciPy and adds a set of algorithms for data mining tasks, including classification, regression, and clustering. It is also capable of implementing tasks like feature selection, transforming data and ensemble methods in only a few lines.

In 2007, David Cournapeau developed the foundational code of "Scikit-Learn" as part of a "Summer of Code" project for "Google." Scikit-learn has become one of Python's most famous open-source machine learning libraries since its launch in 2007. But it wasn't until 2010 that Scikit-Learn was released for public use. Scikit-Learn is "an open-sourced and BSD licensed data mining and data analysis tool used to develop supervised and unsupervised machine learning algorithms" build on Python." Scikit-learn offers various "machine learning algorithms" such as "classification," "regression," "dimensionality reduction," and "clustering." It also offers modules for feature extraction, data processing, and model evaluation.

Designed as an extension to the "SciPy" library, Scikit-Learn is based on "NumPy" and "matplotlib," the most popular Python libraries. NumPy expands Python to support efficient operations on big arrays and multidimensional matrices. Matplotlib offers visualization tools and science computing modules are provided by SciPy. For scholarly studies, Scikit-Learn is popular because it has a well-documented, easy-to-use, and flexible API. Developers are able to utilize Scikit-Learn for their experiments with various algorithms by only altering a few lines of the code. Scikit-Learn also provides a variety of training datasets, enabling developers to focus on algorithms instead of data collection and cleaning. Many of the algorithms of Scikit-Learn are quick and scalable to all but huge datasets. Scikit-learn is known for its reliability, and automated tests are available for much of the library. Scikit-learn is extremely popular with beginners in machine learning to start implementing simple algorithms.

Prerequisites for application of Scikit-Learn library

The "Scikit-Learn" library is based on the "SciPy (Scientific Python)," which needs to be installed before using "SciKit-Learn." This stack involves the following:

NumPy (Base n-dimensional array package)
"NumPy" is the basic package with Python to perform scientific computations. It includes, among other things: "a powerful N-dimensional array object; sophisticated (broadcasting) functions; tools for integrating C/C++ and Fortran code; useful linear algebra, Fourier transform, and random number capabilities." The predecessor of NumPy called "Numeric" was initially developed by Jim Hugunin. In 2005, Travis Oliphant developed "NumPy" by integrating the functionalities of the "Numarray" into "Numeric" and making additional enhancements to it. NumPy is widely reckoned as an effective multi-dimensional container of generic data in addition to its apparent scientific uses. It is possible to define arbitrary data types. This enables NumPy to integrate with a wide variety of databases seamlessly and quickly. NumPy assists the "CPython reference implementation" of Python, which is a "non-optimizing bytecode interpreter." NumPy can partially address the issue of slow execution of mathematical algorithms, by offering multidimensional arrays, functions, and operators that work effectively on arrays by rewriting the code pertaining to the internal loops using NumPy.

Python bindings of "OpenCV's" commonly used computer vision library uses "NumPy arrays" for data storage and operation. Since pictures with various channels are merely depicted as 3-D arrays, indexing, slicing, or masking with other arrays are highly effective methods to access relevant pixels of the picture. The "NumPy array" as a universal data structure in "OpenCV" for pictures, extracted functionality points, filter kernels, and several other, to simplify the "programming workflow and debugging." The primary objective of NumPy is the homogeneity of the multidimensional array. It consists of an element table (generally numbers), all of which are of the same sort and are indicated by tuples of non-negative integers.

The dimensions of NumPy are called "axes," and the array class is called "ndarray." These arrays are considered "stridden views on memory." Unlike the built-in list data structure of Python (also a dynamic array), the "NumPy arrays" can be typed uniformly, which means that "all the elements of a single array must be of the same type." Such arrays could also be "views of memory buffers assigned to the CPython interpreter by C / C++, Cython, and Fortran extensions without the need to copy data around," making them compatible with current numerical libraries. The "SciPy package" that incorporates a multitude of such libraries (particularly "BLAS" and "LAPACK") utilizes this capability. NumPy also offers built-in support for "memory-mapped ndarrays."

To develop "NumPy array" from "Python lists" while accessing elements, use the code below:

"import numpy as np

a = np.array([1, 2, 3])
print(type(a))
print(a.shape)
print(a[0], a[1], a[2])
a[0] = 5
print(a)

b = np.array([[1,2,3],[4,5,6]])
print(b.shape)
print(b[0, 0], b[0, 1], b[1, 0])"

Now, if you would like to index the "NumPy arrays," you should start with slicing the multidimensional "array" into one dimension with the code below:

"import numpy as np

a = np.array([[1,2,3,4], [5,6,7,8], [9,10,11,12]])
b = a[:2, 1:3]
print(a[0, 1])
b[0, 0] = 77
print(a[0, 1]) "

This will result in a "sub-array" of the original "NumPy array" but if you would like to generate an "arbitrary array," you can do so by utilizing "integer array indexing" which enables the generation of arbitrary arrays with the data from another array, as shown in the code below:

```
"import numpy as np
a = np.array([[1,2], [3, 4], [5, 6]])
print(a[[0, 1, 2], [0, 1, 0]])
print(np.array([a[0, 0], a[1, 1], a[2, 0]]))
print(a[[0, 0], [1, 1]])
print(np.array([a[0, 1], a[0, 1]]))"
```

Basic mathematical operations can be applied to arrays, as shown in the code below, and can be found in "NumPy" as "functions" and "operator overloads."

```
"import numpy as np

x = np.array([[1,2],[3,4]], dtype=np.float64)
y = np.array([[5,6],[7,8]], dtype=np.float64)

print(x + y)
print(np.add(x, y))

print(x - y)
print(np.subtract(x, y))

print(x * y)
print(np.multiply(x, y))

print(x / y)
print(np.divide(x, y))

print(np.sqrt(x))"
```

Matplotlib (Comprehensive 2D/3D plotting)

"Matplotlib" is a 2-dimensional graphic generation library from Python that produces high-quality numbers across a range of hardcopy formats and interactive environments. The "Python script," the "Python," "IPython shells," the "Jupyter notebook," the web app servers, and select user interface toolkits can be used with matplotlib. Matplotlib attempts to further simplify easy tasks and make difficult tasks feasible. With only a few lines of code, you can produce tracks, histograms, scatter plots, bar graphs, error graphs, etc.

A MATLAB-like interface is provided for easy plotting of the Pyplot Module, especially when coupled with IPython. As a power user, you can regulate the entire line styles, font's properties, and axis properties through an object-oriented interface or a collection of features similar to the one provided to MATLAB users.

SciPy (Fundamental library for scientific computing)

SciPy is a "collection of mathematical algorithms and convenience functions built on the NumPy extension of Python," capable of adding more impact to interactive Python sessions, by offering high-level data manipulation and visualization commands and courses for the user. An interactive Python session with SciPy becomes an environment that rivals data processing and system prototyping technologies, including "MATLAB, IDL, Octave, R-Lab, and SciLab."

Another advantage of developing "SciPy" on Python is the accessibility of a strong programming language in the development of advanced programs and specific apps. Scientific apps using SciPy benefit from developers around the globe, developing extra modules in countless software landscape niches. Everything produced has been made accessible to the Python programmer, from database subroutines and classes as well as "parallel programming to the web." These powerful tools are provided along with the "SciPy" mathematical libraries.

IPython (Enhanced interactive console)

"IPython (Interactive Python)" is an interface or command shell for interactive computing using a variety of programming languages. "IPython" was initially created exclusively for Python, which supports introspection, rich media, shell syntax, tab completion, and history. Some of the functionalities provided by IPython include: "interactive shells (terminal and Qt-based); browser-based notebook interface with code, text, math, inline plots, and other media support;

support for interactive data visualization and use of GUI tool kits; flexible interpreters that can be embedded to load into your own projects; tools for parallel computing". The architecture of "IPython" offers "parallel and distributed computing." IPython" allows the development, execution, debugging, and interactive monitoring of parallel applications, thus the "I (Interactive) in IPython." The underlying architecture can easily separate parallelism, allowing "IPython" to assist with multiple parallelism styles including: "Single program, various information (SPMD) parallelism," "Multiple programs, various data (MIMD) parallelism," "Message passing using MPI," "Task parallelism," "Data parallelism," combinations of these methods and even customized user-defined strategies.

The parallel computing functionality has been rendered optional under the "ipyparallel python package," with the implementation of "IPython 4.0".
"IPython" often derives from "SciPy stack libraries" such as "NumPy" and "SciPy," frequently installed in combination with one of the various "Scientific Python distributions." IPython" can also be integrated with select "SciPy stack libraries," primarily "matplotlib," which produces inline charts upon use with the "Jupyter notebook." For customization of rich object display, Python libraries can be implemented with "IPython-specific hooks." For instance, if used in the context of "IPython," "SymPy" can implement "rendering of mathematical expressions as rendered LaTeX."

SymPy (Symbolic mathematics)
Developed by Ondřej Čertík and Aaron Meurer, SymPy is "an open-source Python library for symbolic computation." It offers algebra computing abilities to other apps as a stand-alone app and/or as a library as well as live on the internet applications with "SymPy Live" or "SymPy Gamma." "SymPy" is easy to install and test, owing to the fact that it is completely developed in Python boasting limited dependencies. SymPy involves characteristics ranging from calculus, algebra, discrete mathematics, and quantum physics to fundamental symbolic arithmetic. The outcome of the computations can be formatted as the "LaTeX" code. In combination with a straightforward, expandable codebase in a widespread programming language, the ease of access provided by SymPy makes it a computer algebra system with a comparatively low entry barrier.

Pandas (Data structures and analysis)

Pandas provide highly intuitive and user-friendly high-level data structures. "Pandas" has achieved popularity in the machine learning algorithm developer community, with built-in techniques for data aggregation, grouping, and filtering as well as results of time series analysis. The Pandas library has two primary structures: one-dimensional "Series" and two-dimensional "Data Frames."

Some of the key features provided by "Pandas" are listed below:

- A quick and effective "Data Frame object" with embedded indexing to be used in data manipulation activities.
- Tools to read and write data between internal memory data structures and multiple file formats, such as "CSV" and text, "Microsoft Excel," "SQL databases," and quick "HDF5 format".
- Intelligent data alignment and integrated management of incomplete data by achieving automatic label driven computational alignment and readily manipulating unorganized data into an orderly manner.
- Flexible reconstructing and pivoting of datasets.
- Smart label-based slicing and indexing of big data sets, as well as the creation of data subsets.
- Columns can be added to and removed from data structures to achieve the desired size of the database.
- Aggregation or transformation of data using a sophisticated "Group By" system enabling execution of the "split-apply-combine" technique on the data.
- Highly efficient merge and join functions of the data set.
- "Hierarchical axis indexing" offers a simple way to work in a low dimensional data structure even with high dimensional data.
- Time-series functionalities, including "date range generation and frequency conversion, moving window statistics, moving window linear regressions, date shifting, and lagging." Also, the creation of "domain-specific time offsets" and the capability of joining time series with no data loss.
- Having most of the underlying code in "Cython" or "C," Pandas boasts high performance and efficiency.
- Python, in combination with Pandas is being used in a broad range of academic and industrial sectors, including Financial Services, Statistics,

Neurobiology, Economics, Marketing and Advertising, Online Data Analytics, among others.

The two types of Data Structures offered by Pandas are: "Pandas DataFrame" and "Pandas Series."

Pandas DataFrame

It is defined as "2-D labeled data structure with columns of a potentially different type". It has a high resemblance to the Excel spreadsheet, as shown in the picture below, with multiple similar features for analysis, modification, and extraction of valuable insights from the data. You can create a "Pandas DataFrame" by entering datasets from "Excel," "CSV," and "MySQL database," among others.

	NAME	AGE	DESIGNATION
1	a	20	VP
2	b	27	CEO
3	c	35	CFO
4	d	55	VP
5	e	18	VP
6	f	21	CEO
7	g	35	MD

For instance, in the picture above, assume "Keys" are represented by the name of the columns, and "Values" are represented by the list of items in that column. A "Python dictionary" can be used to represent this as shown in the code below:

```
"my_dict = {
   'name' : ["a", "b", "c", "d", "e","f", "g"],
   'age' : [20,27, 35, 55, 18, 21, 35],
   'designation': ["VP", "CEO", "CFO", "VP", "VP", "CEO", "MD"]
}"
```

The "Pandas DataFrame" can be created from this dictionary by using the code below:

```
"import Pandas as PD
df = pd.DataFrame(my_dict)"
```

The resulting "DataFrame" is shown in the picture below which resembles the excel spreadsheet:

	age	designation	name
0	20	VP	a
1	27	CEO	b
2	35	CFO	c
3	55	VP	d
4	18	VP	e
5	21	CEO	f
6	35	MD	g

If you would like to define index values for the rows, you will have to add the "index" parameter in the "DataFrame ( )" clause as shown below:

"df = pd.DataFrame(my_dict, index=[1,2,3,4,5,6,7])"

To obtain "string" indexes for the data instead of numeric, use the code below:

"df = pd.DataFrame(
   my_dict,
   index=["First", "Second", "Third", "Fourth", "Fifth", "Sixth", "Seventh"]
)"

Now, as these index values are uniform, you could execute the code below to utilize the "NumPy arrays" as index values:

"np_arr = np.array([10,20,30,40,50,60,70])
df = pd.DataFrame(my_dict, index=np_arr)"

Similar to "NumPy", the columns of "DataFrame" are also homogeneous. You can use dictionary like syntax or add the column name with "DataFrame" to view the data type of the column as shown in the code below:

"df['age'].dtype   # Dict Like Syntax
df.age.dtype   # DataFrame.ColumnName

df.name.dtype   # DataFrame.ColumnName"

You can use the code below to selectively view the record or rows available within the "Pandas DataFrame" by using the "head ( )" function for the first five rows and "tail ( )" function for the last five rows. For example, to see the data's first three rows, you can use the code below:

"df.head(3)   # Display first 3 Rows"

Pandas Series

It can be defined as a "one-dimensional labeled array capable of holding data of any type (integer, string, float, python objects)." Simply put, it is like a column in an excel spreadsheet. To generate a "Pandas Series" from an array, a "NumPy" module must be imported and used with "array ()" function as shown in the code below:

"# import pandas as pd
import pandas as pd"

"# import numpy as np
import numpy as np"

"# simple array
data = np.array (['m','a','c','h','T','n','e'])"

"ser = pd.Series(data)
print(ser)"

Seaborn (data visualization)
Seaborn is derived from the Matplotlib Library and an extremely popular visualization library. It is a high-level library that can generate specific kinds of graph including heat maps, time series, and violin plots.

TensorFlow
TensorFlow can be defined as a Machine Learning platform providing end-to-end service with a variety of free and open sources. It has a system of multilayered nodes that allow for quick building, training, and deployment of artificial neural networks with large data sets. It is touted as a "simple and flexible architecture to

take new ideas from concept to code to state-of-the-art models and to publication at a rapid pace." For example, Google uses TensorFlow libraries in its image recognition and speech recognition tools and technologies.

Higher-level APIs such as "tf.estimator" can be used for specifying predefined architectures, such as "linear regressors" or "neural networks." The picture below shows the existing hierarchy of the TensorFlow tool kit:

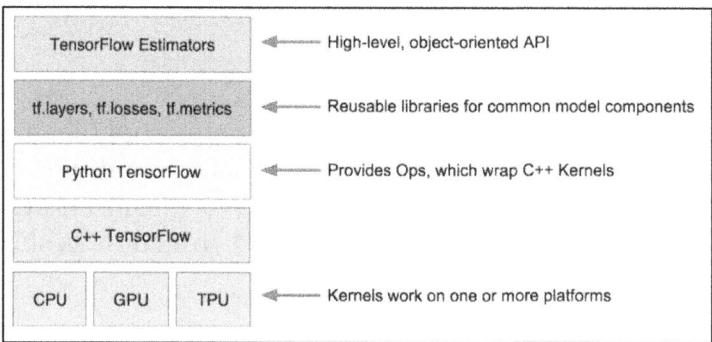

The picture shown below provides the purposes of the different layers:

Toolkit(s)	Description
Estimator (tf.estimator)	High-level, OOP API.
tf.layers/tf.losses/tf.metrics	Libraries for common model components.
TensorFlow	Lower-level APIs

The two fundamental components of TensorFlow are:
1. A "graph protocol buffer"
2. A "runtime" that can execute the graph

The two-component mentioned above are similar to the "Python" code and the "Python interpreter." Just as the "Python interpreter" can run Python code on several hardware systems, TensorFlow can be operated on various hardware systems, like CPU, GPU, and TPU.

To make a decision regarding which API(s) should be used, you must consider the API offering the highest abstraction level to solve the target problem. Easier to use, but (by design) less flexible, are the greater abstract levels. It is recommended to first begin with the highest-level API and make everything work. If for certain unique modeling issues, you need extra flexibility, move one level down. Notice that each level is constructed on the lower-level APIs. It should thus be quite simple to decrease the hierarchy.

For the development of the majority of Machine Learning models, we will use "tf.estimator" API, which significantly lowers the number of code lines needed for development. Also, "tf.estimator" is compatible with Scikit-Learn API.

Chapter 3: Predictive Modeling, Data Visualization and Creation of Training Data Set

Machine Learning

Artificial intelligence is the manifestation of the idea that machines are capable of human-like intelligence and can mimic human thought processing and learning capabilities to adapt to new inputs and perform tasks without requiring human assistance. Machine learning is integral to the concept of artificial intelligence. Machine learning can be defined as a concept of artificial intelligence technology that focuses primarily on the engineered capability of machines to learn and self-train, by identifying data patterns to improve upon the underlying algorithm and make independent decisions. Machine learning hypothesizes that modern-day computers have an ability to be trained using a training data set that can be easily customized to meet desired functionalities. Machine learning is driven by the pattern recognition technique wherein the machine records and revisit past interactions and results that are deemed in alignment with its current situation. Given the fact that machines are required to process the endless amount of data, with new data always pouring in, they must be equipped to adapt to the new data without needing to be programmed by a human speaks to the iterative aspect of machine learning.

Machines are capable of learning from and self-training by utilizing previous computations and underlying algorithms to produce high-quality decisions and results that are easily reproducible. The concept of machine learning has been around for decades, but recent advancements in machine learning algorithms have made it possible for the machines to process and analyze big data. This is accomplished by the application of advanced and complex mathematical calculations using automation at high speed and frequency.

Advanced computing machines of today are capable of rapidly analyzing the humongous amount of data and delivering faster and more accurate results. Companies that are employing machine learning algorithms have enhanced flexibility to modify the training data set to meet their business requirements and train the machines accordingly. These customized machine learning algorithms allow businesses to identify potential risks as well as growth opportunities. Machine learning algorithms are typically used in collaboration with artificial intelligence technology and cognitive technologies to make the machines highly effective and efficient in processing large volumes of data or big data and produce highly accurate results.

Given the intrinsic link between artificial intelligence and machine learning, going forward to make this book easier to understand, we will be using the terms "machine learning" and "artificial intelligence" interchangeably.

There are four types of machine learning algorithms available today:

Supervised Machine Learning Algorithms

These algorithms are widely used in predictive big data analysis, owing to its capability of assessing and applying the lessons learned from previous iterations and interactions to new input data set. These algorithms can label all their ongoing runs based on the instructions provided to successfully predict and forecast future events. For example, humans can program the machine to label its data points as "R" (Run), "N" (Negative), or "P" (Positive). The machine learning algorithm will then label the input data as programmed and receive data inputs with corresponding correct outputs. The algorithm will run a comparison of its own generated output against the "expected or correct" output, to identify potential improvements that can be made and errors that can be fixed to make the model more accurate and smarter.

By applying methods like "regression," "prediction," "classification," and "ingredient boosting" to well train the machine learning algorithms, any new input data can be fed into the machine as "target" data set to orchestrate the learning program as desired. This "known training data set" jump-starts the analytical process, which is followed by the learning algorithm to produce and "inferred function" that can be used to generate forecasts and predictions for future events based on the output values. For example, financial institutions and banks are heavily dependent on supervised machine learning algorithms to detect fraudulent credit card transactions and predict the likelihood of a potential credit card customer failing to make their credit payments on time.

Unsupervised Machine Learning Algorithms

Companies often run into a situation where data sources required to generate a labeled and classified training data set are unavailable. In these situations, the use of unsupervised machine learning algorithms is ideal. Unsupervised machine learning algorithms are used to identify ways in which machines can create "inferred functions" to elucidate a hidden structure from the pile of the unlabeled and unclassified data set. These algorithms are capable of exploring the data to identify a structure within the mass of information.

Unlike the supervised machine learning algorithms, the unsupervised algorithms fail out to identify the correct output, although they are just as efficient at exploring the input data and drawing inferences as the supervised learning algorithms. These algorithms can be used for identification of data outliers, generation of customized and personalized product recommendations, and classification of text topics using techniques like "self-organizing maps," "singular value decomposition," and "k-means clustering." For example, the identification of customers with shared shopping attributes that can be segmented into specific groups and targeted with similar marketing strategies and campaigns. As a result, the unsupervised learning algorithms are extremely popular in the online marketing space.

Semi-Supervised Machine Learning Algorithms

The semi-supervised machine learning algorithms are highly versatile and capable of utilizing labeled as well as unlabeled data set to learn from and train themselves. These algorithms are a "hybrid" of supervised and unsupervised learning algorithms. Typically, the training data set is composed of predominantly unlabeled data with a small amount of label data. The use of analytical methods including "prediction," "regression," and "classification" in combination with semi-supervised learning algorithms allows the Machine to significantly improve its learning accuracy and training abilities.

These algorithms are widely used in cases where generating labeled training data set from raw data highly resource-intensive and less cost-effective for the company. So to avoid additional personnel and equipment cost, companies use semi-supervised learning algorithms on their systems. For example, the facial recognition application requires a large volume of facial data spread across multiple input sources. The preprocessing, processing, classification, and labeling of the raw data obtained from sources like web cameras, requires a lot of manpower, and thousands of hours of work in order to be used as a training data set.

Reinforcement Machine Learning Algorithms

The reinforcement machine learning algorithms are much more unique in that it learns from the environment. These algorithms perform actions and diligently record the results of each action that would have either been a failure resulting in an error or reward for successful execution. The two main characteristics that distinguish the reinforcement learning algorithms are "trial and error" research method and "delayed reward." The machine repeatedly analyzes input data by using a variety of calculations and sending a reinforcement signal for every correct or expected output, to eventually optimize the end result. Simple action and reward feedback loop are developed by the system to assess, record, and learn which actions were successful and led to accurate results in a shorter period of time. The use of these algorithms allows the automatic determination of ideal behaviors within the constraints of a specific context by the system to, and hence, its capabilities and maximize its performance. As a result, the reinforcement machine learning algorithms are heavily used in the gaming industry, robotics engineering as well as in navigation systems.

Big Data Analytics vs. Machine Learning

"Machine learning," "Big Data," as well as "Big Data Analytics" fall under the umbrella of "Artificial Intelligence" technology, which rolls up into the field of "Data Science." Here are some key differences between machine learning and big data or big data analytics:

Applications

Machine learning is used in the development of advanced recommendation engines and models that can predict and forecast future events by analyzing and existing data. For example, "Google" is using advanced machine learning algorithms and the development of their self-driving cars. Virtual personal and home assistance devices such as "Amazon Alexa," "Google Home," and "Apple HomePod" are all driven by advanced machine learning algorithms, working in close collaboration with artificial intelligence technology.

Big data has much wider applicability and can be used for general research purposes to gather information regarding specific business queries such as collecting sales data, building consumer profiles, and financial research, among other applications across industrial domains.

Learning capability

Machine learning algorithms are self-sufficient and capable of learning from a training data set as well as new input data without human assistance. They are powerful enough to create the foundation required for the system to learn and improve upon itself. Big data analytics is capable of gathering existing data and analyzing it for the identification of emerging patterns that can be used in its decision-making process. It is always powered by human-controlled analytical tools and technologies with no scope of self-learning.

Pattern recognition

Big data analytics utilizes statistical methods like regression, clustering, and classification, to recognize data patterns that can be analyzed to produce logical information.

Machine learning can not only recognize emerging data patterns but apply advanced algorithms on these patterns to learn from the data patterns and maximize the system performance with every successive iteration.

Data volume and Data type

Big data pertains to the humongous amount of unstructured, semi-structured, and structured data. Advanced analytical tools and technologies are required to process these large data sets with a majority of unstructured data to gather valuable information.

Machine learning utilizes relatively smaller data sets that are classified and labeled to serve as guiding instructions for the algorithms to learn and improve upon itself.

Fundamental Purpose

The main goal of machine learning is self-improvement solely on the basis of input data with little to no human assistance. The promising use of these algorithms and the development of smart machines could someday assist in providing answers to daunting challenges facing humanity, such as global warming.

Big data is designed to collect and store the skyrocketing data generated by our evolving digital lives. The big data analytics uses pattern recognition technology to uncover hidden patterns and insight that can be easily lost in this mass of information.

Customer Analytics

According to SAS, customer analytics can be defined as "processes and technologies bad gives organizations the customer insight necessary to deliver offers that are anticipated, relevant and timely." Customer analytics is at the heart of all marketing activities and is an umbrella term used for techniques such as "predictive modeling," "data visualization," "information management," and "segmentation."

Importance of Customer Analytics

Customer analytics has evolved as the backbone of the marketing industry. This is a direct result of the advent of "smart consumer" who is more aware and connected to one another than ever before and willing to take their business elsewhere at a moment's notice. The smart customer has seamless access to a variety of information including the best products and services available in the market and where can they find the best deals to make the most of their money. Therefore, companies are required to be proactive and be able to predict consumer behavior when interacting with their products and to be in a position to take the required action to convert the prospective customer into a paying client. To generate more accurate forecasts and predictions of customer behavior, companies must have a solid understanding of their customers' buying habits and lifestyle choices. These near accurate predictions will provide the company with an edge over the competition and help achieve higher conversion rates in their sales and marketing funnel.

One of the best customer analytics solution in the market today is "SAS Customer Intelligence," which claims to have the following applications:

- Achieve higher customer loyalty and response rates.
- Generate personalized customer offers and messages to reach the right customer at the right time.
- Identify prospective customers with similar attributes and a high likelihood of conversion so the company can reduce costs on their targeted marketing strategies and campaigns.
- Reduce customer attrition by generating accurate predictions on customers that are more likely to take their business somewhere else and developing proactive marketing campaigns to retain them.

"The insights derived from our new analytics capabilities are allowing us to find the sweet spots that will continue to drive loyalty, profitability, and sustainable growth."
- Carrie Gray, Executive Director for Medium Business Marketing, Verizon

Predictive Analytics Marketing

According to SAS, predictive analytics is the *"use of data, statistical algorithms, and machine learning techniques to identify the likelihood of future outcomes based on historical data. The goal is to go beyond knowing what has happened to provide the best assessment of what will happen in the future"*. Today, companies are digging through their past with an eye on the future, and this is where artificial intelligence for marketing comes into play, with the application of predictive analytics technology. The success of predictive analytics is directly proportional to the quality of big data collected by the company.

Here are some of the widely used predictive analytics applications for marketing:

Predictive Analysis for Customer Behavior

For the industrial giants like "Amazon," "Apple," and "Netflix," analyzing customer activities and behavior is fundamental to their day-to-day operations. Smaller businesses are increasingly following in their footsteps to implement predictive analysis in their business model. The development of a customized suite of predictive models for a company is not only capital-intensive but also requires extensive manpower and time. Marketing companies like "AgilOne" offer relatively simple predictive model types with wide applicability across industrial domains. They have identified three main types of predictive models to analyze customer behavior, which are:

"Propensity models" – These models are used to generate "true or accurate" predictions for customer behavior. Some of the most common propensity models include: "predictive lifetime value," "propensity to buy," "propensity to turn," "propensity to convert," "likelihood of engagement," and "propensity to unsubscribe."

"Cluster models" – These models are used to separate and group customers based on shared attributes such as gender, age, purchase history, and demographics. Some of the most common cluster models include "product-based or category base clustering," "behavioral customs clustering," and "brand based clustering."

"Collaborative filtering" – These models are used to generate products and services and recommendations as well as to recommended advertisements based on prior customer activities and behaviors. Some of the most common collaborative filtering models include "upsell," "cross-sell," and "next sell" recommendations.

The most significant tool used by companies to execute predictive analytics on customer behavior is "regression analysis," which allows the company to establish correlations between the sale of a particular product and the specific attributes displayed by the purchasing customer. This is achieved by employing "regression coefficients," which are numeric values depicting the degree to which the customer behavior is affected by different variables and developing a "likelihood score" for the future sale of the product.

Predictive Data Analysis using Scikit-Learn library

To understand how Scikit-Learn library is used in the development of the "Predictive Data Analysis" or machine learning model, let us use the "Sales_Win_Loss data set from IBM's Watson repository" containing data obtained from sales campaign of a wholesale supplier of automotive parts. We will build a machine learning model to predict which sales campaign will be a winner and which will incur a loss.

The data set can be imported using Pandas and explored using Pandas techniques such as "head (), tail (), and dtypes ()." The plotting techniques from "Seaborn" will be used to visualize the data. To process the data Scikit-Learn's "preprocessing.LabelEncoder ()" will be used and "train_test_split ()" to divide the data set into a training subset and testing subset.

To generate predictions from our data set, three different algorithms will be used, namely, "Linear Support Vector Classification and K-nearest neighbor classifier." To compare the performances of these algorithms, Scikit-Learn library technique, "accuracy_score," will be used. The performance score of the models can be visualized using "Yellowbrick" visualization and Scikit-Learn.

Installing Scikit-Learn

The latest version of Scikit-Learn can be found on "Scikit-Learn.org" and requires "Python (version >= 3.5); NumPy (version >= 1.11.0); SciPy (version >= 0.17.0); joblib (version >= 0.11)". The plotting capabilities or functions of Scikit-learn start with "plot_" and require "Matplotlib (version >= 1.5.1)". Certain Scikit-Learn examples may need additional applications: "Scikit-Image (version >= 0.12.3), Pandas (version >= 0.18.0)".

With the prior installation of "NumPy" and "SciPy," the best method of installing Scikit-Learn is using "pip: pip install -U scikit-learn" or "conda: conda install scikit-learn."

One must make sure that "binary wheels" are utilized when using pip and that "NumPy" and "SciPy" have not been recompiled from source, which may occur with the use of specific OS and hardware settings (for example, "Linux on a Raspberry Pi"). Developing "NumPy" and "SciPy" from source tends to be complicated (particularly on Windows); therefore, they need to be set up carefully, making sure the optimized execution of linear algebra routines is achievable.

Importing the Data Set

To import the "Sales_Win_Loss data set from IBM's Watson repository," the first step is importing the "Pandas" module using "*import pandas as pd.*"

Then, we leverage a variable URL as *"https://community.watsonanalytics.com/wp content/uploads/2015/04/WA_Fn-UseC_-Sales-Win-Loss.csv"* so that the data set can be stored and downloaded on the URL.

Now, *"read_csv() as sales_data = pd.read_csv(url)"* technique will be used to read the above "CSV or comma-separated values" file, which is supplied by the Pandas module. The CSV file will then be converted into a Pandas data framework with the return variable as "*sales_data,*" where the framework will be stored.

For new 'Pandas' users, the *"pd. read CSV()"* technique in the code mentioned above will generate a tabular data structure called "data framework", where an index for each row is contained in the first column, and the label/name for each column in the first row are the names taken from the data set located in the initial column. In the above code snippet, the *"sales data"* variable results in a table depicted in the picture below.

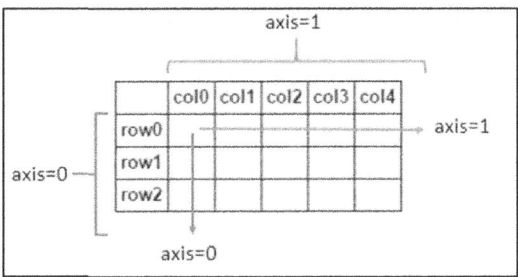

In the above diagram, the individual column is represented by the "row0, row1, row2," and the names for the features of the data set or individual columns are represented by "col0, col1, col2".

With this step, you have successfully stored a copy of the data set and transformed it into a "Pandas" framework!

Now, using the *"head() as Sales_data.head()"* technique, the records from the data framework can be displayed as shown below to get a "feel" of the information contained in the data set.

Data Exploration

We can quickly explore the data to understand what information can tell can be gathered from it and accordingly to plan a course of action.

In any machine learning project, data exploration tends to be a very critical phase. Even a fast data set exploration can offer us significant information that could be easily missed otherwise, and this information can propose significant questions that we can then attempt to answer using our project.

Some third-party Python libraries will be used here to assist us with the processing of the data so that we can efficiently use this data with the powerful algorithms of Scikit-Learn. The same *"head()"* technique that we used to see some initial records of the imported data set in the earlier section can be used here. As a matter of fact, *"(head)"* is effectively capable of doing much more than displaying data records and customize the "head()" technique to display only a selected record with commands like *"sales_data.head(n=2)"*. This command will selectively display the first 2 records of the data set. At a glance, it's obvious that string data is contained in columns such as "Supplies Group" and "Region," while columns such as "Opportunity Resultthe "Opportunity Number," et cetera. are comprised of integer values. It can also be seen that there are unique identifiers for each record in the' Opportunity Number' column.

Similarly, to display select records from the bottom of the table, the *"tail() as sales_data.tail()"* can be used.

To view the different data types available in the data set, the Pandas technique *"dtypes() as sales_data.dtypes"* can be used. With this information, the data columns available in the data framework can be listed with their respective data types. We can figure out, for example, that the "object" data type is in the column "Supplies Subgroup" and that the "integer data type" is in the column "Client Size By Revenue." So, we have an understanding of columns that either contains integer values or string data.

Data Visualization

At this point, we are through with basic data exploration steps, so we will not attempt to build some appealing plots to portray the information visually and discover other concealed narratives from our data set.

Of all the available Python libraries providing data visualization features; "Seaborn" is one of the best available options, so we will be using the same. Make sure that python plots module provided by "Seaborn" has been installed on your system and ready to be used. Now, follow the steps below generate the desired plot for the data set:

Step 1 – Transfer the module "Seaborn" with the command *"import seaborn as sns."*
Step 2 – Transfer the module "Matplotlib" with command *"import matplotlib.pyplot as plt."*
Step 3 - Use the command *"sns.set(style="whitegrid", color_codes=True)"* in setting to white the "background color" of the plot.
Step 4 - To set the "plot size" for all plots, use command *"sns.set(rc={'figure.figsize':(11.7,8.27)})"*.
Step 5 – To generate a "countplot", use command *"sns.countplot('Route To Market', data=sales_data, hue = 'Opportunity Result')"*.
Step 6 – To eliminate the bottom and top margins, use command *"sns.despine(offset=10, trim=True)"*.
Step 7 – To display the plot, use the command *"plotplt.show()."*

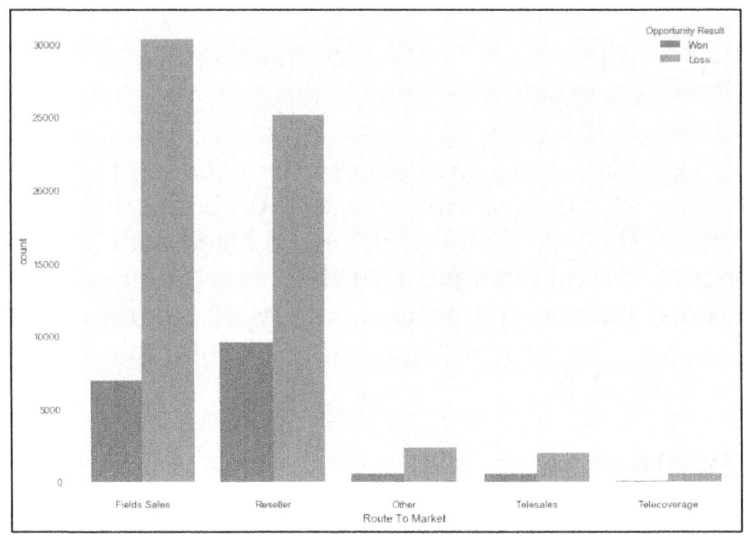

Quick recap - The "Seaborn" and "Matplotlib" modules were imported first. Then the *"set()"* technique was used to define the distinct characteristics for our plots, such as plot style and color. The background of the plot was defined to be white using the code snippet

"sns.set(style= "whitegrid", color codes= True)".

Then the plot size was define using command *"sns.set(rc={'figure.figsize':(11.7,8.27)})"* that define the plot's size as "11.7px and 8.27px".

Next, the command *"sns.countplot('Route To Market',data= sales data, hue='Opportunity Result')"* was used to generate the plot. The "countplot()" technique enables the creation of a count plot, which can expose multiple arguments to customize the count plot according to our requirements. As part of the first *"countplot()"* argument, the X-axis was defined as "Route To Market" column from the data set. The next problem concerns the origin of the data set, which would be the "sales_data" data framework we imported earlier. The third argument is the color of the bar graphs that were defined as "blue" representing the "won" column and "green" for the "loss" column."

Data Pre-processing

By now, you should have a clear understanding of what information is available in the data set. To transform categorical labels from the data set such as "won" and "loss" into numerical values, we will use the *"LabelEncoder()"* technique.

Let's look at the pictures below to see what we are attempting to accomplish with the *"LabelEncoder()"* technique. The first image contains "color" column with 3 records, namely, "Red," "Green," and "Blue." Using the *"LabelEncoder()"* technique, the record in the same "color" column can be converted to numerical values, as shown in the second image.

	Color
0	Red
1	Green
2	Blue

	Color
0	1
1	2
2	3

Let's begin the real process of conversion now. Using the *"fit transform()"* technique given by *"LabelEncoder(),"* the categorical column's label like "Route To Market" can be encoded and converted to numerical labels comparable to those shown in the diagrams above. The function *"fit transform()"* requires input labels identified by the user and consequently returns encoded labels.

To know how the encoding is accomplished, let's go through an example quickly. The code instance below constitutes string data in the form of a cities' list such as ["Paris," "Paris," "Tokyo," "Amsterdam"] that will be encoded into something comparable to "[2, 2, 1,3]".

Step 1 - To import the required module, use the command *"from sklearn import preprocessing."*
Step 2 – To create the Label encoder object, use command *"le = preprocessing.LabelEncoder()".*
Step 3 – To convert the categorical columns into numerical values, use command:

"encoded_value = le.fit_transform(["Paris", "Paris", "Tokyo", "Amsterdam"])"
"print(encoded_value) [1 1 2 0]"

We just transformed our labels for string data into numerical values. The first step was importing the preprocessing module that offers the *"LabelEncoder()"*

technique. Followed by the development of an object representing the *"LabelEncoder()"* type. Then, the *"fit_transform()"* function of the object was used to distinguish between the list's distinct classes ["Paris," "Paris," "Tokyo," "Amsterdam,"] and output the encoded values of "[1 1 2 0]".

The technique of *"LabelEncoder()"* assigns the numerical values with regards to the classes' initial letter, alphabetically to the classes, for example "(A)msterdam" was assigned code "0", "(P)aris" was assigned code "1" and "(T)okyo" was assigned code "2".

Creating Training and Test subsets

To know the interactions between distinct characteristics and how these characteristics influence the target variable, a collection of information must be learned by a machine learning algorithm. We need to split the complete data set into two subsets to accomplish this. One subset will serve as the training data set, which will be used to train our algorithm to construct machine learning models. The other subset will serve as the test data set, which will be used to test the accuracy of the predictions generate by the machine learning model.

The first phase in this stage is the separation of feature and target variables using the steps below:

Step 1 – To select data excluding select columns, use command *"select columns other than 'Opportunity Number', 'Opportunity Result'cols = [col for col in sales_data.columns if col not in ['Opportunity Number','Opportunity Result']]"*.
Step 2 – To drop these select columns, use the command *"dropping the 'Opportunity Number' and 'Opportunity Result' columns
data = sales_data[cols]"*.
Step 3 – To assign the Opportunity Result column as "target", use command *"target = sales_data['Opportunity Result']
data.head(n=2)"*.

The "Opportunity Number" column was removed since it just acts as a unique identifier for each record. The "Opportunity Result" contains the predictions we want to generate, so it becomes our "target" variable and can be removed from the data set for this phase. The first line of the above code will select all the columns except "Opportunity Number" & "Opportunity Result" in. These columns are then assigned to the "cols" variable. Then using the columns in the "cols" variable, a new data framework was developed. This is going to be the "feature set." Next, the column "Opportunity Result" from the *"sales_data"* data frame was used to develop a new data framework called "target."

The second phase in this stage is to separate the date frameworks into training and testing subsets using the steps below. Depending on the data set and desired predictions, it needs to be split into training and testing subset accordingly. For this exercise, we will use 75% of the data as a training subset, and the rest 25% will be used for the testing subset. We will leverage the *"train_test_split()"* technique in "Scikit-Learn" in order to separate the information using steps and code as below:

Step 1 – To import the required module, use the command *"from sklearn.model_selection import train_test_split"*.
Step 2 – To separate the data set, use command *"split data set into train and test setsdata_train, data_test, target_train, target_test = train_test_split(data, target, test_size = 0.30, random_state = 10)"*.

With the code above, the *"train_test_split"* module was first imported, followed by the use of *"train_test_split()"* technique to generate "training subset *(data_train, target_train)"* and "testing subset *(data_test, data_train)."* The *"train_test_split()"* technique's first argument pertains to the features that were divided in the preceding stage, the next argument relates to the ("Opportunity Result") target. We are using 30% for this example, although it can be any amount. The fourth 'random state' argument is used to make sure that the results can be reproduced every time.

Building the Machine Learning Model

The "machine_learning_map" provided by Scikit-Learn is widely used to choose the most appropriate ML algorithm for the data set. For this exercise, we will be using "Linear Support Vector Classification" and "K-nearest neighbors' classifier" algorithms.

Linear Support Vector Classification

"Linear Support Vector Classification" or "Linear SVC" is a sub-classification of "Support Vector Machine (SVM)" algorithm, which we have reviewed in chapter 2 of this book titled "Machine Learning Algorithms." Using Linear SVC, the data can be divided into different planes so the algorithm can identify the optimal group structure for all the data classes.

Here are the steps and code for this algorithm to build our first ML model:

Step 1 – To import the required modules, use commands *"from sklearn.svm import LinearSVC"* and *"from sklearn.metrics import accuracy_score"*.
Step 2 – To develop an LinearSVC object type, use command *"svc_model = LinearSVC(random_state=0)"*.
Step 3 – In training the algorithm and and generating predictions from the testing data, use command *"pred = svc_model.fit(data_train, target_train).predict(data_test)"*.
Step 4 – To display the model accuracy score, use command *"print ('LinearSVC accuracy:', accuracy_score(target_test, pred, normalize = True))"*.

With the code above, the required modules were imported in the first step. We then developed a type of Linear SVC using the "svc_model" object with "random_state" as '0'. In step 3, the "Linear SVC" algorithm is trained on the training data set and subsequently used to generate predictions for the target from the testing data. The *"accuracy_score()"* technique was used in the end to verify the "accuracy score" of the model, which could be displayed as "LinearSVC accuracy: 0.777811004785", for instance.

K-nearest Neighbors Classifier

The "k-nearest neighbors (k-NN)" algorithm is referred to as "a non-parametric method used for classification and regression in pattern recognition." In cases of classification and regression, "the input consists of the nearest k closest training examples in the feature space." K-NN is a form of "instance-based learning," or "lazy learning," in which the function is only locally estimated, and all calculations are delayed until classification. The output is driven by the fact, whether the classification or regression method is used for "k-NN":

- "k-nearest neighbors classification" - The "output" is a member of the class. An "object" is classified by its neighbors' plurality vote, assigning the object to the most prevalent class among its nearest "k-neighbors," where "k" denotes a small positive integer. If k= 1, the "object" is simply allocated to the closest neighbor's class.

- "k-nearest neighbors regression" - The output is the object's property value, which is computed as an average of the k-nearest neighbors' values.

A helpful method for both classification and regression can be assigning weights to the neighbors' contributions to allow closer neighbors to make more contributions in the average compared to the neighbors located far apart. For instance, a known "weighting scheme" is to assign each neighbor a weight of "$1/d$", where "d" denotes the distance from the neighbor. The neighbors are selected from a set of objects for which the "class" (for "k-NN classification") or the feature value of the "object" (for "k-NN regression") is known.

Here are the steps and code for this algorithm to build our next ML model:

Step 1 – To import required modules, use the command *"from sklearn. neighbors import KNeighborsClassifier"* and *"from sklearn.metrics import accuracy_ score".*

Step 2 – In creating the object of the classifier, use command *"neigh = KNeighborsClassifier(n_ neighbors=3)".*

Step 3 – In training the algorithm, use command *"neigh.fit(data_train, target_train)."*

Step 4 – To generate predictions, use command *"pred = neigh.predict(data_test)".*

Step 5 – To evaluate the accuracy, use command *"print ('KNeighbors accuracy score:,' accuracy_score(target_test, pred))."*

Now that our preferred algorithms have been introduced, the model with the highest accuracy score can be easily selected. In Scikit-Learn, the "Yellowbrick library" can be used, which offers techniques to depict various scoring techniques visually.

Data Visualization with Scatter Plots

A scatter plot can be defined as "a two-dimensional data visualization that uses dots to represent the values obtained for two different variables-one plotted along the x-axis, and the other plotted along the y-axis." It is also known as a "scatter graph" or "scatter chart." For instance, the "scatter plot" seen in the picture below depicts a fictional set of height and weight measures for children. Each "dot" in the plot is used to represent an individual with measures of their height along the "x-axis" and weight along the "y-axis."

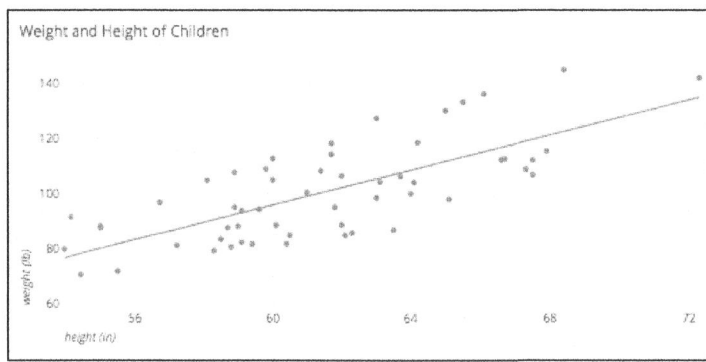

"Scatter plots" are highly useful when you are interested in representing the relationship that exists between two distinct variables. "Scatter plots" are often referred to as "plots of correlation," given the fact that they demonstrate how two distinct variables are related to each other. In the "scatter plot" above, the chart depicts much more than a simple log of the height and weight of children. It also offers a visual of the relationship between the two measures, denoting that as the height increases, the child's weight is also increasing. Now, you can easily conclude that this height and weight relationship isn't ideal, as some taller kids can weigh less than some shorter kids, but the overall trend is fairly satisfactory, and it can be observed that there is a direct relationship between the height and weight of children.

It is important to remember that not all relationships can be linear. For instance, the chart in the picture below indicates an "average of daily high temperature" measured over 7 years, demonstrating a familiar parabolic relationship between these variables as the daily high temperature tends to peak during summer.

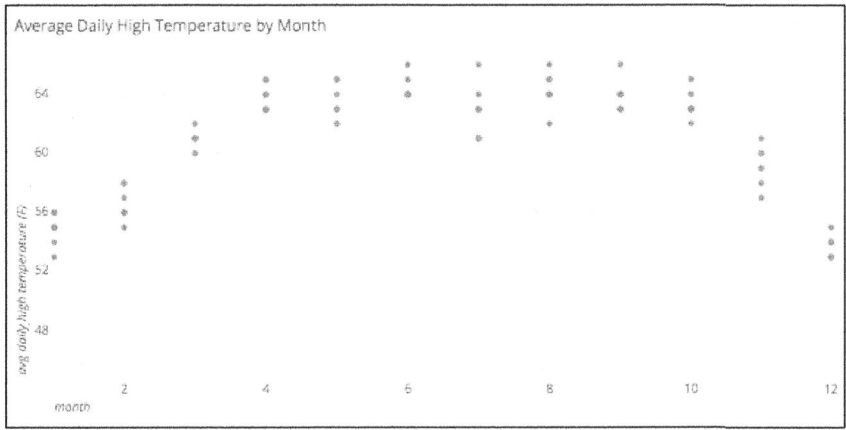

Scatter plots" often contain a trend-line to clarify the relationship between the variable, as shown in the picture below.

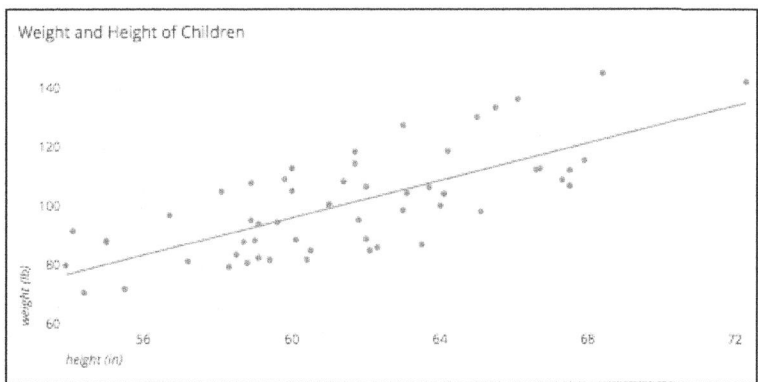

Moreover, the shape, size, and color of the "dot" can be considered and utilized as additional data variables. For instance, the plot below represents the data on the height and weight of the children, but by adding the color of the "dot" to depict the gender of the child, we have acquired a third variable for our analysis.

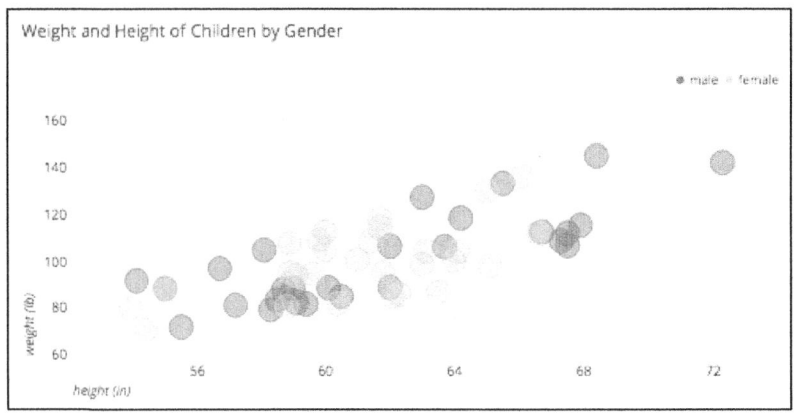

Chapter 4: Applications of Big Data Analysis

Industrial Applications

The applications of Big data and Big Data Analytics are benefiting, both small and big companies across various industrial domains. Some of the widely used industrial applications are:

eCommerce

Over 2.6 billion and counting active social media users include customers and potential customers for every company out there. The race is on to create more effective marketing and social media strategies, powered by machine learning, aimed at providing enhanced customer experience to turn prospective customers into raving fans. The process of sifting through and analyzing a massive amount of data has not only become feasible, but it's easy now. The ability to bridge the gap between execution and big data analysis has been supplemented by artificial intelligence marketing solutions.

Artificial Intelligence (AI) marketing can be defined as a method of you using artificial intelligence consonants like machine learning on available customer data to anticipate customer's needs and expectations while significantly improving the customer's journey. Marketers are able to boost their campaign performance and return on investment read a little to no extra effort in the light of big data insights provided by artificial intelligence marketing solutions. The key elements that make AI marketing as powerful are:

- Big data - A marketing company's ability to aggregate and segment a huge dump of data with minimal manual work is referred to as Big Data. The marketer can then leverage the desired medium to ensure the appropriate message is being delivered to the target audience at the right time.
- Machine learning - Machine learning platforms enable marketers to identify trends or common occurrences and gather effective insights and responses, thereby deciphering the root cause and probability of recurring events.
- Intuitive platform – Super fast and easy to operate applications are integral to AI marketing. Artificial intelligence technology is capable of interpreting

emotions and communicating like a human, allowing AI-based platforms to understand open form content like email responses and social media.

Predictive Analysis

All artificial intelligence technology-based solutions are capable of extracting information from data assets to predict future trends. AI technology has made it possible to model trends that could previously be determined only retroactively. These predictive analysis models can be reliably used in decision-making and to analyze customers' purchase behavior. The model can successfully determine when the consumer is more likely to purchase something new or reorder an old purchase. The marketing companies are now able to reverse engineer customer's experiences and actions to create more lucrative marketing strategies. For example, FedEx and Sprint are using predictive analytics to identify customers who are at potential risk of deflecting to the competitor.

Smart searches

Only a decade ago, if you type in "women's flip flops" on Nike.com, the probability of you finding what you were looking for would be next to zero. But today's search engines are not only accurate but also much faster. This upgrade has largely been brought on by innovations like "semantic search" and "natural language processing" that enable search engines to identify links between products and provide relevant search results, recommend similar items, and auto-correct typing errors. The artificial intelligence technology and big data solutions are able to rapidly analyze user search patterns and identify key areas that the marketing companies should focus on.

In 2015, Google introduced the first Artificial Intelligence-based search algorithm called "RankBrain." Following Google's lead, other major e-commerce websites, including Amazon has incorporated big data analysis and artificial intelligence into their search engines to offer smart search experience for their customers, who are able to find desired products even when they don't know exactly what they're looking for. Even small e-commerce stores have access to Smart search technologies like "Elasticsearch." The data-as-a-service companies like "Indix" allow companies to learn from other larger data sources to train their product search models.

Recommendation Engines

Recommendation engines have quickly evolved into fan favorites and are loved by the customers just as much as the marketing companies. "Apple Music" already knows your taste in music better than your partner, and Amazon always presents you with a list of products that you might be interested in buying. This kind of discovery aide that is able to sift through millions of available options and hone in on an individual's needs are proving indispensable for large companies with huge physical and digital inventories.

In 1998, Swedish computational linguist, Jussi Karlgren, explored the practice of clustering customer behaviors to predict future behaviors in his report titled "Digital bookshelves." The same here, Amazon implemented collaborative filtering to generate recommendations for their customers. The gathering and analysis of consumer data paired with individual profile information and demographics, by the predictive analysis based systems allow the system to continually learn and adapt based on consumer activities such as likes and dislikes on the products in real-time. For example, the company "Sky" has implemented a predictive analysis based model that is capable of recommending content according to the viewer's mode. The smart customer is looking for such an enhanced experience not only from their Music and on-demand entertainment suppliers but also from all other e-commerce websites.

Product Categorization and Pricing

E-commerce businesses and marketing companies have increasingly adopted artificial intelligence in their process of categorization and tagging of the inventory. The Marketing companies are required to deal with awful data just as much, if not more than amazingly organized, clean data. This bag of positive and negative examples serves as training resources for predictive analysis based classification tools. For example, different detailers can have different descriptions for the same product, such as sneakers, basketball shoes, trainers, or Jordan's, but the AI algorithm can identify that these are all the same products and tag them accordingly. Or if the data set is missing the primary keyword like skirts or shirts, the artificial intelligence algorithm can identify and classify the item or product as skirts or shirts based solely on the surrounding context.
We are familiar with the seasonal rate changes of the hotel rooms, but with the advent of artificial intelligence, product prices can be optimized to meet the demand with a whole new level of precision. The machine learning algorithms are

being used for dynamic pricing by analyzing customer's data patterns and making near accurate predictions of what they are willing to pay for that particular product as well as their receptiveness to special offers. This empowers businesses to target their consumers with high precision and calculated whether or not a discount is needed to confirm the sale. Dynamic pricing also allows businesses to compare their product pricing with the market leaders and competitors and adjust their prices accordingly to pull in the sale. For example, "Airbnb" has developed its dynamic pricing system, which provides 'Price Tips' to the property owners to help them determine the best possible listing price for their property. The system takes into account a variety of influencing factors such as geographical location, local events, property pictures, property reviews, listing features, and most importantly, the booking timings and the market demand. The final decision of the property owner to follow or ignore the provided 'price tips' and the success of the listing are also monitored by the system, which will then process the results and adjust its algorithm accordingly.

Predictive Analysis

All artificial intelligence technology-based solutions are capable of extracting information from data assets to predict future trends. AI technology has made it possible to model trends that could previously be determined only retroactively. These predictive analysis models can be reliably used in decision-making and to analyze customers' purchase behavior. The model can successfully determine when the consumer is more likely to purchase something new or reorder an old purchase. The marketing companies are now able to reverse engineer customer's experiences and actions to create more lucrative marketing strategies. For example, FedEx and Sprint are using predictive analytics to identify customers who are at potential risk of deflecting to the competitor.

Customer Targeting and Segmentation

For the marketing companies to be able to reach their customers with a high level of personalization, they are required to target increasingly granular segments. The artificial intelligence technology can draw on the existing customer data and train Machine learning algorithms against "gold standard" training sets to identify common properties and significant variables. The data segments could be as simple as location, gender, and age, or as complex as the buyer's persona and past behavior. With AI, Dynamics Segmentation is feasible which accounts for the fact that customers' behaviors are ever-changing, and people can take on different personas in different situations.

Sales and Marketing Forecast

One of the most straightforward artificial intelligence applications in marketing is in the development of sales and marketing forecasting models. The high volume of quantifiable data such as clicks, purchases, email responses, and time spent on webpages serve as training resources for the machine learning algorithms. Some of the leading business intelligence and production companies in the market are Sisense, Rapidminer, and Birst. Marketing companies are continuously upgrading their marketing efforts, and with the help of AI and machine learning, they can predict the success of their marketing initiatives or email campaigns. Artificial intelligence technology can analyze past sales data, economic trends as well as industrywide comparisons to predict short and long-term sales performance and forecast sales outcomes. The sales forecasts model aid in the estimation of product demand and to help companies manage their production to optimize sales.

Programmatic Advertisement Targeting

With the introduction of artificial intelligence technology, bidding on and targeting program based advertisement has become significantly more efficient. Programmatic advertising can be defined as "the automated process of buying and selling ad inventory to an exchange which connects advertisers to publishers." To allow real-time bidding for inventory across social media channels and mobile devices as well as television, artificial intelligence technology is used. This also goes back to predictive analysis and the ability to model data that could previously only be determined retroactively. Artificial intelligence is able to assist the best time of the day to serve a particular ad, the probability of an ad turning into sales, the receptiveness of the user, and the likelihood of engagement with the ad.

Programmatic companies have the ability to gather and analyze visiting customers' data and behaviors to optimize real-time campaigns and to target the audience more precisely. Programmatic media buying includes the use of "demand-side platforms" (to facilitate the process of buying ad inventory on the open market) and "data management platforms" (to provide the marketing company an ability to reach their target audience). In order to empower the marketing rep to make informed decisions regarding their prospective customers, the data management platforms are designed to collect and analyze the big volume of website "cookie data." For example, search engine marketing (SEM) advertising practiced by channels like Facebook, Twitter, and Google. To efficiently manage huge inventory of the website and application viewers, programmatic ads provide a significant edge over competitors. Google and Facebook serve as the gold standard for efficient and effective advertising and are geared to words providing a user-friendly platform that will allow non-technical marketing companies to start, run and measure their initiatives and campaigns online.

Visual Search and Image Recognition

Leaps and bounds of the advancements in artificial intelligence-based image recognition and analysis technology have resulted in uncanny visual search functionalities. With the introduction of technology like Google Lens and platforms like Pinterest, people can now find results that are visually similar to one another using visual search functionality. The visual search works in the same way as traditional text-based searches that display results on a similar topic. Major retailers and marketing companies are increasingly using the visual search to offer an enhanced and more engaging customer experience. Visual search can be used to improve merchandising and provide product recommendations based on the style of the product instead of the consumer's past behavior or purchases.

Major investments have been made by Target and Asos in the visual search technology development for their e-commerce website. In 2017, Target announced a partnership with interest that allows integration of Pinterest's visual search application called "Pinterest lens" into Target's mobile application. As a result, shoppers can take a picture of products that they would like to purchase while they are out and about and find similar items on Target's e-commerce site. Similarly, the visual search application launched by Asos called "Asos' Style Match" allows shoppers to snap a photo or upload an image on the Asos website or application and search their product catalog for similar items. These tools attract shoppers to retailers for items that they might come across in a magazine or while out and about by helping them to shop for the ideal product even if they do not know what the product is.

Image recognition has tremendously helped marketing companies to gain an edge on social media by allowing them to find a variety of uses of their brand logos and products in keeping up with the visual trends. This phenomenon is also called "visual social listening" and allows companies to identify and understand where and how customers are interacting with their brand, logo, and product even when the company is not referred directly by its name.

Healthcare Industry

With the increasing availability of healthcare data, big data analysis has brought on a paradigm shift to healthcare. The primary focus of big data analytics in the healthcare industry is the analysis of relationships between patient outcomes and the treatment or prevention technique used. Big data analysis driven Artificial Intelligence programs have successfully been developed for patient diagnostics, treatment protocol generation, drug development, as well as patient monitoring and care. The powerful AI techniques can sift through a massive amount of clinical data and help unlock clinically relevant information to assist in decision making.

Some medical specialties with increasing big data analysis based AI research and applications are:

- Radiology – The ability of AI to interpret imaging results supplements the clinician's ability to detect changes in an image that can easily be missed by the human eye. An AI algorithm recent created at Stanford University can detect specific sites in the lungs of the pneumonia patients.
- Electronic Health Records – The need for digital health records to optimize the information spread and access requires fast and accurate logging of all health-related data in the systems. A human is prone to errors and may be affected by cognitive overload and burnout. This process has been successfully automated by AI. The use of Predictive models on the electronic health records data allowed the prediction of individualized treatment response with 70-72% accuracy at baseline.
- Imaging – Ongoing AI research is helping doctors in evaluating the outcome of corrective jaw surgery as well as in assessing the cleft palate therapy to predict facial attractiveness.

Entertainment Industry

Big data analysis, in coordination with Artificial intelligence, is increasingly running in the background of entertainment sources from video games to movies and serving us a richer, engaging, and more realistic experience. Entertainment providers such as Netflix and Hulu are using big data analysis to provide users personalized recommendations derived from individual user's historical activity and behavior. Computer graphics and digital media content producers have been leveraging big data analysis based tools to enhance the pace and efficiency of their production processes. Movie companies are increasingly using machine learning algorithms in the development of film trailers and advertisements as well as pre- and post-production processes. For example, big data analysis and an artificial intelligence-powered tool called "RivetAI" allows producers to automate and excellently read the processes of movie script breakdown, storyboard as well as budgeting, scheduling, and generation of shot-list. Certain time-consuming tasks carried out during the post-production of the movies such as synchronization and assembly of the movie clips can be easily automated using artificial intelligence.

Marketing and Advertising

A machine learning algorithm developed as a result of big data analysis can be easily trained with texts, stills, and video segments as data sources. It can then extract objects and concepts from these sources and recommend efficient marketing and advertising solutions. For example, a tool called "Luban" was developed by Alibaba that can create banners at lightning speed in comparison to a human designer. In 2016, for the Chinese online shopping extravaganza called "Singles Day," Luban generated a hundred and 17 million banner designs at a speed of 8000 banner designs per second.

The "20th Century Fox" collaborated with IBM to use their AI system "Watson" for the creation of the trailer of their horror movie "Morgan." In order to learn the appropriate "moments" or clips that should appear in a standard horror movie trailer, Watson was trained to classify and analyze input "moments" from audio-visual and other composition elements from over a hundred horror movies. This training resulted in the creation of a six-minute movie trailer by Watson in a mere 24 hours, which would have taken human professional weeks to produce.

With the use of Machine learning, computer vision technology, natural language processing, and predictive analytics, the marketing process can be accelerated exponentially through an AI marketing platform. For example, the artificial intelligence-based marketing platform developed by Albert Intelligence Marketing is able to generate autonomous campaign management strategies, create custom solutions and perform audience targeting. The company reported a 183% improvement in customer transaction rate and over 600% higher conversation efficiency credited to the use of their AI-based platform.

In March 2016, the artificial intelligence-based creative director called "AI-CD ß" was launched by McCann Erickson Japan as the first robotic creative director ever developed. "AI-CD ß" was given training on select elements of various TV shows and the winners from the past 10 years of All Japan Radio and Television CM festival. With the use of data mining capabilities, "AI-CD ß" can extract ideas and themes fulfilling every client's individual campaign needs.

Personalization of User Experience

The expectations of the on-demand entertainment users for rich and engaging personal user experience is ever-growing. One of the leading on-demand entertainment platforms, Netflix, rolled out artificial intelligence-based workflow management and scheduling application called "Meson," comprised of various "machine learning pipelines" that are capable of creating, training, and validating personalization algorithms to provide personalized recommendations to users. Netflix collaborated with the University of Southern California to develop a new Machine learning algorithms that can compress video for high-quality streaming without degrading image quality called "Dynamic Optimizer." This artificial intelligence technology will address streaming problems in developing nations and mobile device users by optimizing video fluency and definition.

IBM Watson recently collaborated with IRIS.TV offers a business-to-business service to media companies such as CBS, The Hollywood Reporter, and Hearst Digital Media by tracking and improving the introduction of their customers with their web content. IBM Watson is boosting IRIS.TV company's Machine learning algorithms that can 'learn' from users search history and recommend similar content. Reportedly, a 50% increase in view or retention or a small PDF three months was achieved by the Hollywood reporter with the use of IRIS.TV application.

Search Optimization and Classification

The ability to transform text, audio, and video content into digital copies has led to an explosion of media availability on the Internet, making it difficult for people to find exactly what they're looking for. To optimize the accuracy of search results, advancements are being made in machine learning technology. For example, Google is using artificial intelligence to augment its platform for accurate image searching. People can now simply upload a sample picture to Google Image instead of typing in keywords for their search. The image recognition technology used by Google image will automatically identify and manage features of the uploaded user image and provide search results with similar pictures. Google is also using artificial intelligence technology in advertisement positioning across the platform. For example, a pet food ad will only appear on the pet-related website, but a chicken wings advertisement will not appear on a site targeted to vegetarians.

The company Vintage Cloud has partnered with an artificial intelligence-based startup called "ClarifAI" to develop a film digitalization platform. With the use of computer vision API provided by ClarifAI, Vintage Cloud succeeded in burgeoning the speed of movie content classification and categorization.

A visual assets management platform integrated with machine learning algorithms has been developed by a company called "Zorroa." This platform enables users to search for specific content within large databases called an "Analysis Pipeline." The database contains processors that can tag each visual asset uniquely and Machine learning algorithms that have been 'trained' to identify specific components of the visual data. This visual content is then organized and cataloged to deliver high-quality search results.

Conclusion

Thank you for making it through to the end of *Python for Data Analysis: A Basic Guide for Beginners to Learn the Language of Python Programming Codes Applied to Data Analysis with Libraries Software Pandas, Numpy, and IPython*. Let's hope it was informative and able to provide you with all of the tools you need to achieve your goals, whatever they may be.

The next step is to make the best use of your new-found wisdom on the cutting-edge technology of "Big Data Analytics" and its applications in the world of healthcare and eCommerce. The smart and savvy customers today can be easily swayed by modern companies with a whimsical edge offering consumers a unique, rich, and engaging experience. It is getting increasingly challenging for traditional businesses to retain their customers without adopting the big data analytics technology explained in this book.

You are now ready to make your own predictive analysis model by leveraging all the free and open-source data libraries described in this book. To make the best use of this book, I recommend that you download these free resources and perform hands-on exercises to solidify your understanding of the concepts explained. The skillset of data analysis is always in demand with a lot of high pay job opportunities. Here's hoping this book has taken you a step closer to your dream job!

Finally, if you found this book useful in any way, a review on Amazon is always appreciated!

Python Data Science for Beginners

A Complete Crash Course To Become A Data Scientist From Scratch And Increase Your Skills For A Successful Career

By

Oliver R. Simpson

Code Developer Academy

Table of Contents

INTRODUCTION **145**

CHAPTER 1: A SHORT INTRODUCTION TO PYTHON **146**

CHAPTER 2: INTRODUCTION TO DATA SCIENCE **159**

CHAPTER 3: RAW DATA **165**

CHAPTER 4: INFERENTIAL STATISTICS **184**

CHAPTER 5: PYTHON LIBRARIES-PYGAL **204**

CHAPTER 6: DATA ANALYSIS **222**

CHAPTER 7: EXPLORE MACHINE LEARNING **231**

CHAPTER 8: DEEP DIVE- MACHINE LEARNING **242**

CHAPTER 9: PREDICTIONS USING LINEAR REGRESSION **260**

CHAPTER 10: DATA ANALYSIS-DEEP DIVE **274**

CONCLUSION **283**

Introduction

Data is considered as the concept that is critical to developing the next-level future community. Nowadays, multiple open-source information technology environments are accessible to everyone.

But choosing the tools and learning how to make use of them is not easy. The fact is that there are a lot of languages developed, and most newcomers have a problem of selecting the best one.

Python started around 25 years ago and now has become a language that is taught at universities as an introductory language.

The ability to analyze data using Python is important in data science. Learn the basics and move on to build powerful visualizations.

Chapter 1: A Short Introduction to Python

If you want to master Data Science, you'll need to first develop a basic knowledge of Python programming. All new employees at DataSciencester have to go through orientation; the most exciting part of this orientation is a short introduction in Python.

While this is not a detailed Python guide, but its main focus is to highlight the sections that will be most critical.

Installing Python

To install Python, visit https://www.python.org/. Navigate to the Downloads field where you'll proceed to download the latest Python version depending on your Operating system.

The Zen of Python

These refer to guidelines designed by Tim Peters. The Zen of Python contains 20 guidelines that direct the design of Python language. It's not necessary for your Python code to follow these guidelines, but they're important to remember. The Zen of Python is a hidden joke that appears if you execute import this;

Don't forget that these guidelines are just opinions that can be argued for or against. Like all good sets of moral codes, sometimes they contract each other to deliver the highest flexibility.

Whitespace Formatting

Most programming languages rely on curly braces to separate blocks of code. However, the Python language uses indentation. As a result, it's easy to read Python. However, you must be careful with your formatting. Whitespace is not considered inside parentheses and brackets, which can be useful for long-winded calculations.

Still, you can use a backslash to show that a given statement continues onto the next line, even if you'll rarely do this.

One effect of whitespace formatting is that it can be difficult to copy and paste code into the Python shell. For example, if you attempt to paste the following code inside the Python shell:

```
for i in [1, 2, 3, 4, 5]:
# notice the blank line
    print i
```

The following error will pop up:
IndentationError: expected an indented block
This error pops up because the interpreter assumes that the blank lines indicate the end of the for loop's block.
IPython features a magic function %paste, which accurately pastes everything that's on the clipboard, whitespace and all. This is why you should use IPython.

Modules
Specific properties of Python language don't appear by default. These include both the ones considered as part of the languages as well as third-party features that you can download yourself. To apply these features, you'll require to import the modules that hold them.

```python
import re
my_regex = re.compile("[0-9]+", re.I)
```

In this example, re is the module carrying functions and constants for working with regular expressions. After this import, you can only access those functions by prefixing them using re...
If you already have a separate re in the code, you can use an alias. You can still do this if the module contains an unwieldy name or if you're going to type it a lot. For instance, if you visualize data using matplotlib, then the standard convention to use is:

```python
import matplotlib.pyplot as plt
```

Functions
A function is a directive for accepting zero or more inputs and returning an equivalent output. In Python, functions are defined using the def keyword:

```python
def double(x):
    """this is where you put an optional docstring
    that explains what the function does.
    for example, this function multiplies its input by 2"""
    return x * 2
```

Functions in Python are first-class. In other words, you can allocate them to variables and pass them into functions like any other argument.
It is also easy to define short anonymous functions:

```
y = apply_to_one(Lambda x: x + 4) # equals 5
```

You can allocate lambdas to variables, although most people prefer to use the def keyword. Parameters of a function can also be assigned using a default argument, which is only relevant when you want a value other than the default. Sometimes, it is important to specify arguments using names.

Strings
A string can be defined by single or double quotation marks:
Num-1= "welcome"
Num_2 = 'welcome'
Python makes use of backlashes to encode specific characters. For instance:
tab_string = "\t"
 len(tab_string)

Exceptions
When something is wrong, Python throws an exception. When not addressed, these exceptions will crash your program. So to prevent your program from crashing, you need to use try and except:

```
try:
print 0 / 0
except ZeroDivisionError:
print "cannot divide by zero"
```

Exceptions don't work well in all languages, but in the case of Python, exceptions make your code cleaner. So you should make a habit of writing exceptions in Python.

Lists

Perhaps the most important data structure in Python language is the list. A list can be defined as an ordered collection. Lists in python share a lot of features with lists in other languages.

To check for list membership in Python, you use the in operator as shown below:

```
1 in [1, 2, 3] # True
0 in [1, 2, 3] # False
```

It's a straightforward process to concatenate lists:

```
x = [1, 2, 3]
x.extend([4, 5, 6]) # x is now [1,2,3,4,5,6]
```

Still, you have the option to use x,
If you don't want to alter x, you can use list addition.

```
x = [1, 2, 3]
y = x + [4, 5, 6] # y is [1, 2, 3, 4, 5, 6]; x is unchanged
```

Most of the time, you'll append to lists a single item at a time.
It is effective to unpack lists if you already understand the total number of elements they can store. However, if the number of elements on both sides isn't the same, you will see a valueError.
It's common to write the underscore for a value you want to throw away:

```
_, y = [1, 2] # now y == 2, didn't care about the first element
```

Dictionaries

The dictionary, also referred to as a hashtable, is one of the most robust data structures Python has available to apply. Fortunately, because it's built into the Python language, you don't need to run it yourself.

The dictionary is a useful data structure that features a 'key' and a 'value.' Every key is special within the dictionary and has a connected value. However, the connected value doesn't need to be special.

Some of the practical examples of the dictionary include:

- Your Subway Loyalty Card
- A student identification number at the university
- A phone book
- A physical dictionary

The key within the dictionary can be a number or a string. In fact, it can be any data type. The main point is that the key should be unique!

On learning programming, a dictionary is one of the many data structures present that is built into the Python language. In fact, there are many other data structures and algorithms available that we always have at our disposal. It might even get intimidating.

To create a dictionary to model a phone book, you will need to choose whether your key will contain a value or a name. In the previous example, you can use a phone number. Phone numbers are unique, and hence they're the best candidate for a key. Still, you can use a name as a key, because it is easier to recall a person's number.

```
phoneBook = {'Mike': 55555555} # 'Mike' is the key
```

In this example, you can only have a friend named Mike. If you need more Mike's, you will need to store them as Mike01, Mike03, etc.

But you can print a specific entry from the phonebook using the example below:

Print phonebook {'Mike'}

If you want to display the whole details of the phonebook, you can apply the print command.

With time, you'll want to expand and change the dictionary, so that you can add more entries.

```
if 1 > 2:
message = "if only 1 were greater than two…"
elif 1 > 3:
message = "elif stands for 'else if'"
else:
message = "when all else fails use else (if you want to)"
```

You can still use a tertiary if-then-else on a single line, which you'll perform occasionally:

```
parity = "even" if x % 2 == 0 else "odd"
```

Python features a while loop:

```
x = 0
while x < 10:
print x, "is less than 10"
x += 1
```

While in most cases, you'll apply for and in:

```
for x in range(10):
print x, "is less than 10"
```

However, if you want a complex logic, you can apply to continue and break.

Boolean

Booleans in Python work like in other languages, except that they're capitalized:
In Python, the value None reveals a nonexistent value. It is same as other language's null:
Python allows you to apply any value where it needs a Boolean. The following examples represent falsy:

- None
- ""

- Set()
- 0
- 0.0
- None
- {} (an empty dict)

Fairly common anything else is treated as True. This allows you to apply if statements to search for empty lists or empty strings and so forth. It may also trigger tricky bugs if you're not ready for this behavior.

A simpler way of achieving the same is:

```
first_char = s and s[0]
```

And it will return the second value when the first is "truthy," and the first value when it's not. Also, when x is either a number or None.

safe_x= x or 0

Python has a one-stop function that accepts a list and returns True accurately when every element is truthy, and any function, which returns True when at least one element is truthy:

```
x = [4,1,2,3]
y = sorted(x) # is [1,2,3,4], x is unchanged
x.sort() # now x is [1,2,3,4]
```

By default, the sort method will organize a list from smallest to largest by comparing the elements to one another.

If you want elements to be organized from largest to smallest, you can describe a reverse = true parameter. Rather than comparing the elements themselves, you can compare the outcome of a function that you describe with key:

List Comprehensions

Often, you'll want to change a list into another list, by selecting only specific elements, or by changing elements, or both. The pythonic style of achieving this is through list comprehensions:

```python
even_numbers = [x for x in range(5) if x % 2 == 0] # [0, 2, 4]
squares = [x * x for x in range(5)] # [0, 1, 4, 9, 16]
even_squares = [x * x for x in even_numbers] # [0, 4, 16]
```

You can still convert lists into dictionaries or sets.
If you don't want the value from the list, it's okay to apply an underscore as the variable.

A list of comprehension can comprise of multiple for:

```python
pairs = [(x, y)
for x in range(10)
for y in range(10)] # 100 pairs (0,0) (0,1) ... (9,8), (9,9)
```

And later for can use previous results.
You will apply for comprehensions a lot.

Generators and Iterators

An issue with lists is that they can easily grow very large, for instance, range (1000000) generates an actual list containing 1 million elements. If you only want to deal with them one at a time, this can be a great source of inefficiency. If you only want the first few values, then computing them all is a waste.

A generator is something that you can go over and over, but whose values are generated only as required.

To create generators, you can use functions and the yield operator:

```python
def lazy_range(n):
    """a lazy version of range"""
    i = 0
    while i < n:
        yield i
        i += 1
```

The above loop will accept the yielded values one at a time until none are left:

```
for i in lazy_range(10):
    do_something_with(i)
```

Python has a lazy_range function known as xrange, and in python 2, the range is lazy. In other words, you can even come up with an infinite sequence.
However, you should not iterate over it without using some form of break logic.
The opposite end of laziness is that you can only go over it once. If you want to iterate through something different times, you'll need to recreate the generator every time or apply a list.
Another way to build a generator is to apply the for comprehensions surrounded in parentheses.
Keep in mind that every dict contains items () method that will return a list of key-value pairs. Most frequently, you'll apply the iteritems () method, which lazily generates the key-value pairs every time you go over it.

Randomness

As you learn data science, you'll constantly want to generate random numbers, which you can accomplish using the random module:

```
import random
four_uniform_randoms = [random.random() for _ in range(4)]
# [0.8444218515250481,  # random.random() produces numbers
# 0.7579544029403025,   # uniformly between 0 and 1
# 0.420571580830845,    # it's the random
```

The random module generates pseudorandom numbers depending on an internal state that you can set using random. seed if you want to attain reproducible outcomes.
In some cases, you'll apply random.randrange, which accepts either 1 or 2 arguments and returns an element selected randomly from the corresponding range ():

```
random.randrange(10)    # choose randomly from range(10) = [0, 1, ..., 9]
random.randrange(3, 6)  # choose randomly from range(3, 6) = [3, 4, 5]
```

There are a few more methods that you'll find useful. For example, convenient. random.shuffle randomly reorganizes the elements of a list:
If you want to randomly select a single element from a list you can apply the random.choice:

```
my_best_friend = random.choice(["Alice", "Bob", "Charlie"]) # "Bob" for me
```

And if you want to randomly select a sample of elements without replacement, you can apply random.sample:
To select a sample of elements with replacement, you can set multiple calls to random.choice:

```
four_with_replacement = [random.choice(range(10))
for _ in range(4)]
# [9, 4, 4, 2]
```

Regular Expressions

Regular expressions provide a means of searching text. There are probably helpful but also complex, so much so that there are a bunch of books written about them. You will learn more about them; the few times we encounter them; here are a few examples, below are some examples of how to apply them in Python:

```
import re

print all([ # all of these are true, because
not re.match("a", "cat"),  # * 'cat' doesn't start with 'a'
re.search("a", "cat"),  # * 'cat' has an 'a' in it
not re.search("c", "dog"),  # * 'dog' doesn't have a 'c' in it
3 == len(re.split("[ab]", "carbs")),  # * split on a or b to ['c','r','s']
"R-D-" == re.sub("[0-9]", "-", "R2D2")  # * replace digits with dashes
]) # prints True
```

Object-oriented Programming

Python allows you to define classes that wrap data and the functions that work on them. Sometimes, you'll use them to make your code cleaner and simpler. It's probably easier to describe them by creating a heavily annotated example.
For example, if you don't have the built-in Python set, you may want to build your own Set class.

What behavior should the class hold? Provided an instance of Set, you'll need to add items to it, remove items from it, and confirm whether it has a certain value. You'll generate all these as member functions, which means you'll access them using a dot after Set object.

Functional Tools

When you pass functions around, sometimes, you may want to partially use functions to build new functions. As a simple example, say you have a function of two variables:

```python
def exp(base, power):
    return base ** power
```

And you want to use it to create a function of one variable two_to_the whose input is power and whose output is the outcome of exp(2, power)
Of course, you can achieve this using the def, but this can sometimes become unwieldy:

```python
def two_to_the(power):
    return exp(2, power)
```

A different way is to apply functools.partial:

```python
from functools import partial
two_to_the = partial(exp, 2) # is now a function of one variable
print two_to_the(3) # 8
```

You can still apply partially to fill in later arguments if you describe their names:

```python
square_of = partial(exp, power=2)
print square_of(3) # 9
```

Things begin to get messy once you curry arguments in the middle of the function, so you'll try to avoid doing that.

Typically, you will apply map, reduce, and filter, which present functional alternatives to list comprehensions:

```python
def double(x):
    return 2 * x
xs = [1, 2, 3, 4]
twice_xs = [double(x) for x in xs] # [2, 4, 6, 8]
twice_xs = map(double, xs) # same as above
list_doubler = partial(map, double) # *function* that doubles a list
twice_xs = list_doubler(xs) # again [2, 4, 6, 8]
```

You can apply a map with multiple-argument functions if you create multiple lists. Likewise, the filter performs the task of list-comprehension if:

```python
def is_even(x):
    """True if x is even, False if x is odd"""
    return x % 2 == 0
x_evens = [x for x in xs if is_even(x)] # [2, 4]
x_evens = filter(is_even, xs) # same as above
list_evener = partial(filter, is_even) # *function* that filters a list
x_evens = list_evener(xs) # again [2, 4]
```

And reduce will combine the first two elements of a list, then that outcome with the third, that result with the fourth, and so on, generating a single result.

Enumerate

Not you may want to go over a list and apply both its elements and their indexes. The pythonic style is to enumerate, which generates tuples (index, element):

```python
for i, document in enumerate(documents):
    do_something(i, document)
```

Similarly, if you only need the indexes:

```
for i in range(len(documents)): do_something(i) # not Pythonic
for i, _ in enumerate(documents): do_something(i) # Pythonic
```

Zip and Argument Unpacking

Typically, you will want to zip two or more lists together. Zip changes multiple lists into a single list of tuples of corresponding elements. In case the lists are of different lengths, zip stops immediately at the first list ends.
Still, you can "unzip" a list using a unique trick:

```
pairs = [('a', 1), ('b', 2), ('c', 3)]
letters, numbers = zip(*pairs)
```

The asterisk computes argument unpacking, which relies on the elements of pairs as individual arguments to zip. It finishes as if you'd called.

```
zip(('a', 1), ('b', 2), ('c', 3))
```

Argument unpacking can be applied with any function:

```
def add(a, b): return a + b
add(1, 2) # returns 3
add([1, 2]) # TypeError!
add(*[1, 2]) # returns 3
```

It is rare that you'll find this handy, but once you do, it's a powerful trick.

Chapter 2: Introduction to Data Science

Data Science is an emerging field of work-related to the collection, analysis, preparation, visualization, management, and maintenance of large information. While the name Data Science appears to connect strongly with fields such as databases and computer science, various skills are required.

For some people, when they hear the term Data Science, they think of people dressed in white lab coats seated on a computer. But this is not true.

First, most of the data around the world is unstructured. In other words, the data is not organized in clean rows and columns. Imagine a web page full of short messages and photographs among friends having very few numbers to work on there. While it's probably true that schools, companies, and governments apply numeric information, tax assessments, sales of products are a few examples. However, there is a lot of information in the world that statisticians consider. So, while it is important to have excelled math skills, there is a lot to be done in the world of data science for those who are comfortable working with sounds, words, photographs, and other types of information.

Additionally, data science is more than just analyzing data. There are many people who prefer to analyze data, and probably they can spend the whole day reviewing histograms and averages, but for those who like other activities, data science has different roles and demands a range of skills. Let's explore this idea by looking at the data required to buy a box of cereal.

Whatever your choice of cereal-fibrous, nutty, or fruity-you plan for the purchase by noting down "cereal" on your shopping list. Now, your planned purchase is a piece of data. When you arrive at the grocery store, you use that data as a reminder to grab your favorite choice and put it in your cart. At the checkout point, the cashier scans the barcode on your cereal box, and the cash register inputs the price. Now, in the warehouse, a computer notifies the stock manager that it's time to ask for another order from the distributor because your purchase was the last box in the store. Also, you have a coupon for your box, and the cashier scans that, handing you a specific discount. Towards the end of the week, a report of all the scanned manufacturer coupons is loaded to the cereal company so that they can release a reimbursement to the grocery store for all of the coupon discounts they have given out to customers. Lastly, when the month ends, the store manager stares at the beautiful collection of pie charts revealing all the different types of cereal that were sold. And because of the large sales of fruity cereals, they decide to offer more choices on the store's limited shelf space next month.

So this small detail that started as a scribble on your shopping list ended up in many different places, but the most important on the manager's desk as a decision making aid. The step-wise process from your shopping list to the manager's desk, the data passed through different conversions. Apart from the computers where the data may have stayed for some time, most pieces of hardware such as the barcode scanner were involved in gathering, transforming, and storing the data. Additionally, many different forms of software were involved in organizing, visualizing, and presenting the data. Lastly, different "human systems" interacted with the data. People decided on the type of systems to purchase and install, who should access what type of data, and what may happen to the data after its instant purpose was attained. The individuals at the grocery chain and its partners came up with detailed decisions and negotiations before the cases explained above could become true.

Overall, data scientists do not participate in all of these processes. They don't design and develop computer or barcode readers. Well, where would the data scientists play the most critical role? In general, data scientists serve in the most active roles within the following fields: data acquisition, data archiving, data analysis, and data architecture.

Using the cereal example, let's explore them one by one. With respect to architecture, it was vital in the design of the 'point of sale' system to consider how different people may take advantage of the data originating from the system. The architect of the system, for instance, acknowledges that both the stock manager and the store manager would need to access the data scanned at the register for different reasons. A data scientist would assist the system architect by presenting input on how the data should be routed and organized to boost the analysis, data presentation, and visualization of the data to the right personnel.

Next, the acquisition is concerned with how the data is collected and represented before analysis and presentation. For example, every barcode represents a number that is not descriptive of the product it represents. Different barcodes are used to point to the same product. When should you write a small note that purchase X and purchase Y are the same product, just in separate packages? Representing, grouping, converting, and associating the data are all jobs that need to happen before the data can be profitably reviewed, and these are all jobs that the data scientist is actively involved in.

The analysis stage is where data scientists are intensively involved. In this example, you will use analysis to summarize data, using samples to make inferences about the bigger context, and data visualization by highlighting it in tables, and even animations. While there are a lot of mathematical, technical, and statistical features to these activities, remember that the final audience for data analysis are people. These people are the "users" of this data. Therefore, satisfying their needs is the most significant duty of a data scientist. This point underlines the need for great communication skills in data science. The most advanced statistical analysis ever created will be of no use unless the outcome can be effectively translated to the data user.

Finally, the data scientist must participate in the data archiving process. Preservation of collected data in a manner that makes it reusable-what you may consider as "data curation" is a complex problem because it's so difficult to predict all of the future applications of the data. For instance, when Twitter developers worked on how to store tweets, they perhaps never expected that tweets would be used to highlight earthquakes and tsunamis, but they had enough data to understand that "geocodes" data displays the geographical location from which a tweet was sent.

After all, the cereal box and grocery store example shows places where data scientists should remain active and the skills they require. Below are skills that the example pinpoints:

- Communicate with data users-a data scientist should have good communication skills for learning the preferences of users. Translating back and forth between the technical terms of statistics and the vocabulary of the application domain is a great skill.

- Mastering the application domain. The data scientist must quickly master how the data will be applied in a specific environment.

- Visualizing the big picture of a multifaceted system. Once you gain some knowledge about the application domain, the data scientist must look into how data will travel around among all the critical systems and people.

- Understand how data can be represented. It's important for data scientists to have a clear knowledge about how data is kept and connected.

- Data transformation and analysis. Once data is in the hands of decision-makers, data scientists must be aware of how to change, summarize, and make inferences from the data. As said above, knowing how to release the results of analyses to users is also a great skill.

- Attention to quality. Regardless of how good a piece of data may be, there's no perfect data. As a data scientist, it's your role to know the limitations of the data you work with, understand how you will quantify its accuracy, and be able to recommend ways to increase the data quality in the coming years.

- Ethical reasoning. If data is significant enough to collect, then it's vital to impact people's lives. Thus, data scientists must realize important ethical matters such as security, and must be able to channel the limitations of data to attempt to prevent misuse of data.

The skills and abilities highlighted above are only a tip of the iceberg but recognize what a broad range is represented here. Although mastery of numbers and mathematics is critical, especially for data analysis, the data scientist also requires to demonstrate good communication skills. The data scientist should be an excellent system thinker, be able to think critically about how data will be used to come up with decisions and impact people's lives. Of course, there are a few people who demonstrate great skill at these things, so the people interested in data will concentrate on one field, and others will become specialists in a different area. This demonstrates the significance of teamwork.

In this introduction to Data Science, several data problems of various complexity will be used to reveal the skills and abilities expected by data scientists.

Exploring Data Problems

Data science is unique from other fields, such as statistics or mathematics. Data science is an applied process, and data scientists fulfill the desires and solve the issues of data users. Before you can find a solution to a problem, you need to identify it, and this process is not straightforward as it might appear. This section will look at the identification of data problems.

Apple farmers live in fear because of their blossoms and later their fruit. A late spring frost can destroy the blossoms. Extreme wind or hail in the summer can destroy the fruit. Overall, farming is an activity that is commonly affected by physical elements in the world.

In the current physical world of unpredictable natural forces, is there an opportunity for data science? Of course, there is. But how can you know that? Having a hint for spotting data problems demands openness, creativity, curiosity, and willingness to ask many questions. In fact, if you remove the notion that data scientists sit in front of a computer desk all day and operates a crazy program like Python, that's a mistake. Each data scientist must be quenched in the problem domain where she is working. The data scientist may never become a farmer, but if you're going to look for data problems that a farmer experiences, you have no option but to wear the shoes of the farmer. In other words, you must learn to think like a farmer to some level.

To acquire this domain knowledge, you can decide to read or watch videos, but the right way is to ask "subject matter specialists" about what they do. The entire process of asking questions requires its own treatment, but for now, there are three things to consider when asking questions. First, you need the subject matter specialists to narrate stories of what they do. Then you want to interview them about anomalies: the abnormal things that occur for better or for worse. Lastly, you want to understand the risks and uncertainty: what are the scenarios where it is difficult to tell what will happen next and what happens next may have a profound impact on whether the situation finishes badly or well. Each of the following areas of questioning describes an approach to highlighting data problems that may transform something better that could be accomplished with data, information, and the correct decision at the perfect time.

The reason for asking stories is that people normally think in stories. From farmers to CEOs, people know and narrate stories about their success and failure in their specific domain. Stories are significant ways of spreading wisdom between different members of the same profession, and they're methods of gaining a sense of identity that differentiates one profession from another. The only challenge is that stories can be false.

If you can get a professional to narrate the main stories that describe how she completes her work, you can then consider how to prove those stories. Without doubting the veracity of the individual that narrates the story, you can consider methods of measuring the different features of how things occur in the story with a focus towards confirming the stories that direct professional work.

Another strategy for discovering a problem is to look for unique cases, both good and bad. Highlighting abnormal cases is a great way of understanding how things work, but it's important first to define the most common occurrences to have an accurate idea of what institutes an abnormal case.

Returning to our farmer friend, a powerful wind descended on the orchard, causing the fruits to fall off the trees. Most of the trees lost some bit of fruit. The dropped apples could be seen close to the base of the tree. Another small grouping of trees appeared to lose a lot of fruit, and the drops were typically scattered further from the trees. Is it possible that some weird wind conditions worsened the situation in this particular spot? Or is it a matter of chance that a few trees in the same location lost some fruit than would be normal.

An organized count of lost fruit underneath a random sample of trees would help respond to this question. The bulk of the following trees would perhaps have each lost the same amount, but more importantly, that "typical" group would deliver a yardstick against which we could determine what would actually count as unusual. Once you find an unusual set of cases that is beyond the limits of typical, you can shift your attention to these to try to understand the anomaly.

A third approach to define data problems is to determine the risk and uncertainty. The basic function of information is to cut down on uncertainty. It is always important to eliminate uncertainty because of the way risk impact the things you do. At home, at school, at work, life is full of risks. Making a decision or failing to decide invites a chain of events that may result in something good or not so good. It's hard to say, but in general, you prefer to narrow things down in a way that optimizes the probability of a bad one. To accomplish this, you need to make helpful decisions, and better decisions need to cut down on uncertainty. By asking questions related to risks and uncertainty, a data scientist can zero in on the issues that matter. You can even refer to the previous two strategies-asking about stories that demand professional wisdom and about anomalies.

Chapter 3: Raw Data

In the world of Data Science, raw data occurs in many different types and sizes. Overall, there are many different types of information that can be mined from this raw data. For example, Amazon has a record of click stream data that each and every user clicks on the website. This data can be analyzed to understand whether a user is a price-sensitive customer or prefers popular products. You must have realized the recommended products on Amazon. These products are generated by basing on such data.

The first step of analysis is to parse raw data. Data parsing involves the following stages:

- Data extraction from the source. Data appears in many different types, such as CSV, Excel, and so on. Python simplifies the data from these sources with the help of some relevant packages.

- Data cleaning. Once you perform a sanity check, next is to clean the data properly so that it can be optimized for analysis. You might have a dataset about students of a class and details about their weight, height, and marks. There might also be specific rows with the height missing. Based on the analysis done, these rows with missing values can either be ignored or replaced with the average weight or height.

Arrays with NumPy

By default, Python comes with a data structure, such as a List, which can be optimized for array operations, but a Python list on its own isn't the best to perform complex mathematical operations.

NumPy is a great Python package generated by Travis Oliphant, which has been designed fundamentally for scientific purposes. It supports large matrices, plus a large library of high-level mathematical functions to work on these arrays.

A NumPy array would demand much less memory to store a similar amount of data than a Python list, which enables reading and writing from the array in a quick manner.

Building an Array

A collection of numbers can be passed to the next array function to generate a NumPy array object:

```
>>> import numpy as np
>>> n_array = np.array([[0, 1, 2, 3],
[4, 5, 6, 7],
[8, 9, 10, 11]])
```

A NumPy array object contains different attributes, which help in presenting information about the array. Here are its common attributes:
- Ndim: This shows the number of dimensions of the array. For example,

>>> n_array.ndim
2
- Shape: This indicates the size of every dimension of the array:

>>> n_array.shape
(3,4)
The first dimension of n_array contains a size of 3, and the second dimension features a size of 4. This can be visualized as three rows and four columns.
- Size. This reveals the number of elements:

>>> n_array.size
12
The sum of elements in n_array is 12

- Dtype: This represents the data type of the elements within the array:

>>> n_array.dtype.name
Int64

Mathematical Operations
When you have an array of data, you may want to conduct specific mathematical operations on it. This section will explore a few crucial ones.

Array Subtraction
This command subtracts an array from the b array to get the resultant c array. The subtraction takes place element by element. Kindly note that when you subtract two arrays, they must be of equal dimensions.

Squaring an Array
This command raises each element to the power of 2 to get the following result:
>>> b**2
[1 4 9 16]

A Trigonometric Function Conducted on the Array
This command uses cosine to every value within the b array to attain the following result:

```
>>> np.cos(b)
[ 0.54030231 -0.41614684 -0.9899925 -0.65364362]
```

Conditional Operations
The conditional command applies a conditional operation to every element of the b array to generate the required Boolean values:
>>> b<2
[True False False False]

Matrix Multiplication
Two matrices can be multiplied element by element or using a dot product. The commands below will evaluate element-by-element multiplication:
>>> A1 = np.array([[1, 1],
[0, 1]])
>>> A2 = np.array([[2, 0],
[3, 4]])
>>> A1 * A2
[[2 0]
[0 4]]
The dot product can be computed using the following command:
>>> np.dot(A1, A2)
[[5 4]
[3 4]]

Indexing and Slicing
If you would like to select a given element of an array, you can complete this step using indexes:
>>> n_array[1, 2]

This will select the second array and then select the third value in the array. It can also be considered as an intersection of the first row and the second column of the matrix.

In case a range of values has to be highlighted in a row, then you can write the following command:

```
>>> n_array[ 0 , 0:3 ]
[0 1 2]
```

The 0.3 value represents the first three values of the first row.
The entire row of values can be highlighted using the following command:
>>> n_array[0 , :]
[0 1 2 3]
By using this command, the whole column of values require to be selected:
>>> n_array[: , 1]
[1 5 9]

Shape Modification

When the array is created, it can change the shape of it too. The command below flattens the array.
>>> n_array.ravel()
[0 1 2 3 4 5 6 7 8 9 10 11]
The above command changes the shape of the array into six rows and two columns format. Additionally, remember that when reshaping, the new shape should have an equal number of elements as the initial one:

```
>>> n_array.shape = (6,2)
>>> n_array
[[ 0  1]
 [ 2  3]
 [ 4  5]
 [ 6  7]
 [ 8  9]
 [10 11]]
```

The above array can be transposed to become:

```
>>> n_array.transpose()
[[ 0  2  4  6  8 10]
 [ 1  3  5  7  9 11]]
```

Authorizing Data Analysis Using Pandas

Pandas is an open-source library. The library is designed specifically for data analysis. Pandas is built on NumPy, and hence, it is easy to work with data.
The panda's library contains efficient data structures to process data, complete fast joins, and read data from different sources.

The Data Structure of Pandas

The panda's library basically has three data structures:
1. Panel
2. Series
3. DataFrame

Series

Series is a single-dimensional array, which can store any type of data such as floats, strings, integers, and Python objects too. A series can be generated by writing the following functions:

```
>>> import pandas as pd
>>> pd.Series(np.random.randn(5))
0  0.733810
1 -1.274658
2 -1.602298
3  0.460944
4 -0.632756
dtype: float64
```

The index of the series can be personalized by calling the functions below:

```
>>> pd.Series(np.random.randn(5), index=['a', 'b', 'c', 'd', 'e'])
a   -0.929494
b   -0.571423
c   -1.197866
d    0.081107
e   -0.035091
dtype: float64
A series can be derived from a Python dict too:
>>> d = {'A': 10, 'B': 20, 'C': 30}
>>> pd.Series(d)
A    10
B    20
C    30
dtype: int64
```

DataFrame

The DataFrame refers to a 2D data structure containing columns that can be of different data types. This can be viewed as a table. A DataFrame can be generated from the above data structures:

- A NumPy array
- A 2D NumPy array
- Dicts
- Lists

A DataFrame can be generated from a dict of series when you write the following commands:

```
>>> d = {'c1': pd.Series(['A', 'B', 'C']),
'c2': pd.Series([1, 2., 3., 4.])}
>>> df = pd.DataFrame(d)
>>> df
  c1  c2
0  A   1
1  B   2
2  C   3
3 NaN  4
```

Panel

A Panel refers to a data structure that deals with 3D data. The command below demonstrates an example of a panel:

```
>>> d = {'Item1': pd.DataFrame(np.random.randn(4, 3)),
'Item2': pd.DataFrame(np.random.randn(4, 2))}
>>> pd.Panel(d)
<class 'pandas.core.panel.Panel'>
Dimensions: 2 (items) x 4 (major_axis) x 3 (minor_axis)
Items axis: Item1 to Item2
Major_axis axis: 0 to 3
Minor_axis axis: 0 to 2
```

The previous commands indicate that there are 2DataFrames represented by two items. There are four rows represented by four great axes and three columns represented by three minor axes.

Inserting and Exporting Data

The data is kept in different forms, such as databases, CSV, tsv, and so forth. The panda's library makes it relevant to read data from these formats to export to the following formats. You'll use a dataset containing the weight statistics of the students from the U.S school.

You'll use a file with the structure below:

Column	Description
LOCATION CODE	Unique location code
COUNTY	The county the school belongs to
AREA NAME	The district the school belongs to
REGION	The region the school belongs to
SCHOOL YEARS	The school year the data is addressing
NO. OVERWEIGHT	The number of overweight students
PCT OVERWEIGHT	The percentage of overweight students
NO. OBESE	The number of obese students
PCT OBESE	The percentage of obese students
NO. OVERWEIGHT OR OBESE	The number of students who are overweight or obese
PCT OVERWEIGHT OR OBESE	The percentage of students who are overweight or obese
GRADE LEVEL	Whether they belong to elementary or high school
AREA TYPE	The type of area
STREET ADDRESS	The address of the school
CITY	The city the school belongs to
STATE	The state the school belongs to
ZIP CODE	The zip code of the school
Location 1	The address with longitude and latitude

CSV

To read data from a.csv file, enter the following read_csv function:

```
>>> d = pd.read_csv('Data/Student_Weight_Status_Category_Reporting_Results__Beginning_2010.csv')
>>> d[0:5]['AREA NAME']
```

The read_csv function accepts the path of the .csv file to input the data. The command after this prints the first five rows of the Location column in the data. To write data to the .csv file, you can use the to_csv function.

```
>>> d = {'c1': pd.Series(['A', 'B', 'C']),
'c2': pd.Series([1., 2., 3., 4.])}
>>> df = pd.DataFrame(d)
>>> df.to_csv('sample_data.csv')
```

The DataFrame is written to a .csv file by applying the to_csv method. The path and the filename where the file requires to be built should be mentioned.

XLS

Besides the panda's package, the xlrd package should be installed for pandas to read the data from an Excel file.

The preceding function resembles the CSV reading command. To write to an Excel file, the xlwt package has to be installed.

>>> df.to_excel('sample_data.xls')

JSON

To read the data from a JSON file, python's standard JSON package can be applied. The commands below are useful in reading the file.

```
>>> import json
>>> json_data = open('Data/Student_Weight_Status_Category_Reporting_Results__Beginning_2010.json')
>>> data = json.load(json_data)
>>> json_data.close()
```

In the previous command, the open() function starts a connection to the file. The JSON.load () function loads the data into Python. The json_data.close() function closes the connection to the file.

The panda's library also generates a function to read the JSON file, which you can access using the pd.read_json ().

Database

To read data from a database, use the following function:
>>> **pd.read_sql_table(table_name, con)**

The previous command creates a DataFrame. Suppose a table name and an SQLAlchemy engine are provided, they return a DataFrame. This function doesn't support the DBAPI connection. Below is the description of the above parameters.

- Table_name. As the name suggests, it refers to the name of the SQL table within a database.

- Con: Refers to the SQLAlchemy engine.

The command below reads SQL query into a DataFrame:
>>> **pd.read_sql_query(sql, con)**

Below is the description of the parameters applied:

- Sql. References the sql query that is supposed to be executed.

- Con. This refers to the SQLAlchemy engine.

Cleansing of Data

Data, while in row form, deserves some cleaning before it can be analyzed or a dashboard builds on it. There are many factors that may make data to have problems. For example, the Point of Sale system at a retail shop may have malfunctioned and entered some data with missing values. This section will teach you how to handle such data.

Search for Missing Data

In general, most data will feature missing values. There could be different reasons for this: the source system which gathers the data might not have collected the values, or the values may never have existed. Once you have data loaded, it is important to search for the missing features in the data. Based on the requirements, the missing data has to be handled. It can be taken care of by eliminating a row or replacing a missing value with an alternative value.

In the case of the Student Weight data, to verify whether the location column has missing value, you can use the command below:

```
>>> d['Location 1'].isnull()
```

The not null () function will display each row of the value as True or False. In case it's false, then there is a missing value. This particular data can be combined to count the number of missing value instances:

```
>>> d['Location 1'].isnull().value_counts()
```

The preceding command illustrates that the Location 1 column contains 24 instances of missing values. These missing values can be taken care of by removing the rows using missing values or substituting it with some values. To eliminate the rows, run the following command:

```
>>> d = d['Location 1'].dropna()
```

To remove all the rows using an instance of missing values, the following command is useful:

```
>>> d = d.dropna(how='any')
```

Complete the Missing Data

Let's define some DataFrames to use:

```
>>> df = pd.DataFrame(np.random.randn(5, 3), index=['a0', 'a10', 'a20', 'a30', 'a40'],
columns=['X', 'Y', 'Z'])
>>> df

     X         Y         Z
a0  -0.854269  0.117540  1.515373
a10 -0.483923 -0.379934  0.484155
a20 -0.038317  0.196770 -0.564176
a30  0.752686  1.329661 -0.056649
a40 -1.383379  0.632615  1.274481
```

Next, add some extra row indexes, which will generate null values within the DataFrame:

```
>>> df2 = df2.reindex(['a0', 'a1', 'a10', 'a11', 'a20', 'a21',
 'a30', 'a31', 'a40', 'a41'])

>>> df2
       X         Y         Z
a0  -1.193371  0.912654 -0.780461
a1   NaN       NaN       NaN
a10  1.413044  0.615997  0.947334
a11  NaN       NaN       NaN
a20  1.583516  1.388921  0.458771
a21  NaN       NaN       NaN
a30  0.479579  1.427625  1.407924
a31  NaN       NaN       NaN
a40  0.455510 -0.880937  1.375555
a41  NaN       NaN       NaN
```

In case you would like to replace the null values in the df2 DataFrame with a zero value, then run the following command:

```
>>> df2.fillna(0)
       X         Y         Z
a0  -1.193371  0.912654 -0.780461
a1   0.000000  0.000000  0.000000
a10  1.413044  0.615997  0.947334
a11  0.000000  0.000000  0.000000
a20  1.583516  1.388921  0.458771
a21  0.000000  0.000000  0.000000
a30  0.479579  1.427625  1.407924
a31  0.000000  0.000000  0.000000
a40  0.455510 -0.880937  1.375555
a41  0.000000  0.000000  0.000000
```

String Operations

Sometimes, you may want to change the string field column in your data. Here's a technique that describes some of the string operations:

- Substring: let's begin by selecting the first five rows of the AREA NAME column within the data as the sample data to edit.

```
>>> df = pd.read_csv('Data/Student_Weight_Status_Category_Reporting_Results__Beginning_2010.csv')
>>> df['AREA NAME'][0:5]
```

To extract the first word from the Area Name column, you will need to apply the extract function as presented in the command below:

```
>>> df['AREA NAME'][0:5].str.extract('(\w+)')
```

In the above command, the str feature of the series is applied. The str class has an extract method, where a common expression can be fed to extract data, which is powerful. It is also possible to fetch the second word in AREA NAME as a separate column:

```
>>> df['AREA NAME'][0:5].str.extract('(\w+)\s(\w+)')
```

To mine data from various columns, the required regular expressions should be surrounded in separate parentheses.

- Filtering: If you want to filter rows using data on ELEMENTARY school, then you can use the command below:

```
>>> df[df['GRADE LEVEL'] == 'ELEMENTARY']
```

- Uppercase: To change the area name to uppercase, you'll type the following command:

```
>>> df['AREA NAME'][0:5].str.upper()
```

Since the strings of data are already in uppercase, there won't be any visible change.

- Lowercase: To change Area Name to lowercase, you'll apply the following command:

```
>>> df['AREA NAME'][0:5].str.lower()
```

- Length. To determine the length of each element of the Area Name column, you'll apply the following command:

```
>>> df['AREA NAME'][0:5].str.len()
0  47
1  47
2  47
3  27
4  27
Name: AREA NAME, dtype: int64
```

- Split: To split Area Name based on whitespace, you'll apply the following command:

```
>>> df['AREA NAME'][0:5].str.split(' ')
```

- Replace: If you want to replace all the area names ending with DISTRIC to DIST, then you can use the following command:

```
>>> df['AREA NAME'][0:5].str.replace('DISTRICT$', 'DIST')
```

The first argument in the replacement method represents the regular expression to be used to highlight the section of the string to replace. The second argument represents the value for it to be replaced with.

Merging Data

To aggregate data sets, the concat function of pandas can be applied. Consider the Area Name and the Country columns featuring the first five rows:

```
>>> d[['AREA NAME', 'COUNTY']][0:5]
```

Still, you can divide the data, as shown below:

```
>>> p1 = d[['AREA NAME', 'COUNTY']][0:2]
>>> p2 = d[['AREA NAME', 'COUNTY']][2:5]
```

The first two rows of the data are in p1, and the last three rows are in p2. These parts can be combined using the concat() function. For example:

>>> **pd.concat([p1,p2])**

The combined parts can be identified by allocating a key:

```
>>> concatenated = pd.concat([p1,p2], keys = ['p1','p2'])
>>> concatenated
```

By applying the keys, the pieces can be extracted back from the combined data. For example:
>>> **concatenated.ix['p1']**

Data Operations

Once you finish with the missing data, the different operations can be conducted on the data.

Aggregation Operations

There are different aggregation operations like sum, average, and so forth, which you would like to conduct on a numerical field. Below are methods used to evaluate it:

- Average. To evaluate the average number of students in the ELEMENTARY school who are obese, first, you need to filter the ELEMENTARY data using the command below:

```
>>> data = d[d['GRADE LEVEL'] == 'ELEMENTARY']
213.41593780369291
```

Now, you can compute the mean using the command below:
>>> **data['NO. OBESE'].mean()**
The elementary grade level data is stored and filtered within the data object. The NO. OBESE column is chosen, which has the number of obese students and applying the mean () method; the average is determined.

- SUM. To determine the total number of elementary students who are said to be obese across all the school, apply the following command:

```
>>> data['NO. OBESE'].sum()
219605.0
```

- MAX. To determine the highest number of students that are obese in an elementary school, apply the command below:

```
>>> data['NO. OBESE'].max()
48843.0
```

- MIN: To determine the minimum number of students that are obese in an elementary school, apply the following command:

```
>>> data['NO. OBESE'].min()
5.0
```

- STD: To find the standard deviation of the number of obese students, apply this command:

```
>>> data['NO. OBESE'].std()
1690.3831128098113
```

- COUNT: To determine the total number of schools with the Elementary grade in the DELAWARE county, apply this command:

```
>>> data = df[(d['GRADE LEVEL'] == 'ELEMENTARY') & (d['COUNTY'] == 'DELAWARE')]
>>> data['COUNTY'].count()
19
```

The tab
le is filtered for the ELEMENTARY grade and the DELAWARE county. See that the conditions are wrapped in parentheses. This is to make sure that individual conditions are computed, and if the parentheses aren't provided, Python will throw an error.

Joins

SQL-like joins can be conducted on the DataFrame using pandas. Let's create a lookup DataFrame, this will assign levels to each of the grades using the command below:

```
>>> grade_lookup = {'GRADE LEVEL': pd.Series(['ELEMENTARY',
'MIDDLE/HIGH', 'MISC']),'LEVEL': pd.Series([1, 2, 3])}

>>> grade_lookup = DataFrame(grade_lookup)
```

Let's consider the first five rows of the GRADE data column as an example for calculating the joins:

```
>>> df[['GRADE LEVEL']][0:5]

GRADE LEVEL
0       DISTRICT TOTAL
1       ELEMENTARY
2       MIDDLE/HIGH
3       DISTRICT TOTAL
4       ELEMENTARY
```

The Inner Join

The image below represents an example of an inner join:

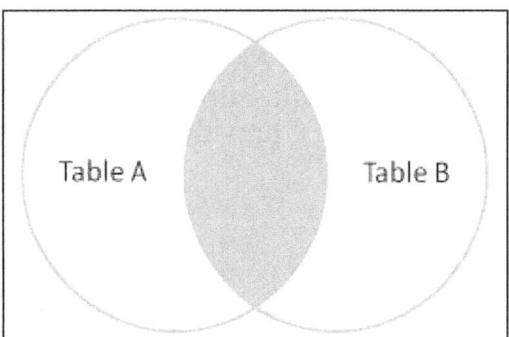

An inner join can be executed using the following command:

```
>>> d_sub = df[0:5].join(grade_lookup.set_index(['GRADE LEVEL']),
on=['GRADE LEVEL'], how='inner')
>>> d_sub[['GRADE LEVEL', 'LEVEL']]
```

The join occurs with the join () method. The first argument selects the DataFrame on which the lookup occurs. Remember that the grade_lookup DataFrame's index is being set using the set_index () method. This is necessary for a join because the join method will not know which column to join the DataFrame to.
The second argument accepts a column of the d DataFrame to join the data. The third argument defines the join as an inner join.

The Left Outer Join
Here's an image illustrating the left outer join.

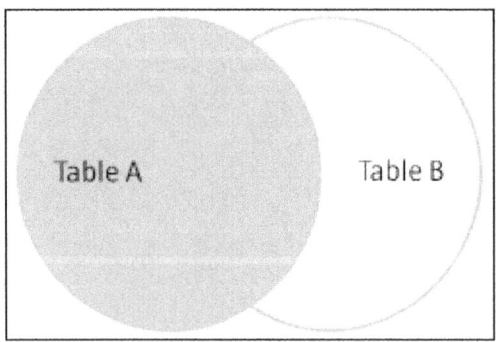

You can complete an outer join by writing the following commands:

```
>>> d_sub = df[0:5].join(grade_lookup.set_index(['GRADE LEVEL']),
on=['GRADE LEVEL'], how='left')
>>> d_sub[['GRADE LEVEL', 'LEVEL']]
```

You can realize that the DISTRICT TOTAL contains missing values for a level column. The grade_lookup DataFrame doesn't have an instance for DISTRICT TOTAL.

The Full Outer Join
The image below is a sample of a full outer join:

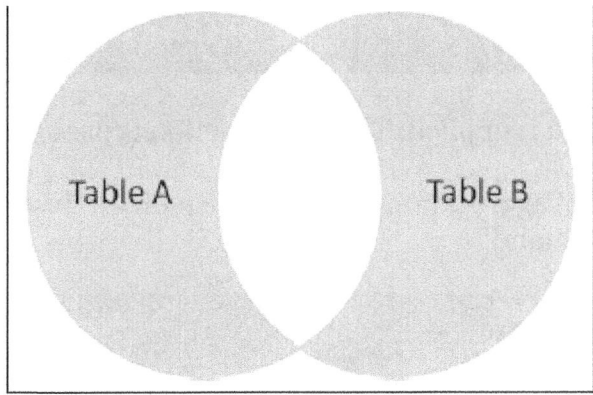

The full outer join can be implemented using the following commands:

```
>>> d_sub = df[0:5].join(grade_lookup.set_index(['GRADE LEVEL']),
on=['GRADE LEVEL'], how='outer')
>>> d_sub[['GRADE LEVEL', 'LEVEL']]
```

The Groupby Function
It is straightforward to execute an SQL-like group by operation using pandas. Say, for instance; you want to determine the sum of the number of obese students in every grade, then you can apply the following command:

```
>>> df['NO. OBESE'].groupby(d['GRADE LEVEL']).sum()
  GRADE              LEVEL

DISTRICT TOTAL      127101
ELEMENTARY           72880
MIDDLE/HIGH          53089
```

This command selects the number of obese students column and then applies the group by a method to group the data-based group level, and lastly, the sum method totals the number. The same can be accomplished using the function below:

```
>>> d['NO. OBESE'].groupby(d['GRADE LEVEL']).aggregate(sum)
```

In the above case, the aggregate method is applied. The sum function is passed on acquiring the results.

It's also possible to get multiple types of aggregations on the same metric. This can be accomplished by the following command:

```
>>> df['NO. OBESE'].groupby(d['GRADE LEVEL']).aggregate([sum, mean, std])sum mean std
```

To summarize, this chapter has explored the basics of NumPy and pandas packages. You have learned the various datatypes in pandas and how to use them. You have learned how to clean data and modify data. This chapter provides you with the foundation for data science, and you can explore deeper into NumPy and pandas. In the next chapter, we shall look at inferential statistics and how you can create meaning from different concepts in inferential statistics.

Chapter 4: Inferential Statistics

Before you understand the inferential statistics, first, let's explore what descriptive statistics is about.

Descriptive statistics is a term assigned to data analysis that summarizes the data in a meaningful style such that patterns are extracted from it. It's a simple way to describe data, but it doesn't help us come up with a conclusion on the hypothesis made. Say, for instance, you have the height of 1,000 people living in Hong Kong. The average of their height would be descriptive statistics, but their average height does not reveal that it's the mean height of entire Hong Kong. In this case, inferential statistics will allow you to define what the average height of the entire Hong Kong would be; this is explained further in the following chapter. In other words, inferential statistics involves an explanation of the bigger picture of the analysis using a limited amount of data and mining conclusions from it.

Different Types of Distribution

There are different types of probability distributions, and every distribution reveals the probability of different results for a random experiment. This section will deal with different probability distributions.

The Normal Distribution

This is the most common type of distribution and widely used form of distribution in statistics. Also known as a "bell curve" and "Gaussian curve" named after the mathematician Karl Friedrich Gauss. A normal distribution happens commonly in nature. Let's consider the example of height we introduced at the start of the chapter. If you have height data for all individuals of a given gender in the city of Hong Kong, and you plot a bar chart where every bar represents the number of people at this specific height, then the curve that is extracted will resemble the following graph. The numbers in the plot represent the standard deviation numbers from the mean. In the following case, it's zero. This concept will become clear as we tackle other chapters.

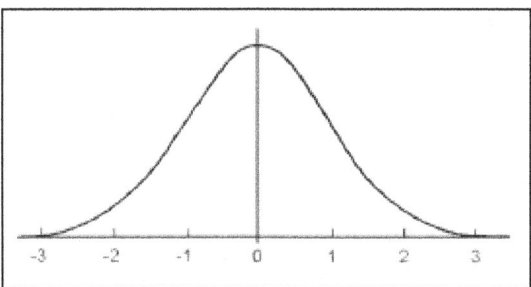

Additionally, if you observe an hourglass the way sand piles up when the hourglass is inverted, it creates a normal distribution curve. This is an excellent example that illustrates how normal distribution exists in nature.

Consider the figure below: It has three curves with a normal distribution. The curve A has a standard deviation of 1, the curve C has a standard deviation of 2, and curve B has a standard deviation of 3. In other words, curve B has the highest spread of values, while curve A has the least spread of values. Another perspective is this, if curve B represents the height of people in a country, then this nation has a lot of people with different heights, whereas the country with the curve A distribution will have people whose heights resemble each other.

Normal Distribution from a Binomial Distribution

If you toss a coin, the likelihood of seeing a head or tail is 50%. If you toss the same coin six times, the probability of seeing ahead three times can be determined using the formula below:

$$P(x) = \frac{n!}{x!(n-x)!} p^x q^{n-x}$$

X is the expected number of successes.

In the above formula, n denotes the number of times the coin is tossed, p stands for the chance of success, and q is (1-p), which is the likelihood of failure.

The python SciPy package has helpful functions to complete statistical computations. You can get if from http://www.scipy.org/. These commands allow you to plot the binomial distribution.

```python
>>> from scipy.stats import binom
>>> import matplotlib.pyplot as plt
>>> fig, ax = plt.subplots(1, 1)
>>> x = [0, 1, 2, 3, 4, 5, 6]
>>> n, p = 6, 0.5
>>> rv = binom(n, p)
>>> ax.vlines(x, 0, rv.pmf(x), colors='k', linestyles='-', lw=1, label='Probablity')
>>> ax.legend(loc='best', frameon=False)
>>> plt.show()
```

The binom function generates binomial distributions and the relevant statistics connected to it. If you take a look at the previous commands, there are parts of it that originate from the matplotlib, which you're going to use now to plot the binomial distribution. You will learn more about the matplotlib library in the later chapters. The plt.subplots function is important in generating plots on a screen. The binom function accepts the number of attempts and the likelihood of success. The ax.vlines function is used to plot vertical lines, and rv.pmf is important in computing the probability at different values of x. The ax.legend function adds a legend to the graph, and lastly, plt.show outputs the graph. The outcome is as follows:

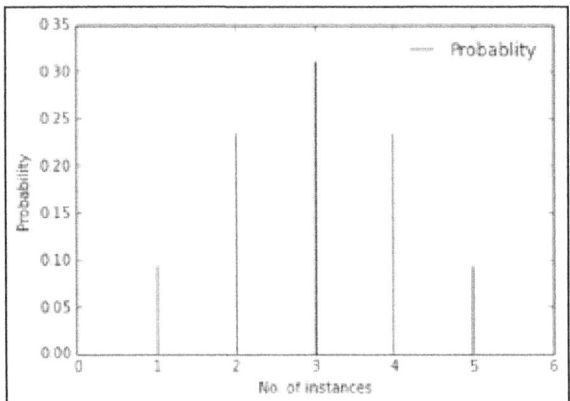

From the above graph, if the coin is tossed six times, then the probability of finding three heads has the highest probability while acquiring a single or five heads has the least probability.

Now, what if we increase the number of attempts to 100. How will the distribution look?

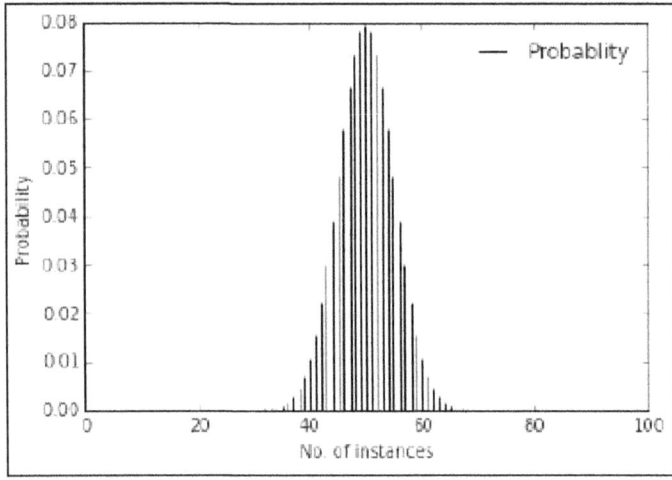

When the likelihood of success is set to 0.4, this is what you will see:

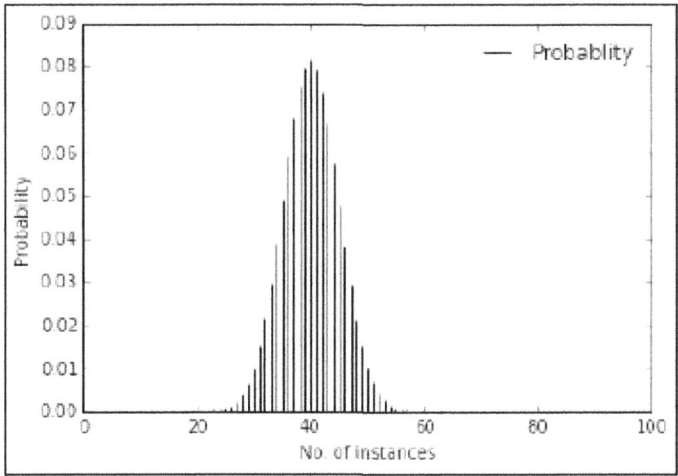

And when you toss the coin 1000 times at 0.5 probability. This is what you will get:

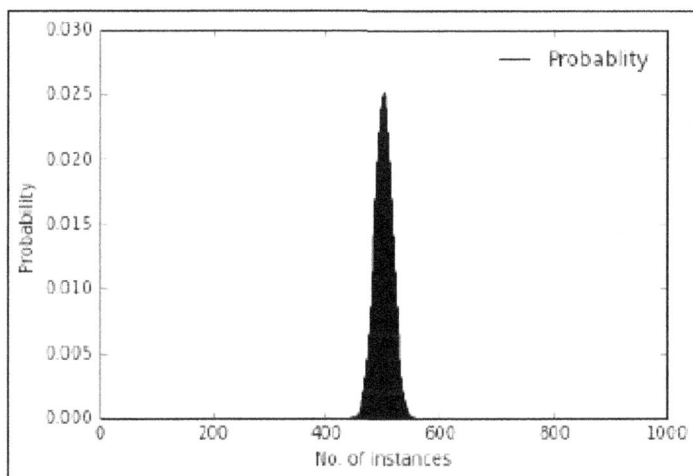

Can you notice that the binomial distribution has started to resemble a normal distribution?

The Poisson Distribution
This refers to the probability distribution of self-determining interval occurrences in an interval. The binomial distribution is used to measure the probability of

binary occurrences, whereas a Poisson distribution is important for count-based distributions. Suppose lambda is the average occurrence of the events per interval, then the probability of getting a k occurrence within a particular interval is provided by this formula:

$$f(k;\lambda) = \Pr(X=k) = \frac{\lambda^k e^{-\lambda}}{k!}$$

In the following formula, e denotes Euler's number, k is the total occurrences for which the probability is going to be determined, and lambda refers to the mean number of occurrences.

Let's explain this with an example. If the number of cars that travel through a bridge within an hour is 20. What is the likelihood of 23 cars traveling through the bridge in an hour?

For this example, we shall apply the Poisson function from SciPy:

```
>>> from scipy.stats import poisson
>>> rv = poisson(20)
>>> rv.pmf(23)
```

With the Poisson function, you define the mean value, which is 20 cars. The rv.pmf function reveals the probability, which is about 6%.

The Bernoulli distribution

You can conduct an experiment based on two possible outcomes: success or failure. The probability of success is denoted by p, and the likelihood of failure is 1-p. Bernoulli distribution is defined as a random variable that takes the value of 1 if there is success and 0 if there is a failure. The probability distribution formula for this is:

$$P(n) = p^n (1-p)^{1-n}$$

Also written as:

$$P(n) = \begin{cases} 1-p & \text{for } n=0 \\ p & \text{for } n=1 \end{cases}$$

Below is a graph representing the Bernoulli distribution:

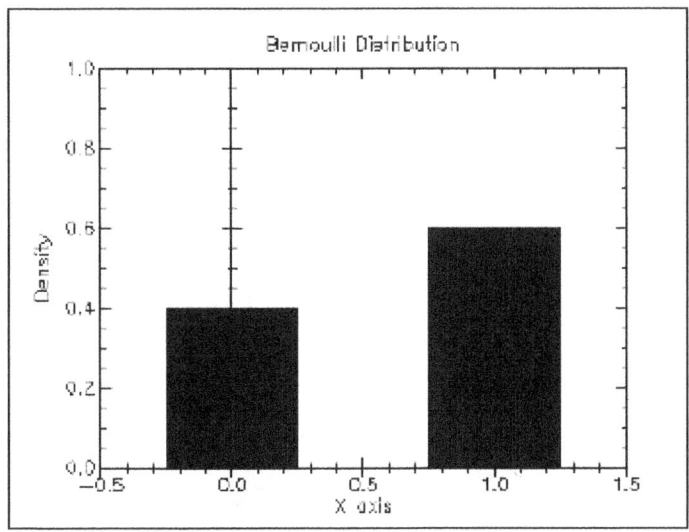

A perfect example of the Bernoulli distribution is voting in an election.
The Bernoulli distribution can be produced using the bernoulli.rvs () function of the SciPY package. This function generates a Bernoulli distribution using a probability of 0.7.

```
>>> from scipy import stats
>>> stats.bernoulli.rvs(0.7, size=100)
array([1, 1, 1, 1, 1, 0, 0, 1, 1, 0, 1, 1, 1, 0, 1, 1, 1, 1, 1, 1, 1,
1, 0,
1, 1, 1, 0, 1, 1, 0, 1, 0, 0, 1, 0, 0, 1, 0, 1, 0, 1, 1, 1, 1,
1, 0,
1, 1, 1, 1, 1, 0, 0, 1, 1, 1, 0, 1, 0, 1, 0, 0, 0, 0, 0, 1, 0,
0, 0,
1, 1, 1, 0, 1, 0, 1, 1, 1, 1, 1, 1, 0, 0, 1, 1, 1, 0, 0, 0, 1,
1, 1,
1, 0, 1, 1, 1, 0, 1, 1])
```

If the above output represents the number of votes for a candidate by people, then the candidate has 70% of the votes.

The A-Z Score

In simple terms, this is a score that describes the value of distribution in standard deviation with respect to the average. Consider the following formula that computes the z-score:

$$z = (X - \mu) / \sigma$$

In the following example, X represents the value in the distribution, u denotes the mean of the distribution, and σ denotes the distribution standard deviation.

Let's explain this concept using a school classroom example.

Assume a classroom of 60 students who have just received their mathematics examination score. Now, we simulate the score of these 60 students using a normal distribution based on the following command:

```
>>> classscore
>>> classscore = np.random.normal(50, 10, 60).round()
[ 56. 52. 60. 65. 39. 49. 41. 51. 48. 52. 47. 41. 60.
 54. 41.
 46. 37. 50. 50. 55. 47. 53. 38. 42. 42. 57. 40. 45.
 35. 39.
 67. 56. 35. 45. 47. 52. 48. 53. 53. 50. 61. 60. 57.
 53. 56.
 68. 43. 35. 45. 42. 33. 43. 49. 54. 45. 54. 48. 55.
 56. 30.]
```

The NumPy package contains a random module that has a normal function, where 50 assigned as the mean of the distribution, 10 is the standard deviation of the distribution, and 60 represents the number of values to be produced. You can plot the normal distribution using the following commands:

```
>>> plt.hist(classscore, 30, normed=True) #Number of breaks is 30
>>> plt.show()
```

The score of each student can be converted to a z-score using the following functions:

```
>>> stats.zscore(classscore)

[ 0.86008868  0.38555699  1.33462036  1.92778497 -1.15667098
  0.02965823
 -0.91940514  0.26692407 -0.08897469  0.38555699 -0.20760761 -
  0.91940514
  1.33462036  0.62282284 -0.91940514 -0.32624053 -1.39393683
  0.14829115
  0.14829115  0.74145576 -0.20760761  0.50418992 -1.2753039  -
  0.80077222
 -0.80077222  0.9787216  -1.03803806 -0.44487345 -1.63120267 -
  1.15667098
  2.16505081  0.86008868 -1.63120267 -0.44487345 -0.20760761
  0.38555699
 -0.08897469  0.50418992  0.50418992  0.14829115  1.45325329
  1.33462036
  0.9787216   0.50418992  0.86008868  2.28368373 -0.6821393  -
  1.63120267
 -0.44487345 -0.80077222 -1.86846851 -0.6821393   0.02965823
  0.62282284
 -0.44487345  0.62282284 -0.08897469  0.74145576  0.86008868 -
  2.22436727]
```

In the following case, a student with a score of 60 out of 100 has a z-score of 1.334. To make a lot of sense from the z-score, you'll apply the standard normal table. This table helps in defining the probability of a score.

It is important to know that the probability of acquiring a score above 60 would be:

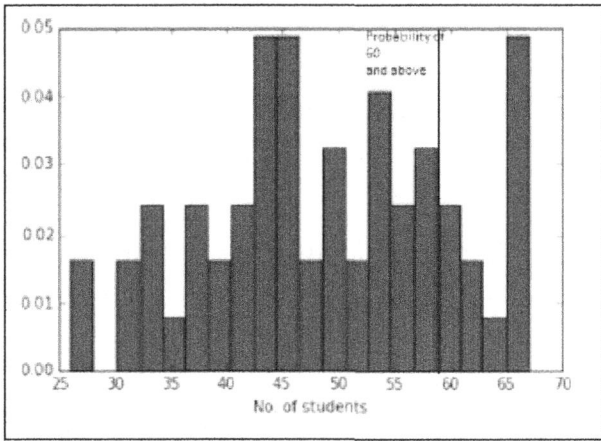

The standard normal table can allow you to compute the probability of the occurrence of the score, but you do not need to conduct the difficult task of identifying the value by searching through the table and determining the probability. This task is simplified by the cdf function, which is the cumulative distribution function:

```
>>> prob = 1 - stats.norm.cdf(1.334)
>>> prob
0.091101928265359899
```

The cdf function reveals the probability of finding values up to the z-score of 1.334 and doing a minus one of it will show the probability of acquiring a z-score, which is above it. This means 0.09 is the probability of getting marks above 60.
Here is a different question, "how many students managed to get to the top 20% of the class?"
For this particular question, you will need to work in reverse to identify the marks which all the students above it are in the top 20% of the class.
So to achieve the z-score at which the top 20% score marks, you can apply the ppf function in SciPy:

```
>>> stats.norm.ppf(0.80)
0.8416212335729143
```

The z-score for the previous output that decides whether the top 20% marks are at 0.84, as shown below:
>>> (0.84 * classscore.std()) + classscore.mean()
55.942594176524267
You multiply the z-score with the standard deviation and then add the result with the average of the distribution. This helps in changing the z-score to a value in the distribution. The 55.83 marks mean that the students who have scored more than this are in the top 20% of the distribution.
The z-score is an important concept in statistics, which is broadly used. Now you can understand that it is basically applied in standardizing any distribution so that it can be compared to it.

A P-value

A p-value refers to the probability of refusing a null-hypothesis when the hypothesis is found to be true. The null hypothesis is a statement that states that there is no difference between the two measures. If the hypothesis is that individuals who clock in 4 hours study daily score of more than 90 marks out of 100. The null hypothesis, in this case, would be that there is no connection between the number of hours clocked in and the marks scored.

In case the p-value is equivalent to or less than the significance level (a), then the null hypothesis is irregular, and it requires to be rejected.

Let's understand this feature using an example where the null hypothesis is that it is common for students to get 68 marks in mathematics.

Let's acquire the z-score of 68 marks:

```
>>> zscore = ( 68 - classscore.mean() ) / classscore.std()
>>> zscore
2.283
```

Now, let's determine the value:

```
>>> prob = 1 - stats.norm.cdf(zscore)
>>> prob
0.032835182628040638
```

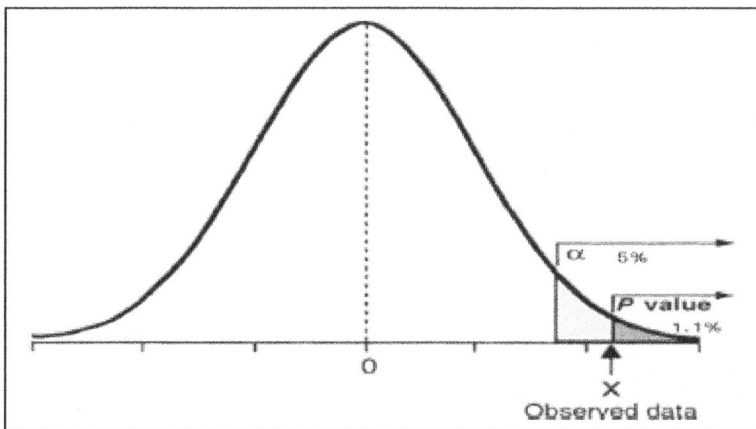

So, you can see that the p-value is at 3.2%, which is lower than the significance level. In other words, the null hypothesis can be rejected, and it can be concluded that it's not common to attain 68 marks in mathematics.

One-Tailed and Two-Tailed Tests

When it comes to a two-tailed test, both the tails of the null hypothesis are used to determine the hypothesis.

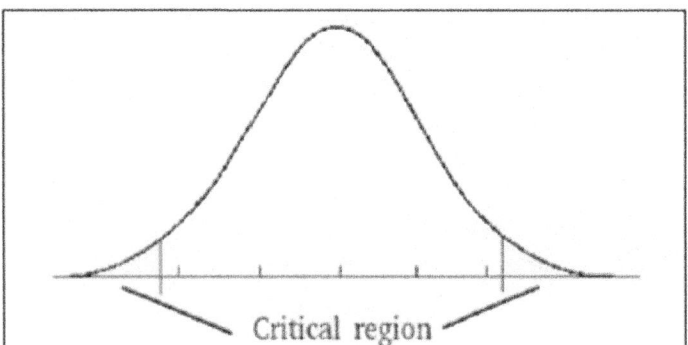

For a two-tailed test, when a given percentage of 5% is used, then it's distributed equally on both sides. In this case, it is 2.5% on one side, and 2.5% on the opposite side.

Here's an example to illustrate this further. The average score of mathematics exam at a national level is 60 marks, and the standard deviation is 3 marks.

The average marks of a class are 53. The null hypothesis refers to the mean marks of the class, similar to the national average. First, let's test the following hypothesis by first finding the z-score 60.

```
>>> zscore = ( 53 - 60 ) / 3.0
>>> zscore
-2.3333333333333335
```

The p-value would be:

```
>>> prob = stats.norm.cdf(zscore)
>>> prob
0.0098153286286453336
```

In this case, the p-value is 0.98%. The null hypothesis is to be rejected, and the p-value should be lower than 2.5% in either direction of the bell curve. Because the p-value is less than 2.5%, you can reject the null hypothesis and clearly define what the average marks of the class are different from the national average.

Type 1 and Type 2 Errors

The type 1 error refers to the error that happens when there is a rejection of the null hypothesis when it's definitely true. This type of error is known as an error of the first kind and is equivalent to false positives.

Let's demonstrate this concept by applying an example. Say for, example, a new drug is being created, and it requires to be tested on whether it's effective in fighting diseases. The null hypothesis is that it's not effective in fighting diseases. The significance level is retained at 5% so that the null hypothesis can be confidently accepted 95% of the time. But, 5% of the time, you'll accept the rejection of the hypothesis even if it had to be accepted. In other words, even if the drug is ineffective, it's assumed to be effective.

The Type 1 error is regulated by controlling the relevance level, which is alpha. Alpha is the highest chance to have a Type 1 error. The lower the alpha, the lower will be the Type 1 error.

The Type 2 error is the type of error that happens when you don't reject a null hypothesis that is false.

This type of error happens in a drug scenario when the drug is said to be ineffective but in a real sense, is effective.

This kind of error can be regulated one at a time. In case one of the errors is minimized, then the other increases. It depends on the application and the problem statement that the analysis tries to focus on, and based on it, the right error should reduce. In the case of this drug scenario, a Type 1 error should be reduced because it is better to ship a drug that is confidently effective.

A Confidence Interval

The confident interval in statistics refers to the population factor. The confidence interval helps to determine the level for computing the population mean can be described.

Assume there are 50 men and their height in centimeters:

```
>>> height_data = np.array([ 186.0, 180.0, 195.0, 189.0, 191.0,
177.0, 161.0, 177.0, 192.0, 182.0, 185.0, 192.0,
173.0, 172.0, 191.0, 184.0, 193.0, 182.0, 190.0, 185.0, 181.0,
188.0, 179.0, 188.0,
170.0, 179.0, 180.0, 189.0, 188.0, 185.0, 170.0, 197.0, 187.0,
182.0, 173.0, 179.0,
184.0, 177.0, 190.0, 174.0, 203.0, 206.0, 173.0, 169.0, 178.0,
201.0, 198.0, 166.0,
171.0, 180.0])
```

When you plot the distribution, it contains a normal distribution:

```
>>> plt.hist(height_data, 30, normed=True)
>>> plt.show()
```

The average of the distribution includes:
>>> **height_data.mean()**
183.24000000000001
Therefore, the mean height of a man from the sample is 183.4 cm.
To compute the confidence interval, you'll now define the standard error of the mean.
The standard error of the mean refers to the derivation of the sample mean from the population mean. It's defined by applying the following formula:

$$SE_{\bar{x}} = \frac{s}{\sqrt{n}}$$

In the following case, s refers to the standard deviation of the sample, and n is the number of elements within the sample.
This can be computed using the following sem() function of the SciPy package:
>>> **stats.sem(height_data)**
1.3787187190005252
Thus, there is a normal error of the mean of 1.38cm. The lower and upper limit of the confidence interval can be computed by entering this formula.

```
Upper/Lower limit = mean(height) + / - sigma * SEmean(x)
```

Thus, for the lower limit:
*183.24 + (1.96 * 1.38) = 185.94*
And for upper limit:
*183.24 - (1.96*1.38) = 180.53*
At 1.96 standard deviation occupies 95% of the area in the normal distribution. We can confidently consider the population mean to be between 180.53 and 185.94cm of the height.

Assume we now take a sample of 50 people, put down their height, and then repeat this process 30 times. We can then plot the averages of every sample and observe the distribution.

The commands used to simulate the preceding plot include:

```python
>>> average_height = []
>>> for i in xrange(30):
>>> sample50 = np.random.normal(183, 10, 50).round()
>>> average_height.append(sample50.mean())
>>> plt.hist(average_height, 20, normed=True)
>>> plt.show()
```

You should realize that the mean ranges from 180 to 187 cm when you simulate the mean height of 50 men, which was measured 30 times.

Suppose you sample 1000 men and repeat the process 30 times:

```python
>>> average_height = []
>>> for i in xrange(30):
>>> sample1000 = np.random.normal(183, 10, 1000).round()
>>> average_height.append(sample1000.mean())
>>> plt.hist(average_height, 10, normed=True)
>>> plt.show()
```

As you may realize, the height changes from 182.4cm and to 183.4 cm. What does this represent?

In other words, the sample size increases, the standard error of the mean decreases, which also means that the confidence interval narrows, and you can tell with surety the interval that the population mean would be.

Correlation

When it comes to statistics, correlation refers to the similarity between two random variables. The most commonly applied correlation is Person correlation and is defined using the following formula:

$$\rho_{X,Y} = \frac{\text{cov}(X,Y)}{\sigma_X \sigma_Y} = \frac{E[(X-\mu_X)(Y-\mu_Y)]}{\sigma_X \sigma_Y}$$

```
>>> mpg = [21.0, 21.0, 22.8, 21.4, 18.7, 18.1, 14.3, 24.4, 22.8,
19.2, 17.8, 16.4, 17.3, 15.2, 10.4, 10.4, 14.7, 32.4, 30.4,
33.9, 21.5, 15.5, 15.2, 13.3, 19.2, 27.3, 26.0, 30.4, 15.8,
19.7, 15.0, 21.4]
>>> hp = [110, 110, 93, 110, 175, 105, 245, 62, 95, 123, 123, 180,
180, 180, 205, 215, 230, 66, 52, 65, 97, 150, 150, 245,
175, 66, 91, 113, 264, 175, 335, 109]
>>> stats.pearsonr(mpg,hp)
(-0.77616837182658638, 1.7878352541210661e-07)
```

The first value of the output assigns the correlation between the horsepower and the mileage, while the second value provides the p-value.

Therefore, the first value indicates that it is highly negatively associated, and the p-value shows that there is a huge correlation between them.

Here is the plot diagram:

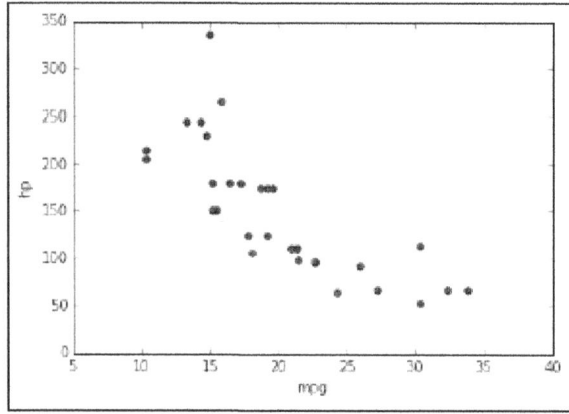

From the above plot, you can notice that the mpg increases, and the horsepower drops.

Let's consider another correlation known as the Spearman correlation. The following correlation applies to the rank order of the values, and so it delivers a monotonic relation between the two distributions. It is important for ordinal data and isn't affected by outliers.

Let's consider the Spearman correlation between miles per gallon and horsepower. You can achieve this using the spearmanr() function within the SciPy package:

```
>>> stats.spearmanr(mpg,hp)
(-0.89466464574996252, 5.085969430924539e-12)
```

You should notice that the Spearman correlation is -0.89, and the p-value is important.

Let's perform an experiment where we introduce different outlier values within the data and notice how the Pearson and Spearman correlation is affected.

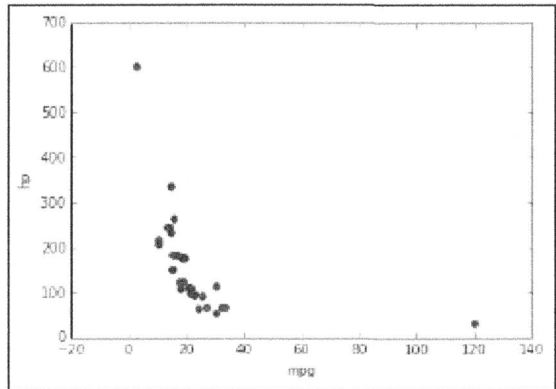

From the previous plot, you can clearly define the outlier values. Let's consider how the correlations are affected by both Pearson and Spearman correlation. The commands below represent the Pearson correlation:

```
>>> stats.pearsonr(mpg, hp)
>>> (-0.47415304891435484, 0.0046122167947348462)
```

Below is the Spearman correlation:

```
>>> stats.spearmanr(mpg,hp)
(-0.89466464574996252, 5.085969430924539e-12)
```

You can now see that the Pearson correlation has been clearly affected because of the outliers, which originate from a correlation of 0.89 to 0.47.

The Spearman correlation doesn't get affected, although it's based on the order instead of the actual value within the data.

Z-test vs T-test

You've already conducted several Z-tests before you validated your null hypothesis.

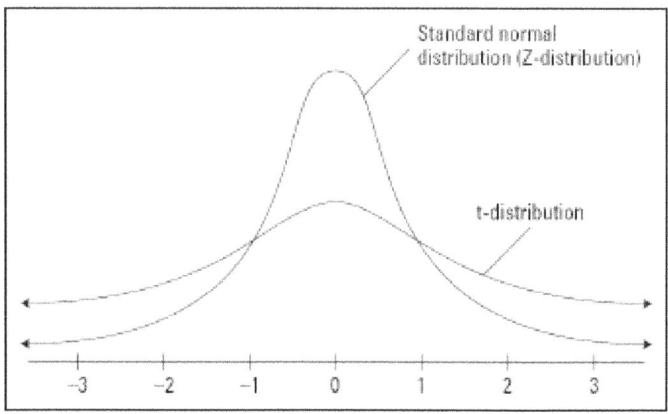

A T-distribution resembles a Z-distribution. The T-distributions' standard deviation is always proportionally larger than the Z.

The t distribution is normally used to analyze the population when the sample is small.

The Z-test is used to make a comparison of the population mean against a sample than the population mean of two distributions using a sample size greater than 30. For example, Z-test would be comparing the heights of men from various ethnicity groups.

The T-test is used to compare the population average against a sample, or compare the population mean of two distributions using sample size less than 30, and when you don't know the population's standard deviation.

The F Distribution
This distribution is also referred to as the Snedecor's F distribution. An F static is provided by the following formula.

$$f = [s_1^2/\sigma_1^2]/[s_2^2/\sigma_2^2]$$

In the following case, s1 refers to the standard deviation of sample 1 with an n1, size, s2, and the standard deviation of sample 2. The distribution of all the possible values of f statistics is referred to as F distribution. The d1 and d2 represent the degrees of freedom in this chart:

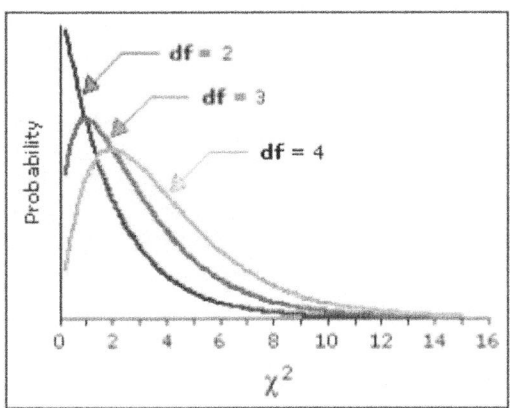

The Chi-Square Distribution
This type of distribution is defined using the following formula:

$$X^2 = [(n-1)*s^2]/\sigma^2$$

In the following case, n refers to the size of the sample, s represents the standard deviation of the sample, and σ is the standard deviation of the population.
If you repeatedly pick samples and define the chi-square statistics, then you can create a chi-square distribution, which is described by the following probability function:

$$Y = Y_0 * (X^2)^{(v/2-1)} * e^{-X2/2}$$

Chi-Square for the Goodness of Fit

The Chi-square test can be applied to test whether the observed data differs significantly from the desired data. For example, the dice is rolled 36 times, and the likelihood that each face should turn upwards is 1/6. Therefore, the expected distribution is as follows:

Expected Frequency	Outcome
6	1
6	2
6	3
6	4
6	5
6	6

The observed distribution consists of the following:

Observed Frequency	Outcome
7	1
5	2
3	3
9	4
6	5
6	6

The null hypothesis within the chi-square test is that the observed value resembles the expected value.

The chi-square can be conducted using the chisquare function within the SciPy package:

```
>>> stats.chisquare(observed,expected)
(3.333333333333333, 0.64874235866759344
```

The first value is the chi-square value, and the second value is the p-value, which is very high. In other words, the null hypothesis is valid, and the observed value resembles the expected value.

Chapter 5: Python Libraries-Pygal

Why Should You Use Pygal?

In Python development, there are a lot of libraries for charts (Matplotlib and plotly are a few examples), and different resources have been created for many of them. Because this is an introduction to data charting, you need a simple to use the library where new developers to Python charting can be able to follow the code provided.

Pygal is a Python-based SVG Charts creator developed by the Kozea Community. This is a community committed to building quality open source libraries, mainly Python-based.

The Pygal library comes with multiple charting options beyond what is defined as standard charts: line charts, pie graphs, and bar charts. It contains a world map, radar charts, box plots, and funnel charts.

It also comes with prebuilt themes and styles, which you don't need to customize if you are not forced to do so. Additionally, because the chart library's output is SVG, this makes it a flexible output for HTML5 or even print media. One problem with certain chart libraries in Python language is that the output defaults to the PNG format with a particular image size. Because SVG is a vector graphic, it is possible to be scaled and resized for any need without damage to quality.

You can navigate to the http://pygal.org/: website.

The Pygal website is made up of a beautiful and easy to read the documentation. One thing that is obvious with third-party Python libraries is that the documentation can comprise of a well-documented, online-searchable wiki to a simple readme.txt file that only reveals how to install the library. Additionally, the Pygal library doesn't need a lot of dependencies, which is important for an introductory book.

A lot of Python frameworks have picky dependencies that you may require for your project, but they may or may not work with your system.

The lxml library is the only library required for pygal, but it has several issues depending on the kind of operating system you are executing your Python code. It is important that you take the time to reread the notes on lxml before you can head straight to pygal installation.

Pygal Installation Using Pip

First, if you're yet to install lxml, and you are working on Windows, you'll want to install the lxml installer. Otherwise, these commands should help you install lxml.

Next, you will need to apply pip and install pygal using the following commands for Mac and Windows systems.
If you are using a windows laptop, enter the following commands:
Pip install pygal
If you are working on Ubuntu, enter the following command:
Sudo pip install pygal
Next, open Eclipse with PyDev and start a new Python project. Once you create the project, create a new file, name it importtest.py, and enter the following command:
Import pygal
Once complete, you should press CTRL + Space bar and see PyDev's code. This screenshot illustrates pygal being rearranged in the system:

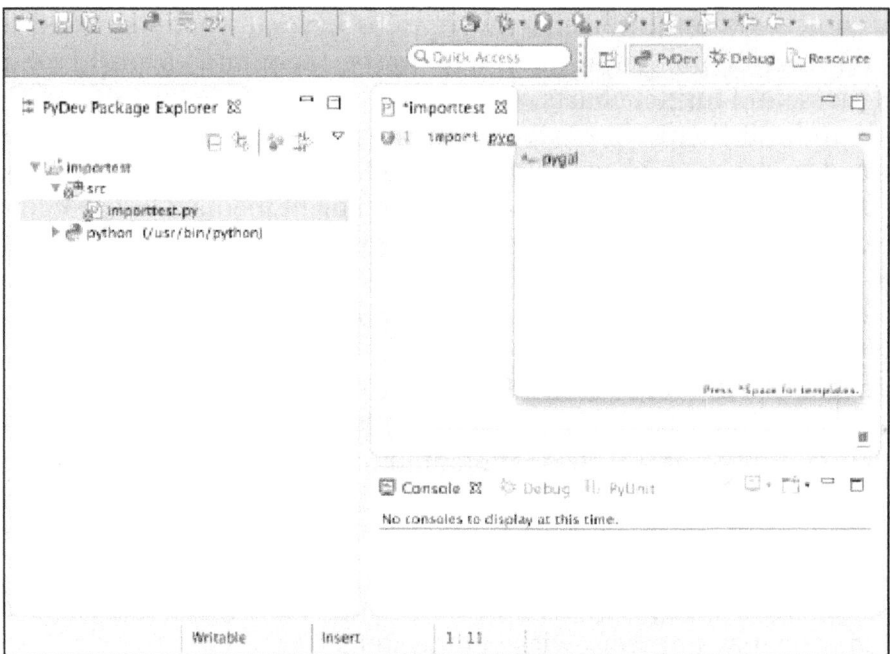

Install Pygal Using Python Tools for Visual Studio

If you plan to use Visual Studio, here's a note on installation. First, if you have not installed lxml, then run easy_install using your Python environment in the install Python Package window, as illustrated in the following screenshot:

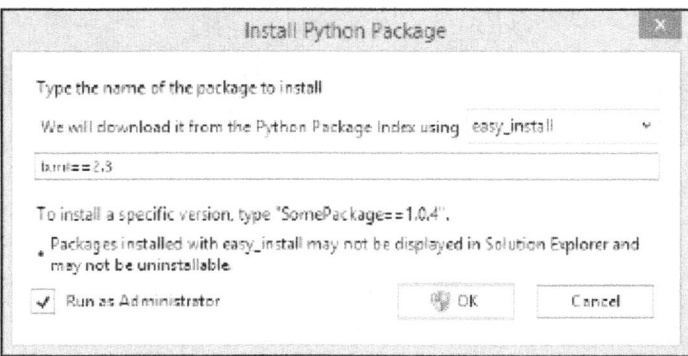

If successful, then install the pygal library. You can right-click inside your environments and choose install python package, this time using pygal, as described in the screenshot:

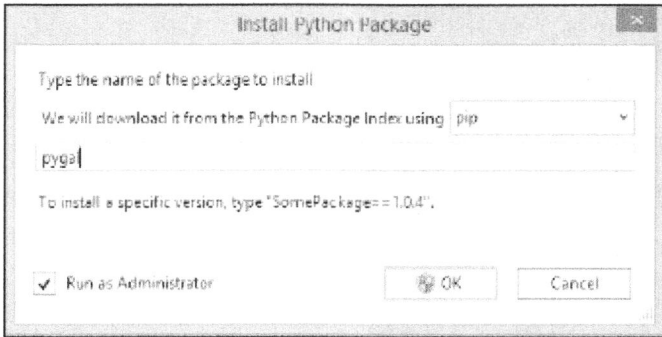

Creating a Line Chart

In general, line charts represent how a given data changes at different time intervals. When it comes to charting, this is the simplest chart that you can create. It is made up of the x and y axes, and each axis on the chart denotes time, value, or a different parameter.

Let's create a simple chart on the number of hits a website has received in the past two years. Take a look at the first line of this code. That is a declarative line by the Python interpreter to describe the string encoding type to the file. Additionally, you'll realize online.x_labels that you apply an inline function known as range (). This allows you to build an array of numbers, beginning from the lowest numbers to the highest number. In this case, 2012 and 2014 would output as 2012, 2013, 2014, in an array. Now, copy this code into your project's main python file:

```python
# -*- coding: utf-8 -*-
import pygal
#create a new line chart.
line = pygal.Line()
line.title = 'Website hits in the past 2 years' #set chart title
line.x_labels = map(str, range(2012, 2014)) #set the x-axis labels.
line.add('Page views', [None, 0, 12, 32, 72, 148]) #set values.
line.render_to_file('linechart.svg') #set filename.
```

The screenshot below demonstrates a basic pygal line chart output:

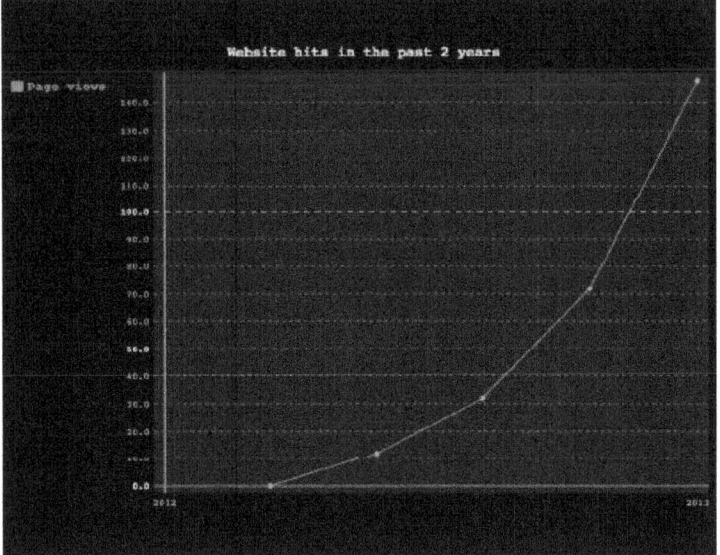

Inside your main project file where you executed your script, you should see the linechart.SVG file created. Open this file, and your char will look like the above screenshot. To identify the file, open the directory your project is in and search the linechart.svg file. Keep in mind that you can hover over the dots and acquire the values of every marker in the chart. These are some of the properties that come prebuilt inside the pygal library.

You will also notice that the timeline of the chars begins from 0.0 in 2013. If you look at the line.add() statement; the first parameter is None. This creates a spacer within the chart to push the chart data out rather than force the chart to begin in 2012. This is a popular trick to setting up chart layouts.

Another property is that if you hover over the line label, the enter line is highlighted, this describes the dataset you're viewing with that label. The pygal library will also review your data and stress-specific lines on the data axis like 0.0, 50.0, and 100.0, to break up several chart lines for easier readability.

Code hinting support for line () function of pygal depends on the type of IDE you are using. The pygal library is written a bit different when compared to most Python libraries. The library generates each type of chart dynamically by applying a for a loop. This loop confirms each chart class in the pygal library. Because of this, IDEs that demand static, hardcoded functions in Python will throw an error, but not break when they are run. This means applying code hinting may or may not work well based on the editor you're using.

Stacked Line Charts

Stacked line charts operate like the traditional line charts. The only exception is that it accumulates numerous sets of data on top of each other. Add the following code into your Python file and execute it.

```python
# -*- coding: utf-8 -*-
import pygal
#create a new stacked line chart.
line = pygal.StackedLine(fill=True)
line.title = 'Web hits in the past 2 years' #set chart title
line.x_labels = map(str, range(2012, 2014)) #set the x-axis labels.
line.add('Site A', [None, 0, 12, 32, 72, 148]) #set values.
line.add('Site B', [2, 16, 12, 87, 91, 342]) #set values.
line.add('Site C', [42, 55, 84, 88, 90, 171]) #set values.
line.render_to_file('linechart.svg') #set filename.
```

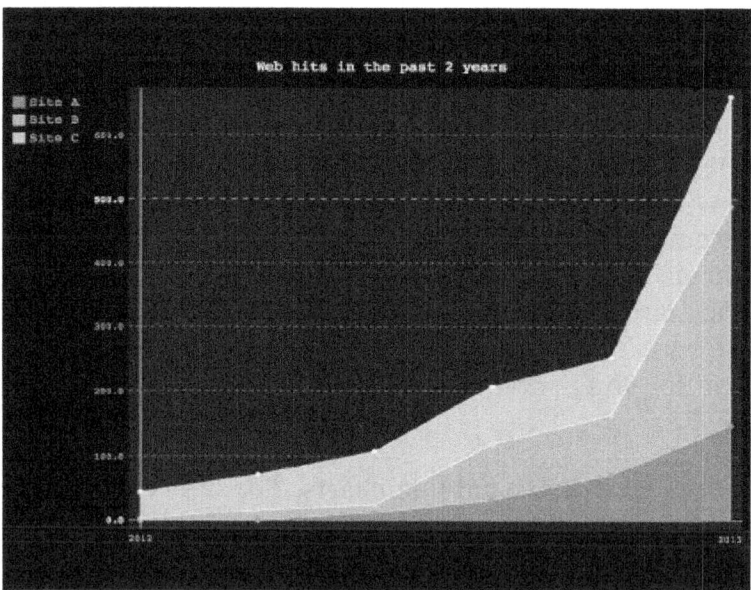

Once deployed, your stacked chart will resemble what's shown in the previous screenshot. Open the directory your project is in to determine the linechart.svg file. Keep an eye on how pygal overrides your first SVG file by default, remember this while working with the following library. Also, you will discover that you added a fill = True parameter to the StackedLine function when you declare your chart; this is a chart parameter.

Simple Bar Charts

The application of simple bar charts resembles line charts. Additionally, it discloses values to information categories. Use the code below to create a simple bar chart.

```
# -*- coding: utf-8 -*-
import pygal
#create a new bar chart.
bar = pygal.Bar()
bar.title = 'Searches for term: sleep'
bar.x_labels = map(str, range(2011, 2015))
bar.add('Searches', [81, 88, 88, 100])
bar.render_to_file('bar_chart.svg')
```

Navigate to your project directory and open bar_chart.svg within your browser. Keep in mind that the code hasn't changed a lot. The screenshot below illustrates the results:

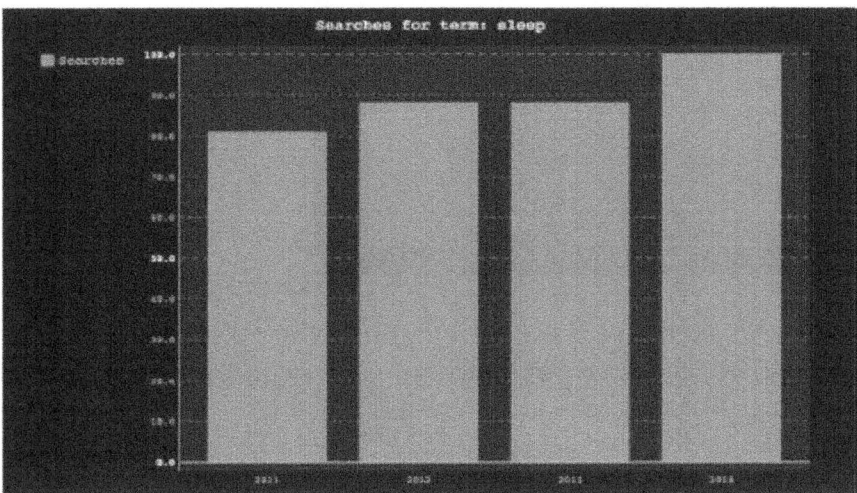

Stacked Bar Charts

Just like the line chart, stacked bar charts overlay different bars one over the other by data order. Add the code below in your python script file.

```
# -*- coding: utf-8 -*-
import pygal

#Create a new stacked bar chart.
bar = pygal.StackedBar()
bar.title = 'Searches for term: sleep'
bar.x_labels = map(str, range(2011, 2015))
bar.add('Men', [81, 88, 88, 100])
bar.add('Women', [78, 84, 69, 92])
bar.render_to_file('bar_chart.svg')
```

Here is the result of the running the above script:

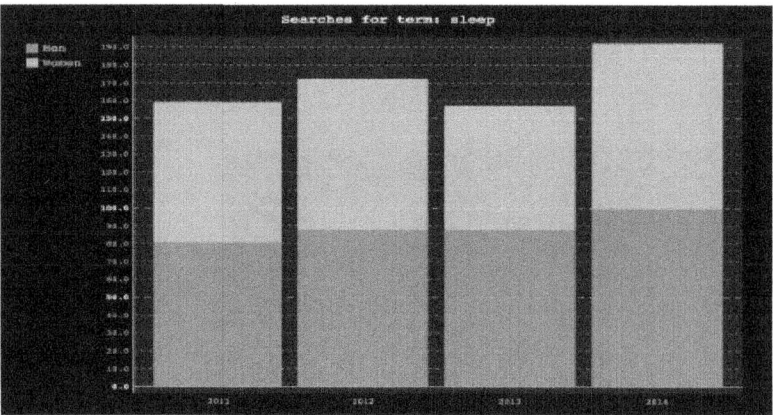

Since this is a stacked value, you have two sets of data. In the following case, men and women searches. The previous screenshot is a complete chart that demonstrates the combined dataset with various segment values of total searches for the term "sleep."

Horizontal Bar Charts

This is the last bar chart provided by pygal, you will apply a horizontal chart and reuse your data from the simple bar chart. A horizontal bar chart is built to demonstrate data at one point in time. For that reason, you will remove your x_labels property because you only want a single month displayed. Now, add the following code, and execute the script:

```
# -*- coding: utf-8 -*-
import pygal
#create a new bar chart.
bar = pygal.HorizontalBar()
bar.title = 'Searches for term: sleep in April'
bar.add('Searches', [81, 88, 88, 100])
bar.render_to_file('bar_chart.svg'
```

Open the bar_chart.svg file, the results are highlighted in the following screenshot:

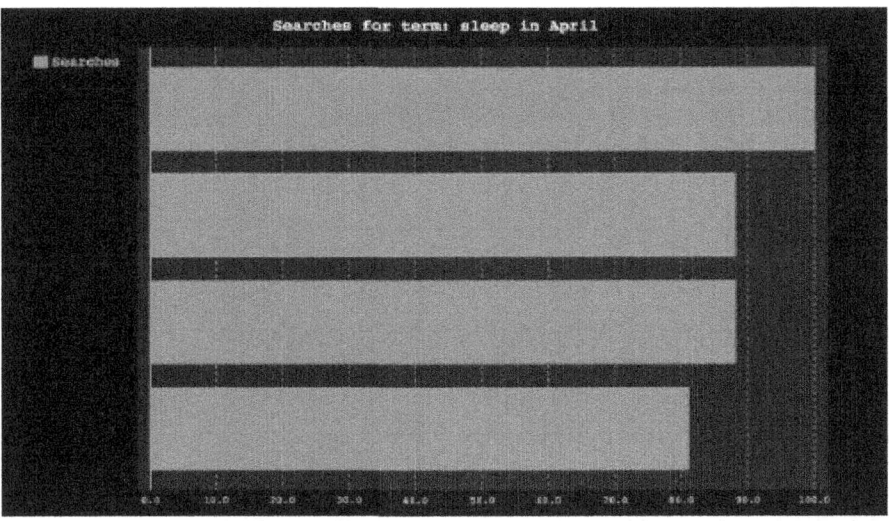

XY Charts

The XY charts are popular in scientific data to represent numerous values at different periods. They can display negative values too. These charts can output various sets to increase readability. Now create a simple xy chart with two points by using the code presented below.

```
# -*- coding: utf-8 -*-
import pygal
xy_chart = pygal.XY()
xy_chart.add('Value 1', [(-50, -30), (100, 45)])
xy_chart.render_to_file("xy_chart.svg")
```

Open the xy_chart.svg file. The results are presented in the screenshot below:

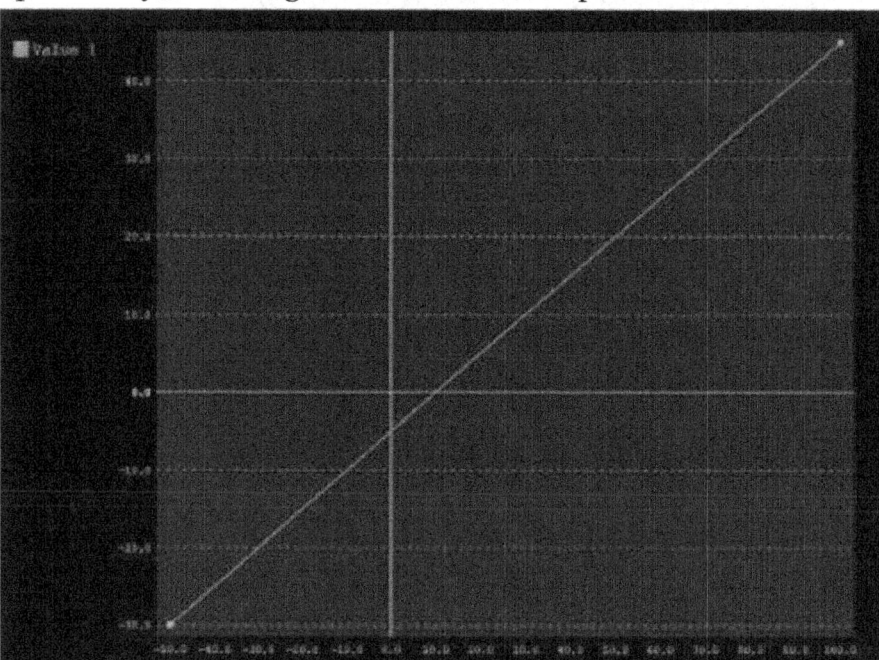

Pay attention to how pygal highlights the 0 lines on both the x and y coordinates. This is a freestyling supported by the pygal library to demonstrate negative values. Additionally, take note of the add () function, and the way each value is underlined as an (x. y) coordinate, classified in an array. Let's create another chart, this time using two plots. In the following case, we will create using Value 1 and Value 2. Add the following code into your Python script and run it.

```python
# -*- coding: utf-8 -*-
import pygal
xy_chart = pygal.XY()
xy_chart.add('Value 1', [(-50, -30), (100, 45)])
xy_chart.add('Value 2', [(-2, -14), (370, 444)])
xy_chart.render_to_file("xy_chart.svg")
```

Open the xy_chart.svg file. Remember that the two-line plots are present as shown in the screenshot:

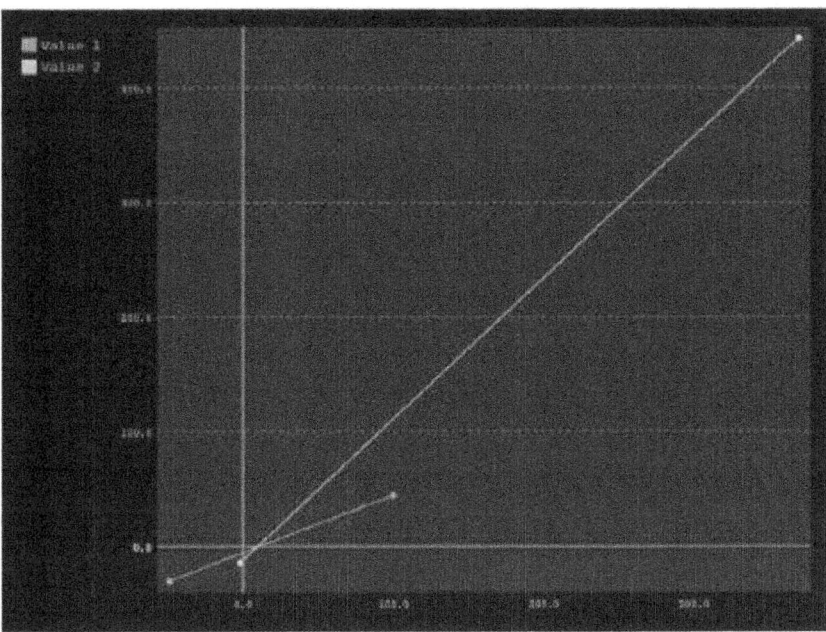

Next, you're going to learn how to set up a basic line plot in an XY chart, but suppose you have multiple values in a single line? You will create another XY chart using three values and six points per value. Copy the following code and run it.

```
# -*- coding: utf-8 -*-
import pygal
xy_chart = pygal.XY()
xy_chart.add('Value 1', [(-50, -30), (100, 45), (120, 56), (168, 102), (211, 192), (279, 211)])
xy_chart.add('Value 2', [(-2, -14), (370, 444), (391, 464), (399, 512), (412, 569), (789, 896)])
xy_chart.add('Value 3', [(2, 10), (142, 164), (184, 216), (203, 243), (208, 335), (243, 201)])
xy_chart.render_to_file("xy_chart.svg")
```

Once it is completed, open the xy_chart.svg file, this should resemble what is shown in the screenshot below:

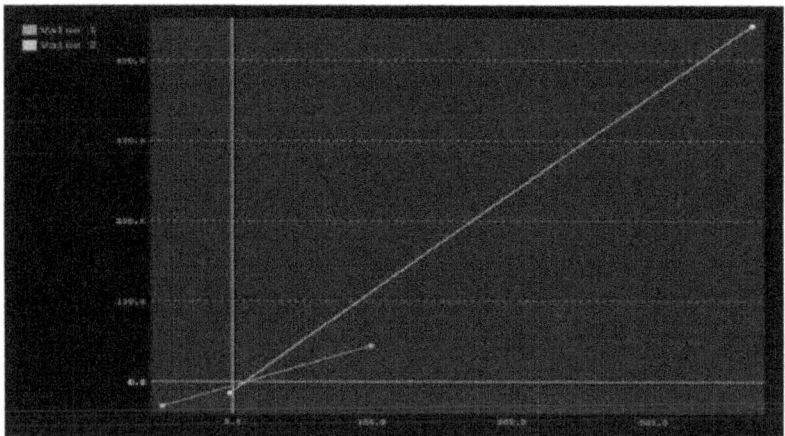

Take a look at how it's easy to read each dataset. You can discern that Value 2 has the highest values that are on the higher side, and also Value 3 has a higher point than Value 1 but dropped down quickly. This makes XY charts powerful for scientific data. Now, consider a variation of XY charts known as scatter plots.

Scatter Plots

This works like XY charts, but they don't have lines that connect together. In the case of the pygal library, the "scatterplot" function doesn't exist. However, you reuse the XY chart function and define a parameter. In the following case, stroke is equivalent to False. Now, let's reuse the XY code from the last chart, and include the stroke parameter.

```python
# -*- coding: utf-8 -*-
import pygal
xy_chart = pygal.XY(stroke=False)
xy_chart.add('Value 1', [(-50, -30), (100, 45), (120, 56), (168, 102), (211, 192), (279, 211)])
xy_chart.add('Value 2', [(-2, -14), (370, 444), (391, 464), (399, 512), (412, 569), (789, 896)])
xy_chart.add('Value 3', [(2, 10), (142, 164), (184, 216), (203, 243), (208, 335), (243, 201)])
xy_chart.render_to_file("xy_chart.svg")
```

Once you're done copying this code, run the file. Your scatter plots should resemble the one in the screenshot below:

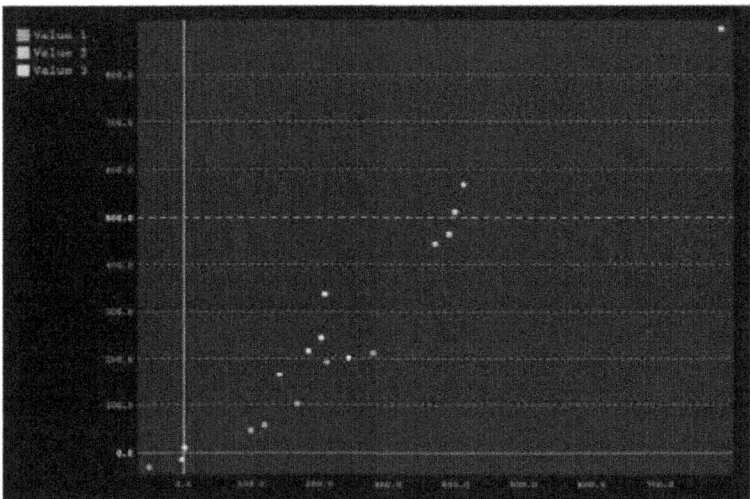

Notice how easy this chart can be to interpret with multiple data points. Typically, a tip for using XY charts versus scatter plots is when your data points are more than 10 per dataset or more than 6 datasets to be displayed.

The last variation of the xy chart library in the pygal is the DateY.

Date Y Charts

This chart operates exactly like the XY chart, with only one difference. Each data point is connected with a date and not a string type in Python with but a physical datetime object within the python code. Each X label will be hooked with a date object within the python code, and Y will either be an integer or a float supplied by us.

Also, the DateY comes with its own function with its own rules to be adhered. Let's create a simple DateY chart to understand what we are working with. First, before you implement the following code, look at the datetime library.

This library is a built-in library for Python and is pretty simple. It facilitates the saving of dates and counts back or forwards in time.

The timedelta function is part of the datetime library. What timedelta () represents is the period, and the difference between two dates or times, with date-based parameters.

```
import datetime
from time import sleep
start = datetime.datetime.now()
sleep(5) #delay the python script for 5 seconds.
stop = datetime.datetime.now()
elapsed = stop - start
if elapsed > datetime.timedelta(minutes=4):
print "Slept for greater than 4 minutes"
if elapsed > datetime.timedelta(seconds=4):
print "Slept for greater than 4 seconds"
```

The result of running the following code is shown below. Remember that 4 seconds is passed inside the script using the sleep () function to set a delay of 5 seconds before setting the stop variable's date.

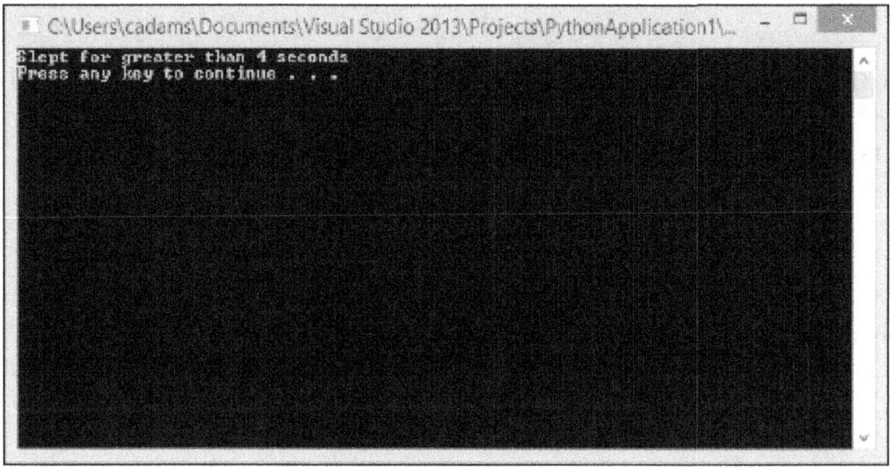

Next, let's build the DateY chart. For this chart, you will need to timestamp an array of dates using values.

```
# -*- coding: utf-8 -*-
import pygal
from datetime import datetime, timedelta
Date_Y = pygal.DateY()
Date_Y.title = "Flights and amount of passengers arriving from St.Louis."
Date_Y.add("Arrival", [
(datetime(2014, 1, 5), 42),
(datetime(2014, 1, 14), 123),
(datetime(2014, 2, 2), 97),
(datetime(2014, 3, 22), 164)
])
Date_Y.render_to_file('datey_chart.svg')
```

Now, let's review this chart. We can notice that a full date-time is linked with each data point as well as our char value. You can also see a range of time on the x-axis label. But, there is a problem with this. Carefully study the following chart and pay attention to the labels on the x-axis.

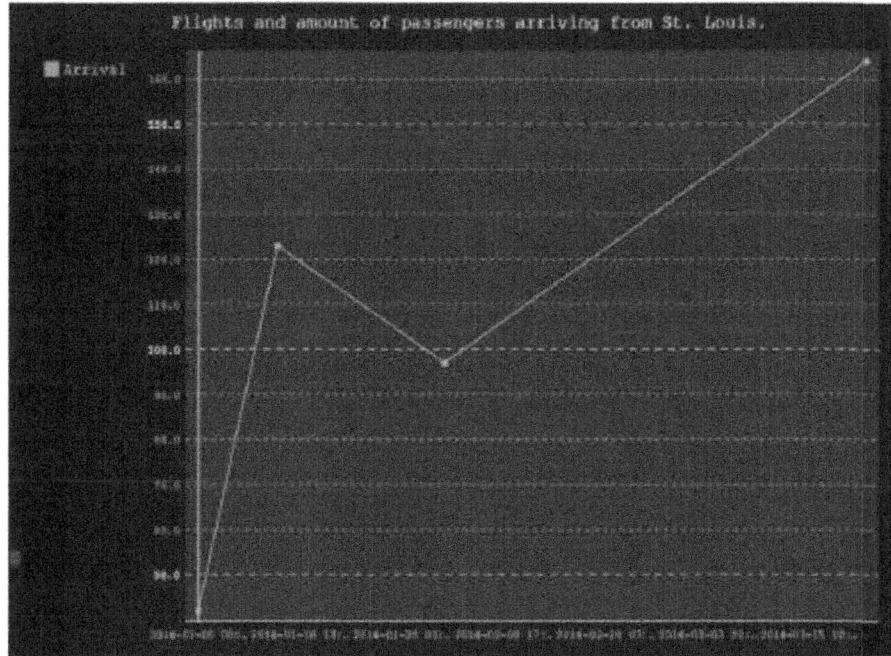

See how the labels bunch up and crop off if they fail to fit. This should not be a problem for you because the DateY chart contains an optional parameter to assist render these labels. You can rotate them along the x-axis using the parameter displayed in the following code:

```python
# -*- coding: utf-8 -*-
import pygal
from datetime import datetime, timedelta
Date_Y = pygal.DateY(x_label_rotation=25)
Date_Y.title = "Flights and amount of passengers arriving from St.Louis."
Date_Y.add("Arrival", [
(datetime(2014, 1, 5), 42),
(datetime(2014, 1, 14), 123),
(datetime(2014, 2, 2), 97),
(datetime(2014, 3, 22), 164)
])
Date_Y.render_to_file('datey_chart.svg')
```

Next, re-render the chart, like in the following screenshot. You can notice that the labels are formatted in a way that supports readability.

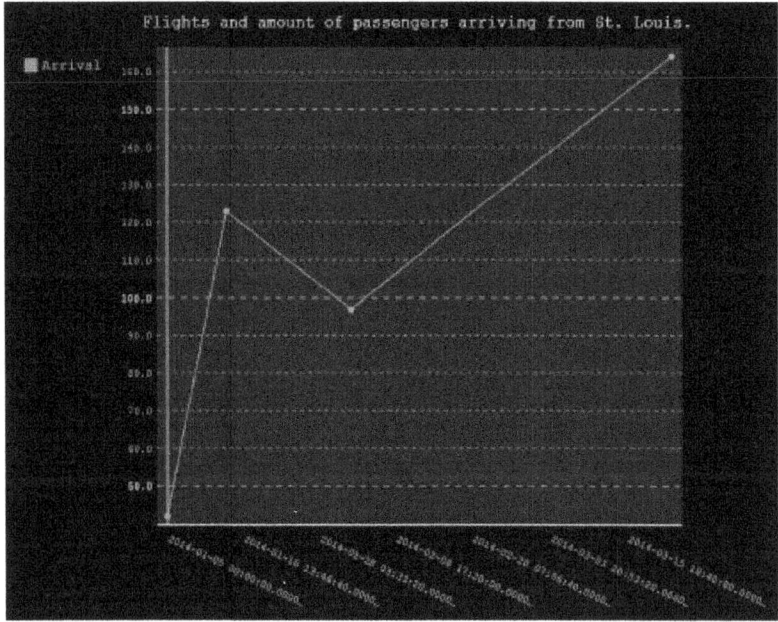

Let's include an additional chart before we complete the following chapter. In the following case, you'll capture two points in time known by your code; one is going to be delayed using a sleep delay similar to the time delta example, you're going to have two flights come in at two different points in time.

Here, you'll set a delay between two arrivals and set the time for every data point. You will apply for time. Sleep () to delay the script. Execute this script. Remember that because the chart has a delay in its code, the SVG file will require 277 seconds to process:

```
# -*- coding: utf-8 -*-
import pygal, time
from datetime import datetime
#Set pre-defined arrival dates for compare.
arrival1 = datetime.now()
time.sleep(277)
arrival2 = datetime.now()
delta = arrival2 - arrival1
result = str(delta.seconds) + ' seconds'
Date_Y = pygal.DateY(x_label_rotation=25)
Date_Y.title = "Flights and amount of passengers arriving from St.Louis."
Date_Y.add("Arrival", [
(datetime(2014, 1, 5), 42),
(datetime(2014, 1, 14), 123),
(datetime(2014, 2, 2), 97),
(datetime(2014, 3, 22), 164)
])
Date_Y.add("Arrivals today (time between flights %s)" % result, [
(arrival1, 14),
(arrival2, 47)
])
Date_Y.render_to_file('datey_chart.svg')
```

Now, let's consider the results. Since the times aren't too far apart, you may want to hover over for a granular appearance at how much time has elapsed. Our label shows that 277 seconds have elapsed.

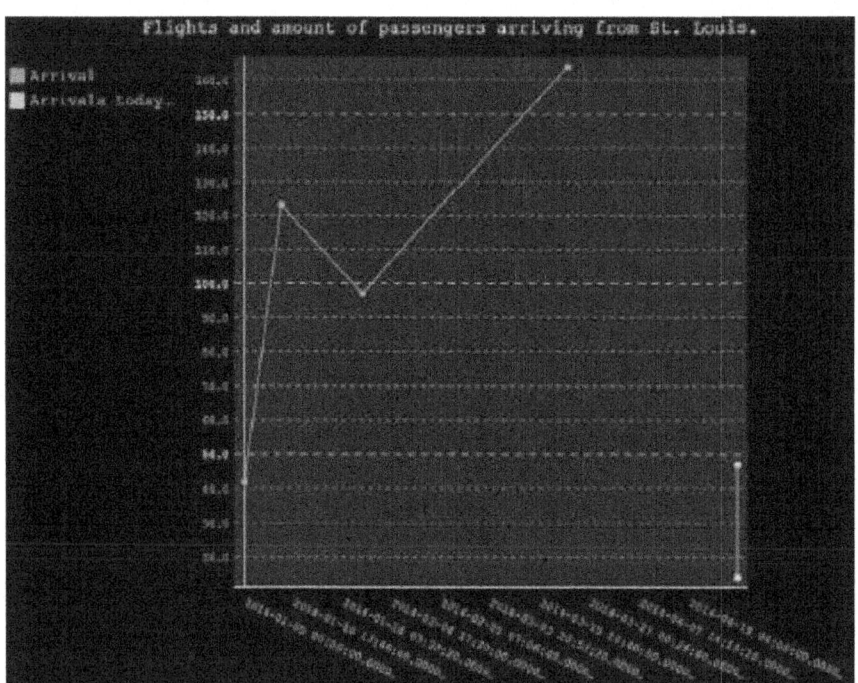

Chapter 6: Data Analysis

Analyzing a dataset to identify patterns is an art. There can be different metrics related to a dataset, and you would like to identify the needle in the following haystack. For your case, the needle is the insight you're searching for in the data that you aren't aware of. In this case, insight may refer to relevant information about people who purchase milk of a certain brand and also purchase cereals of another company. The retail store can then arrange the products close to each other.

Whenever you choose to analyze a dataset, you need to have a deep knowledge of it and also of the domain that is related with. If it's a simple dataset that can be understood easily, then the analysis should be done directly, but if the dataset has some similarities to the sensor data of a turbine, then the field of knowledge of how turbines operate and what is important to their operation will increase richness to your analysis.

The mastery of a domain allows you to navigate your analysis.

What is Data Mining?

Data mining refers to the process of exploring data and discovering patterns in the application of machine learning, database systems, and statistics. The end result of data mining is to extract important information from data, which can be optimized to boost revenue, limit costs, or even save lives through some of its applications.

When you have a dataset that you need to mine, it's not feasible to apply all the data-mining techniques that are available on each column field of the data to extract insights. This will be a difficult task, and it will take a long time to extract any important insights.

To increase the process of data mining, understanding of domains is critical. With the following knowledge, one can understand what the data represents and how to analyze it to gain insights.

The perfect way to begin data mining is to extract themes on which the data requires to be mined. If you have sales data of a Fast Moving Consumer Goods company, then the themes could be as follows:

- Brand behavior
- Outlet behavior

- Growth of products
- Seasonal effect on products

The themes are useful in giving direction to explore data and discover patterns in it.

Once you have the themes, you need to set questions for each to polish the analysis. For example:

- Brand behavior: Here are questions used to enhance the analysis:

-Which are the best brands?
-Which brands have the largest coverage?
-Which companies are cannibalizing the sales of other brands?

- Outlet behavior: The following are questions that polish the analysis.

-What is the percentage of outlets that consume 80% of revenue?
-What type of outlets has the highest number of sales?
-What type of outlets sells major premium products?

- Growth of products: Here are the questions used to streamline the following theme.

-How many brands are seasonal?
- What is the difference based on sales during seasonal and no seasonal times?
-Which holiday generates the highest amount of sales for a specific brand?

The previous questions below these themes offer pinpointed directions to identify patterns and conduct analysis that generates quality results.

The process of data exploration can be summarized by the flow chart below:

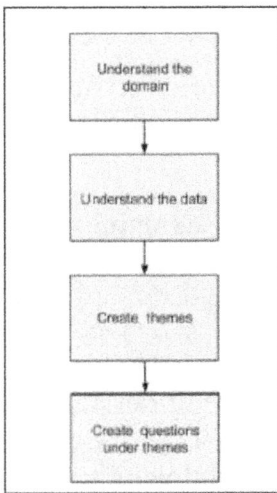

Present an Analysis

After analysis, you will want to present specific observations derived from your analysis. The most popular medium for doing this is using Microsoft PowerPoint presentations. The result of your analysis can be a construct in the form of a chart or table. When you present these constructs, there is particular information that needs to be included in your slides. This is one of the most popular templates applied:

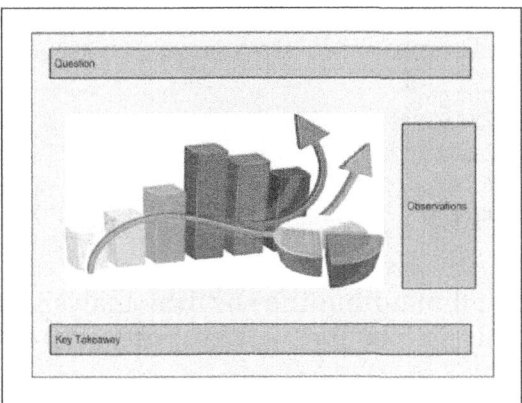

Below are the different parts of the previous image:
- Question: The topmost section of the template should describe the problem statement that a given analysis is trying to focus on.

- Observation: In the following case, observations from the construct are outlined in a vertical column. Sometimes, the observations can be highlighted using arrow marks.

- Key takeaway: At the bottom of the image, you can explain what's concluded from the chart.

Exploring the Titanic

To conduct the data analysis, you'll use the Titanic dataset from Kaggle.
This is easy to understand the dataset and doesn't need any domain understanding to extract insights.
This dataset holds the details of every passenger on the Titanic and whether they survive or not.
Here are the field descriptions:

Field	Descriptions
survival	Survival(0 = No, 1 = Yes)
pclass	Passenger class(1 = 1st, 2 = 2nd, 3 = 3rd)
name	Name of the passenger
sex	Gender of the passenger
age	Age of the passenger
sibsp	Number of siblings/spouses aboard
parch	Number of parents/children aboard
ticket	Ticket number
fare	Passenger fare
cabin	Cabin
embarked	Port of embarkation (C = Cherbourg, Q = Queenstown, S = Southampton)

Because the data is simple to understand, you'll maintain the survival analysis as the major theme that can be used for data analysis. You'll place questions near the themes:
Here are some of the questions that you will respond:
- Which class of passengers has the highest number of survivors?

- What is the distribution of the nonsurvivors among classes that have relative on the ship?

- What is the distribution, depending on the gender of the survivors among the various classes?

- What is the percentage of survival among various age groups?

Which class of passengers has the highest number of survivors?

To respond to this question, you will create a simple bar plot of the number of survivors and the percentage of survivors in every class, respectively.

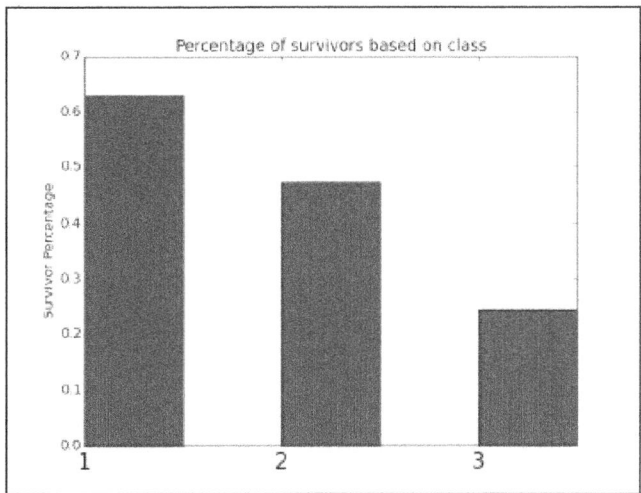

In your code, you need to perform a preliminary check for null values on the fields that are utilized. Next, compute the number of survivors and the percentage of survivors in every class. Then, you can plot two bar charts to get the overall number of survivors and the percentage of survivors.

Here are your observations:

- The highest number of survivors are found in the first and third class, respectively.

- With regard to the overall number of passengers in every class, the first class has the highest survivors at around 61%.

- With regard to the overall number of passengers in every class, the third class has the highest number of survivors at around 25%.

Now, your key takeaway:
- There was obviously a preference toward saving those from the first class as the ship was drowning. Also, it featured the highest percentage of survivors.

What is the distribution of survivors in terms of gender among different classes? Men and women with regard to the class they were in.

The answer to this question, you'll use this code to plot a side-by-side bar chart to compare the different rates and percentage among m

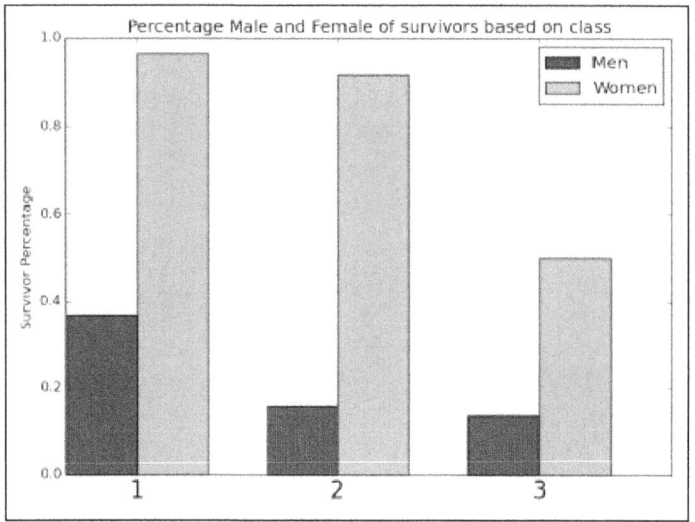

The number of male and female survivors is computed, and then you plot a side-by-side bar plot. After this, the percentage of male and female survivors with reference to the total of males and females in their respective classes are taken and plotted.

Here are our observations:
- Most survivors are females in all the classes.

- More than 90% of female passengers in the first and second class survived.

- The percentage of male passengers who survived in the first and third class are comparable.

Key Takeaway
- Female passengers were assigned preference for lifeboats, and the majority were saved.

What is the distribution of non-survivors among the different classes who have family aboard the ship?

To answer this question, you will write a code to plot bar charts again using the total number of non-survivors in every class that had family aboard, and the percentage with respect to the total number of passengers. The code you write will be similar to the code used in the previous questions. In this case, you can find the number of non-survivors who have a family and then do the typical bar plots.

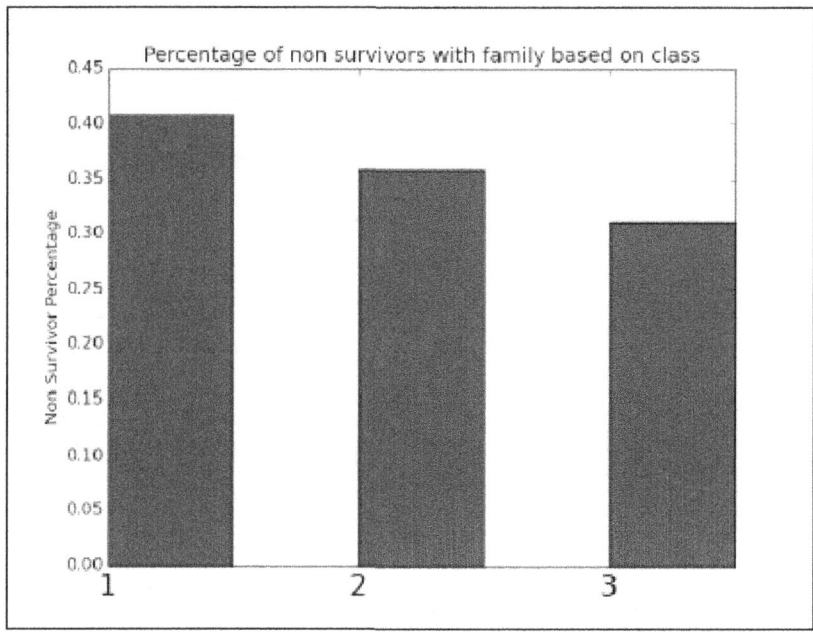

Here are the observations you can deduce:
- There are many non-survivors in the third class

- The second class has the least number of non-survivors with relatives.

- With regard to the total number of passengers, the first class, who have relatives aboard, has the highest number of non-survivors, and the third class has the least.

- Although the third class has the highest number of non-survivors with relatives aboard, it mainly had passengers who did not have relatives on the ship, whereas, in the first class, most people have relatives aboard the ship.

What is the survival ercentage among various age groups?
For this particular question, you will write the following code to plot pie charts to compare the proportion of survivors based on the number and percentage with respect to the different age groups:

```
>>> #Checking for null values
>>> df['Age'].isnull().value_counts()
>>> False 714
>>> True 177
>>> dtype: int64
>>> #Defining the age binning interval
>>> age_bin = [0, 18, 25, 40, 60, 100]
>>> #Creating the bins
>>> df['AgeBin'] = pd.cut(df.Age, bins=age_bin)
>>> #Removing the null rows
>>> d_temp = df[np.isfinite(df['Age'])] # removing all na instances
>>> #Number of survivors based on Age bin
>>> survivors = d_temp.groupby('AgeBin')['Survived'].agg(sum)
>>> #Total passengers in each bin
>>> total_passengers = d_temp.groupby('AgeBin')['Survived'].agg('count')
>>> #Plotting the pie chart of total passengers in each bin
>>> plt.pie(total_passengers, labels=total_passengers.index.values.tolist(), autopct='%1.1f%%', shadow=True, startangle=90)
>>> plt.title('Total Passengers in different age groups')
>>> plt.show()

>>> #Plotting the pie chart of percentage passengers in each bin
>>> plt.pie(survivors, labels=survivors.index.values.tolist(), autopct='%1.1f%%', shadow=True, startangle=90)
>>> plt.title('Survivors in different age groups')
>>> plt.show()
```

In the following code, you defined the bin using the age_bin variable and added a column called AgeBin, where bin values are occupied with the cut function. After this, you filter out all the rows using the age set as null. Next, you create two pie charts: one to represent the total number of passengers in every age group and the other for the number of survivors in every age group.

Here are the observations:

- The 25-40 age group contains the highest number of passengers, and 0-18 has the second maximum number of passengers.

- Among individuals who survived, the 18-25 age group contains the second-highest number of survivors.

- The 60-100 age group has the least proportion among the survivors.

The Key Takeaway

- The 25-40 age group has the highest number of survivors compared to any other age group, and people who were old were either unfortunate or made way for the younger people to take the lifeboats.

This chapter has explored the meaning of data mining. You have learned the significance of domain knowledge in conducting analysis and how to implement data mining in a systematic way. You have also learned the different ways of presenting the results of data mining.

Chapter 7: Explore Machine Learning

Machine Learning is a way of teaching programs that utilize data to generate algorithms rather than explicitly program an algorithm from scratch.
This is a field of computer science that starts from the research into artificial intelligence. It's closely related to statistics and mathematical optimization, which provide methods, application domains, and theories to the field. Machine learning is applied in different computing tasks where programming is infeasible. Examples of applications consist of e-mail spam filters, language translation, search engines, and computer versions. Sometimes, machine learning can be confused with data mining, although it concentrates mainly on exploratory data analysis.
Below are terms that will be applied in the following chapter:

- Features: This describes specific traits that will help define the result.

- Sample: A sample is an item to process. It can be a document, audio, image, or a CSV file.

- Feature Vector: This refers to a numerical feature, like an n-dimensional vector, that represents some object.

- Feature extraction: This describes the processing of a feature vector where data is converted from a high-dimensional space to a lower-dimensional space.

- Training set: This describes a set of data that discovers highly predictive relationships.

- Testing set: This describes a set of data that determines the predications.

Various Types of Machine Learning

Machine learning is divided into three types depending on the nature of the learning target or the feedback present to the learning system:

1. Supervised Learning: The computer is assigned a set of inputs and their respective outputs. The goal of the program is to learn from the inputs to reproduce the outputs.

2. Unsupervised learning. There is no target variable in the case of unsupervised learning. The computer is left on its own to discover patterns inside the data.

3. Reinforcement learning. A program has to interact with its environment in a dynamic style, such as driving a car.

Supervised Learning

As said before, a supervised learning algorithm masters the training data and generates a function, which can be applied in predicting new instances.

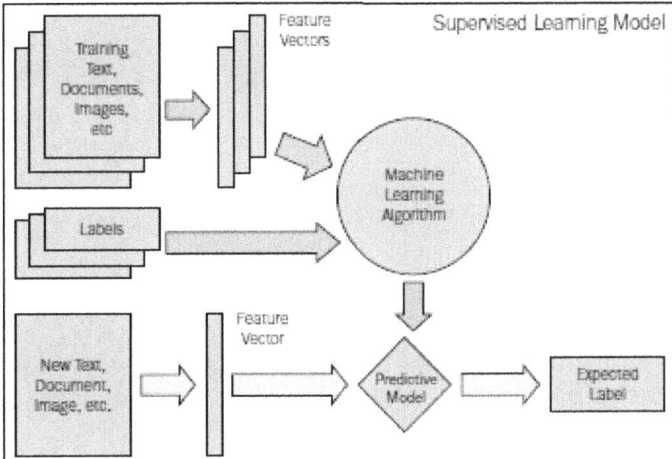

As you can see from the previous diagram, there is training data, which the machine learning model will learn from.
Let's say that the training data contains a set of text that represents different news articles. These news articles can be associated with sports, national, international, and different news categories. These news categories will act as labels. From the following training data, you'll extract feature vectors where each word can be a vector or could be extracted from the text. For example, the number of times of the phrase "Football" can be a vector, or the number of instances of the word "Prime Minister" can be a vector too.
These feature vectors and labels are directed to the machine learning algorithm, which learns from the data. Once the model has been trained, it is later applied to

the new data where the features are again extracted and inputted to the model, which generates the target data.

Below are some examples of supervised machine learning algorithms, which you will briefly study in the following chapter, and some of them will be further described in the later chapters.

1. Decision trees
2. Logistic regression
3. Linear regression
4. The naïve Bayes classifier

Unsupervised Learning

As said before, unsupervised learning attempts to discover hidden structures in unlabeled data. In the following diagram, there is no label that is entered into the algorithm.

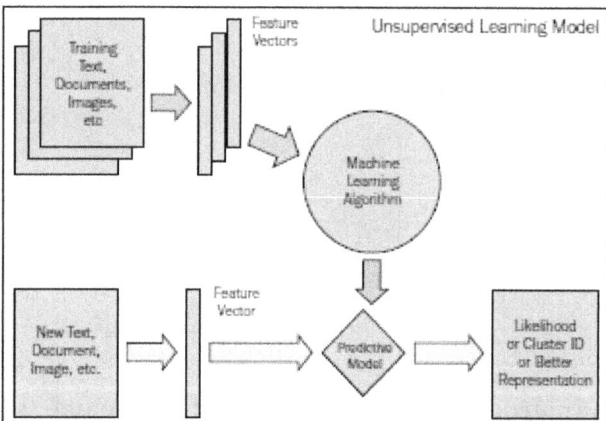

Consider the example of images that will act as the training dataset of inputs. The images have faces of human beings, insects, and horses. From these images, features are derived, which will help discover the group that the images belong to. These features are then added to the unsupervised machine learning algorithm. The algorithm will detect patterns within the data and assist in bucketing these images to the rightful group.

This same algorithm can then be applied for new images and assist in bucketing the images into the correct buckets.

Below are examples of unsupervised machine learning algorithms, which will be introduced in the following chapter.
1. The k-means clustering

2. The hierarchical clustering

Reinforcement Learning
When it comes to reinforcement learning, the data to be inputted is provided as a stimulus to the model from the environment to which the machine learning model must react. Feedback is generated not like a teaching process like the case of supervised learning, but like punishments and rewards in the environment.

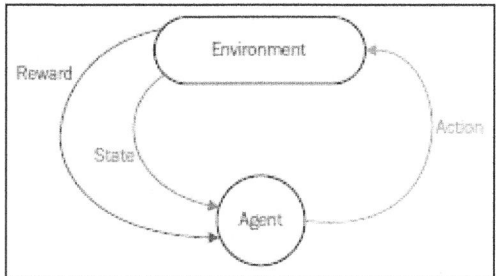

The steps taken by the agent results in learning. Rather than being explicitly taught, and the action it chooses is based on its past experience and also by the fresh choices designed by it, which basically implies it learns from trial and error. The agent acquires the reinforcement signal in terms of numerical reward that encodes the success, and the agent tries to teach itself to take actions that will boost the accumulated reward over time.
Reinforcement learning is heavily applied in robotics and not much in data science. Below are the algorithms that belong to reinforcement learning:
1. Q learning

2. Temporal difference learning

Decision Trees
A simple predictive model maps the results of an item to the input data. It is a popular predictive modeling technique, which is commonly applied in the industry.
Decision tree models are of two types:

1. Classification trees: These point to dependent variables that accept a finite value. In these tree structures, branches represent the rules of the features that result in class labels, and leaves denote the class labels of the results.

2. Regression trees: When dependent variables accept continuous values, then they're referred to as regression trees.

Let's consider an example. The following data determines whether you should play tennis or not, depending on the general appearance of the weather, wind intensity, and humidity.

Play	Wind	Humidity	Outlook
No	Low	High	Sunny
No	High	Normal	Rain
Yes	Low	High	Overcast
Yes	Weak	Normal	Rain
Yes	Low	Normal	Sunny
Yes	Low	Normal	Overcast
Yes	High	Normal	Sunny

If you consider the following data, then apply Play as the target variable, and the remaining as the independent variable, then you'll attain a decision tree model that will comprise of the following structure as the rules:

Therefore, when new data comes in, it will reverse this tree to come to the following conclusion, which will be the result:

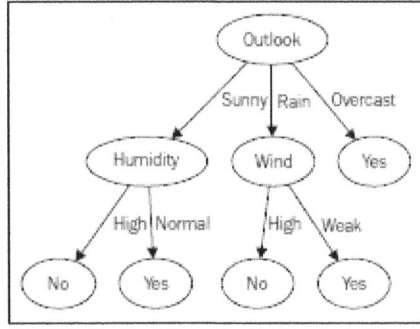

Decision trees are the easiest of the predictive models, and here are some of their advantages:

1. It's easy to communicate and visualize decision trees.

2. It's possible to discover old patterns. Say you want to determine the voting pattern between two parties for an election, and you have data on education, sex, age, and income. You may identify a pattern where highly educated people have a very low income and vote for a certain party.

3. Decision trees make the least assumptions on the data.

Below are the disadvantages of a decision tree
1. There is a large classification error rate, while the training set is small compared to the number of classes.

2. There is an exponential growth in determining when the data and the number of dependent variables increase in size.

3. There is a need for discrete data for a specific construction algorithm

Linear Regression

Linear regression is a modeling method that builds the scalar linear relationship between a scalar dependent variable, and an independent variable, X, which can be one or more in value:

$$y = X\beta + \varepsilon$$

Let's explain this with an example. This table represents both the height and weight of students in a class:

Height (inches)	Weight (pounds)
50	125
58	135
63	145
68	144
70	170
79	165
84	171
75	166
65	160

If you execute the following using simple linear regression function using the weight as a dependent variable, y, and the independent variable, x, which is the height, we will get the following equation:

$$y = 1.405405405\ x + 57.87687688$$

If you plot the above equation as a line using 57.88 as the intercept and the slope of the line being 1.4 cm top of a scatter plot with Weight in the y-axis and Height in the x-axis, then you will get the following plot:

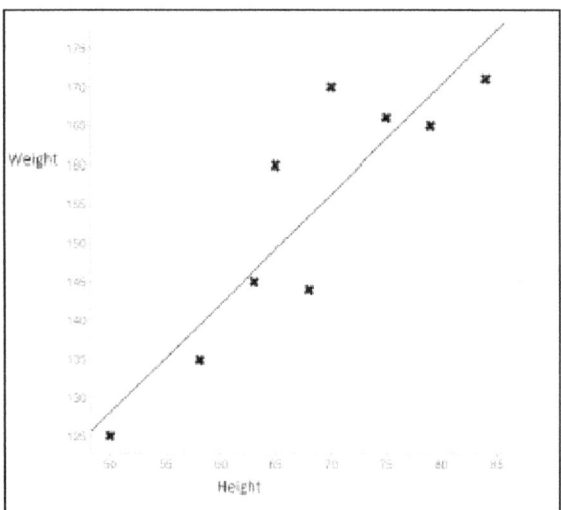

In the above example, the regression algorithm attempts to build the preceding equation, which has the minimum error when predicting the weight of the student. This is an example of simple linear regression.

Logistic Regression

Logistic regression is another supervised learning approach, which is a probabilistic classification model. It is normally used in predicting a binary predictor, such as whether a credit card transaction is fraudulent.

Logistic regression relies on logistics. A logistic function is a useful function that can accept any value from negative infinity to positive infinity, and display values from 0 to 1. Therefore, it is interpretable as a probability. Here is a logistic function that outputs predicted values from 0 to 1 depending on the x variable:

$$F(x) = \frac{1}{1 + e^{-(\beta_0 + \beta_1 x)}}$$

In the above example, x will be the independent variable, and F(x) will be the dependent variable.

If you attempt to plot the logistic function from negative infinity to positive infinity, then you will attain the following S-shaped graph:

Logistic regression can be used in the following cases:

1. Denying a propensity score for a customer in a retail store of purchasing a new product that has been launched.

2. The probability of a transformer not working

3. The probability of a user clicking on an ad that is displayed on a website depending on their behavior.

Logistic regression has a lot of applications, and it will be handled in the later chapters using examples.

The Naïve Bayes Classifier

The naïve Bayes classifier is a simple probabilistic classifier, which dependent on the Bayes theorem. The assumption here is that there is strong interdependence between the features; as a result, it is called naïve. Below is the Bayes theorem:

$$P(A|B) = \frac{P(B|A)P(A)}{P(B)}$$

In the previous formula, A and B are events, p(A), and p(B) denote the probabilities of A and B. Additionally, these are interdependent of each other. P(A|B) refers to the probability of A, provided that B is True, which is a conditional probability. P(B|A) is the probability of B, provided that A is True. The naïve Bayes formula is as follows:

$$P(A_k|B) = P(A_k \cap B)/P(A_1 \cap B) + P(A_2 \cap B) + \ldots + P(A_n \cap B)$$

Let's try to find the solution to the above naïve Bayes formula using the following example:

Ann is going for an engagement tomorrow in Austin at an outdoor event. In the last few years, Austin has only experienced six rainy days in a year. Unfortunately, there has been a rain forecast for tomorrow by the weatherman. 80% of the time, the weatherman accurately predicted the rain. But he incorrectly forecasts the weather 20% of the time when it doesn't rain. Find the likelihood that it will rain on the day of Ann's engagement. Below are some of the scenarios based on which the probability can be computed:

- A1. This event states that it rains on Ann's engagement.

- A2. This event states that it doesn't rain on Ann's engagement.

- B. This event states that weatherman forecasts rain

Here are the probabilities based on the previous events
- P(AI) = 6/365. In other words, it rains six days out of the year.
- P(AII) = 359/365. In other words, it doesn't rain 359 days out of the year.
- P (B| AI). In other words, 80% of the time, it rains as predicted by the weatherman.
- P (B| AII). This means that 20% of the time, it doesn't rain as predicted by the weatherman.

This formula will ensure that you compute the naïve Bayes probability:

$$P(AI \mid B) = P(AI)P(B \mid AI) / (P(AI)P(B \mid AI) + P(AII)P(B \mid AII))$$

$$P(AI \mid B) = (0.0164 * 0.8) / (0.0164 * 0.8 + 0.9834 * 0.2)$$

$$P(AI \mid B) = 0.065$$

Therefore, the preceding computation says that although the weatherman forecasted rain, there is only a 6.5% probability that it will rain with respect to Bayes theorem.

The naïve Bayes is heavily applied in e-mail filtering. It requires the instance of every word in an e-mail and calculates the likelihood of whether the e-mail is spam or not. The naïve Bayes model learns from the previous data of e-mails and marks emails as spam, which is important in coming to the conclusion on whether an e-mail is a spam or not.

The K-means Clustering

The k-means clustering is a technique of unsupervised learning that is important in segregating data of n observations into k buckets of the same observations.

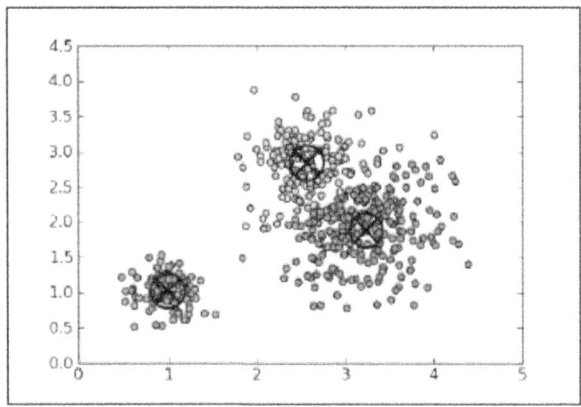

This clustering algorithm called so because it operates by computing the mean of the feature, which represents the dependent variables you cluster things like customer classification on an average transaction amount and the average number of products purchased in a quarter of a year. The average value then becomes the center of a cluster.

The number of k points to the number of clusters. In other words, the technique involves calculating a k number of means, resulting in the clustering of the data around these k-means.

How do We Select this K?

If you've got some idea of what you are searching for or how many clusters you expect, or won't, then you set K to be this number before you start the engines and allow the algorithm to compute along.

If you don't know the number, then your exploration will take a bit longer and involve some trial and error. For example, try k=3, 4, and 5 until you notice that the clusters make sense to the domain.

$$J(V) = \sum_{i=1}^{c} \sum_{j=1}^{c_i} \left(\left\| x_i - v_j \right\| \right)^2$$

||\x1-v1|| describes the Euclidean distance between xi and vj, c1 within the ith cluster, the number of data points, c represents the number of clusters.

The K-means clustering is usually applied in computer visions, geostatistics, and agriculture.

The k-means clustering will be discussed later using real-life examples.

Hierarchical clustering

Hierarchical clustering refers to an unsupervised learning approach where a hierarchy of clusters is derived out of observations.

This clustering collects data at different levels of a cluster tree. It is not a single set of clusters, but a hierarchy of multiple levels where clusters at the specific level are connected as clusters on the next level. This enables you to choose the level of clustering that is most relevant.

The hierarchical clusters consist of two types:
- Agglomerative hierarchical clustering. This is a bottom-up method where every observation begins in its own cluster and two other clusters as they move up a hierarchy.

- Divisive hierarchical clustering. This is a top-down approach where observations begin in a single cluster, and then they are split into two as they move down a hierarchy.

The screenshot below describes Agglomerative and Divisive hierarchical clustering:

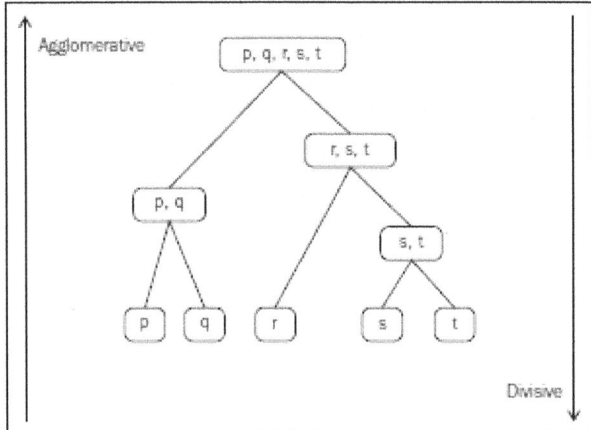

Hierarchical clustering will be described in detail.

Chapter 8: Deep Dive- Machine Learning

This section will concentrate on supervised learning techniques.

Every record or an instance can be written as a set (X, Y), where X is a set of features, and y is a corresponding class label.

Mastering a target function, F that maps every record's property set to one of the predefined class labels, Y is the role of a classification algorithm.

The typical steps for a classification algorithm include the following:

1. Identify the right algorithm.

2. Learn a model using a training set, and verify the model with the help of a test set.

3. Use the model to predict any unseen instance or record

The first thing is to determine the correct classification algorithm. There is no prescribed method of selecting the best algorithm; it arises from repeated trial and error. Once you select the algorithm, a training and test set is developed, which is delivered to the algorithm to train a model, that is, a target function F. After building the model with a training set, a test set is used to verify the model. In general, we apply a confusion matrix to ascertain the model. You will learn more about confusion matrices when it comes to determining the nearest neighbors.

You will start with a method that will describe how to divide the input dataset into training and test sets. You will follow this using a lazy learner algorithm for classification known as the K-Nearest neighbor. Before shifting to Naïve Bayes classifiers. The choice of an algorithm in this section isn't random. All the tree algorithm that you will learn in the following chapter can handle multiclass problems as well as binary problems. For the multiclass problems, there are more than two class labels to which the instances belong.

Preparing Data for Model Creation

In the following section, you will explore how to create a train and a test data set using a dataset for the classification problem. A test dataset is not displayed in the model. In a real-world scenario, you create another dataset know as a dev. Dev represents dataset development: a dataset that you can apply to continuously tune the model during successive runs. The model is trained with the help of a train set, and the model performance metric, such as accuracy, is measured in dev. Based on the following result, the model is further transformed in case changes are needed.

For this particular case, you will apply the Iris dataset. It is easy to illustrate the idea of using the following dataset.

How to Proceed It

```python
# Load the necesssary Library
from sklearn.cross_validation import train_test_split
from sklearn.datasets import load_iris
import numpy as np
def get_iris_data():
    """
    Returns Iris dataset
    """
    # Load iris dataset
    data = load_iris()
    # Extract the dependend and independent variables
    # y is our class label
    # x is our instances/records
    x = data['data']
    y = data['target']
    # For ease we merge them
    # column merge
    input_dataset = np.column_stack([x,y])
    # Let us shuffle the dataset
    # We want records distributed randomly
    # between our test and train set
    np.random.shuffle(input_dataset)
    return input_dataset
# We need 80/20 split.
# 80% of our records for Training
# 20% Remaining for our Test set
train_size = 0.8
test_size = 1-train_size
```

```
# get the data
input_dataset = get_iris_data()
# Split the data
train,test =
train_test_split(input_dataset,test_size=t
est_size)
# Print the size of original dataset
print "Dataset size ",input_dataset.shape
# Print the train/test split
print "Train size ",train.shape
print "Test size",test.shape
```

This was straightforward.

How it Operates

Once you import the relevant library modules, you need to build a convenient function, get_iris_data (), which will output the Iris dataset. Next, column concatenates the x and y arrays into a single array known as input_dataset. Next, shuffle the dataset so that the records can be randomly distributed to the test and the train datasets. The function displays a single array of both the instances and the class labels.

If you want to include 80 percent of the record in the training dataset and apply the rest as the dataset. Both the train_size and test_size variables feature a percentage of the values, which should lie in the testing and training dataset.

You must call the get_iris_data () function to accept the input data. Then, you can leverage the train_test_split function from the scikit-learn's cross_validation model to divide the input dataset into two.

Lastly, you can display the size of the initial dataset, followed by the test and the train datasets.

```
Compare Data Set Size
-----------------------

Original Dataset size   (150, 5)
Train size   (120, 5)
Test   size (30, 5)
```

As you can see, 80 percent of the 150 rows, that is, 120 records, have been allocated to the training set. You have seen how you can easily divide input data into the train and the test sets.

Remember, this is a classification challenge. The algorithm has to be trained to predict the right class label for a specific unknown instance. For this, you need to present the algorithm and equal distribution of all the classes at the time of training. The Iris dataset represents a three-class problem. You need to have equal representation from all three classes. Let's find out whether the method has taken care of this.

It is important to define a function called get_class_distribution, which selects a single y parameter's array of class labels. This function outputs a dictionary, where the key represents the class label, and the value represents the percentage of records for this particular distribution. Therefore, the following dictionary represents the distribution of the class labels. You need to call this function in the following function to understand what the class distribution is on the train and the test datasets.

The print_class_labe_split function is straightforward. You need to pass the train and the test datasets as the argument. Since you have concatenated x and y, the last column is our classical label. Next, you extract the train and test class labels in y_train and y_test. You pass them to attain get_class_distribution to find a dictionary of the class labels and their distribution, and lastly, you print it.

You can then invoke print_class_label_split, and the output should appear as follows:

```
Train data set class label distribution
===========================================
Class label =0, percentage records =0.36
Class label =1, percentage records =0.32
Class label =2, percentage records =0.33

Test data set class label distribution
===========================================
Class label =0, percentage records =0.23
Class label =1, percentage records =0.40
Class label =2, percentage records =0.37
```

Let's now determine the output. As you can see, the training features different distribution of the class labels compared with the test set datasets.

In the last section of code, you make use of stratifiedshufflesplit from scikit-learn to attain equal class distribution in the training and the test sets. Let's look at the parameters of StratifiedShuffleSplit:

```
stratified_split =
StratifiedShuffleSplit(input_dataset[:,-1]
,test_size=test_size,n_iter=1)
```

The first parameter describes the input dataset. You pass all the rows and the last column. The test size is described by the test_size variable, which was initially declared. You can make an assumption that you need only one split applying the n_iter variable. Next, we proceed to trigger the print_class_label_split to display the class label distribution. Let's look at the output:

```
Train data set class label distribution
----------------------------------------
Class label =0, percentage records =0.33
Class label =1, percentage records =0.33
Class label =2, percentage records =0.33

Test data set class label distribution
----------------------------------------
Class label =0, percentage records =0.33
Class label =1, percentage records =0.33
Class label =2, percentage records =0.33
```

Now, you have the class labels distributed uniformly between the test and train sets.
Still, there's more....
You need to prepare the data carefully before it's applied in the machine learning algorithm. Providing a uniform class distribution to both the train and the test sets is necessary for creating a successful classification model.
When it comes to practical machine learning cases, you build another dataset known as dev set to the train and test sets. You might not get your model right during the first iteration. However, you don't want to reveal the test dataset to the model because this may create some bias in the following iteration of model building. Therefore, you create this dev set, which you can apply as you iterate through your model building process.

The 80/20 rule of thumb is a great scenario. But in most practical applications, you may not have sufficient data to leave out that many instances for a test set. There are different practical techniques that come into play in such cases.

Identifying the Nearest Neighbors

Before we dive in, let's take time to understand how to verify whether the classification model is working to our satisfaction. At one point in the chapter, we discussed the confusion matrix.

A confusion matrix refers to the arrangement of the actual versus the predicted class tables. Say, for example, that you have a two-class problem, that is, your y can take either value, T, or F. Assume you have trained a classifier to predict your y. You have predicted the value of y from your model. Then you can complete your confusion matric using like this:

		Predicted	
		T	F
Actual	T	TP	FN
	F	FP	TN

In the above table, it is important to list the results from the test set. Keep in mind that you know the class labels in the test set; thus, you can compare the classification model output with the actual class label.

- Below TP, which stands for True Positive, it has a count of all those records within the test set whose labels feature T, and where the model is predicted T.

- Below the FN, which stands for False Negative, you have a count of all the records whose actual label is T, but the algorithm is predicted as N.

- FP stands for False Positive, where the actual label is F, but the algorithm is predicted as T.

- TN stands for True Negative, where the algorithm predicted both the label and the original class label as F.

With the above knowledge about the confusion matrix, you can extract performance metrics using the measure of the quality of our classification model.

Accuracy is defined as the ration of a correct prediction to the total number of predictions. From the confusion matrix, you know that the sum of TP and TN totals the number of correct predictions.

Accuracy from the training set is normally very optimistic. It is important for someone to consider the test set's accuracy value to define the true performance of the model.

With the above knowledge, the first classification problem that you will consider is the k-nearest neighbor, shortened as KNN. Before jumping to details of KNN, let's consider a simple classification algorithm known as the rote classifier algorithm. The note classifier memorizes the whole training data; it loads all the data within the memory. You need to conduct classification on an unseen new training instance. It will try to march the new training instance using any of the training instances within the memory. It will match each attribute within the training instance. In case it discovers a match, it predicts the class label of the test insurance as the class label of the matched training instance.

So far, you need to know that this classifier will fail in case the test instance isn't similar to any of the training instances loaded into the memory.

KNN resembles the rote classifier, except that instead of searching for an exact match, it applies a similarity measure. Resembling the rote classifier, KNN loads all the training sets into the memory. When it requires to classify a test instance, it determines the distance between the test instance and all the training instances. Using the above distance, it selects K's closest instances within the training set. Next, the prediction for the test set is defined based on the number of classes of the K nearest neighbors.

For example, if you have a two-class classification problem and you select the K value as three, and if the test record's three nearest neighbors have classes, 1,1, and 0, it will categorize the test instance as 1, which the popular.

KNN is part of the family algorithms known as instance-based learning. Besides that, the decision to categorize a test instance is considered last; it is also known as the lazy learner.

For this algorithm, you will generate some data by making use of the scikit's make_classification method. This will produce a matrix of four columns and 100 instances:

The get_data function internally requests make_classification to produce test data for any classification task.

It's always a great practice to visualize the data before beginning to feed it into any algorithm. The plot_data function generates a scatter plot between all the variables.

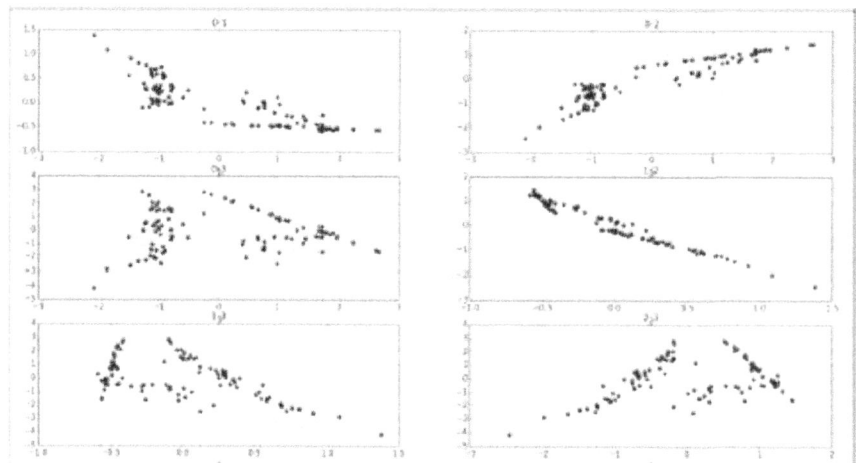

In the above diagram, you have plotted all the variable combinations. The top two charts demonstrate combinations between the 0th and 1st column, followed by 0th and 2nd. The points are also colored using their class labels. This presents a hint of how much information is available for variable combinations to perform a classification task.

How to Achieve It

You will need to divide your dataset preparation and model training into two different methods: get_train_test to find the train and test data, and build your model. Finally, you will apply the test_model to verify the usefulness of the model.

How it Operates

You must start by calling get_data and plotting it using plot_data.

It is also important to separate a section of the training data for the testing that is required to determine the model. Next, invoke the get_train_test method to achieve the same.

Within the get_train_test, you need to train the test split size, which is the standard 80/20. Next, apply 80 percent of the data to train your model. Now, combine both x and y to a single matrix before the split by using NumPy's column_stack method.

Next, leverage StratifiedShuffleSplit discussed previously to attain a uniform class label distribution between the training and test sets.

Armed with the following train and test sets, you should be ready to create a classifier. You must trigger the build model using the training set, class labels y, and attributes x. This function also accepts K, the number of neighbors, as a parameter, with a default value of two.

We apply the scikit-learn's KNN execution, KNeighborClassifier. Then build an object of the classifier and call it fit method to create the model.

You should be ready to test how good the module is by leveraging on the training data. You can pass the training data (x and y) and model to the test_model function.

You know the actual class labels (y). Now invoke the predict function using x to get the predicted labels. Next, print some of the model evaluation metrics. You can then begin with printing the accuracy of the model, follow it up using a confusion matrix, and then display the output of a function known as the classification_report. Scikit-learn's metrics module offers a function called classification_report, which can display different model evaluation metrics.

Let's explore the model metrics:

```
Model evaluation on training set
--------------------------------

Model accuracy - 91.25%

Confusion Matrix
================
array([[40,  0],
       [ 7, 33]])
None

Classification Report
---------------------
             precision    recall  f1-score   support

        0.0       0.85      1.00      0.92        40
        1.0       1.00      0.82      0.90        40

avg / total       0.93      0.91      0.91        80
```

As you can see, the accuracy score is 91.25 percent. You will not repeat the definition accuracy; you can refer to the introduction part.

Let's consider the confusion matrix. The top-left cell represents a true positive cell. You should see that there are no false negatives, but there are seven false positives. Lastly, you have precision, remember an F1 score, and support within the classification report. Let's consider their definitions:

Precision refers to the ratio of the true positive and the sum of the true positive and false positive.

Accuracy refers to the ration of the true positive and the total of the true positive and false negative.

An F1 score describes the harmonic mean of precision and sensitivity.

You will learn more about the above metric. For now, let's assume that we have high precision and recall values.

It is good to understand that we have about 91 percent accuracy for our model, but the actual test will be when it is performed on the test data. Consider the metrics for the test data:

```
Model evaluation on test set
=================================
Model accuracy = 95.00%

Confusion Matrix
------------------
array([[ 9,  1],
       [ 0, 10]])
None

Classification Report
==================
             precision    recall  f1-score   support

        0.0       1.00      0.90      0.95        10
        1.0       0.91      1.00      0.95        10

avg / total       0.95      0.95      0.95        20
```

It is good to understand that our model contains 95 percent accuracy for the test data, which is a sign of a great job in a fitting model.

Let's look deeper into the model that we have created.

First, the function get_params is invoked. This function outputs all the parameters that are passed to the model. Let's define each of the parameters.

The first parameter describes the underlying data structure applied by the KNN implementation. Because each record within the training set has to be compared against another record, brute force implementation may require heavy resources. Therefore, you can decide either kd_tree or ball_tree as the data structure. A brute will apply the brute force method for looping through all the records for each record.

Leaf size represents the parameter passes to the kd_tree or ball_tree method. Metric represents the distance measure applied to determine the neighbors. The p-value of two decreases the Minkowski to Euclidean distance.

Lastly, there is a weight parameter. KNN selects the class label of the test instance, depending on the class label of its K nearest neighbors. The highest vote decides the class label for the test instance. However, if you set the weights to distance, then each neighbor is assigned a weight that is inversely proportional to its distance. Therefore, to choose the class label of a test set, weighted voting is done instead of simple voting.

How to Classify Documents Using Naïve Bayes

You will review a document classification problem for this case. The algorithm that you will use is the Naïve Bayes classifier. The Bayes' rule is the engine driving the Naïve Bayes algorithm.

$$P(X|Y) = \frac{P(Y|X) * P(X)}{P(Y)}$$

It describes how likely it is for the event X to occur, given that you know the event Y has already taken place. Now, you will classify the text. This is a binary classification problem: provide a movie review, you want to categorize whether the review is positive or negative.

In Bayesian terms, you need to identify the conditional probability: the probability that the review is positive, and the probability that the review is negative. Here's an equation:

$$P(class = positive | review), \text{ and } P(class = negative | review)$$

For any given review, if you have the preceding two probability values, you can classify the review as positive or negative by comparing these values. In case the conditional probability for a negative is higher than the conditional probability for positive, you can classify the review as negative, vice versa.

Let's discuss these probabilities with the help of Bayes' rule:

$$P(positive \mid review) = \frac{P(review \mid positive) * P(positive)}{P(review)}$$

$$P(negative \mid review) = \frac{P(review \mid negative) * P(negative)}{P(review)}$$

As you compare these two equations to finalize the prediction, you can ignore the denominator, which is a simple scaling factor.
The LHS (left-hand side) of the preceding equation is known as the posterior probability.
Let's consider the numerator of the RHS (right-hand side)
   P(review\positive) * P (positive)
P (positive) refers to the probability of a positive class. It's the belief about the positive class label distribution depending on the training set.
You will approximate it from the training test. It's computed as follows:

$$P(positive) = \frac{No\ of\ reviews\ with\ positive\ class\ label}{Total\ reviews\ in\ the\ corpus}$$

P(review|positive) is the probability. It addresses the question: what is the odd of getting the review, provided that the class is positive. Again, you will estimate it from the training set.
Before we explore the probability equation further, let's introduce the feature of independence assumption. The algorithm is prefixed as naïve because of this assumption. Contrary to this, you assume that the words occur in a document independent of each other. You will apply this assumption to compute the likelihood.
A look at the list of words. Let's apply some mathematical notation:

$$review = \{word_1, word_2, \ldots\ldots, word_n\}$$

With the independence assumption, you can conclude that the probability of each of these words taking place in a review is the product of all the individual probabilities of the constituent words in the review.

Now you can define the likelihood equation as follows:

$$P(review = \{word_1, word_2, \ldots, word_n\} \mid positive) = \prod_{i=1}^{n} P(word_i \mid positive)$$

So, provided a new review, you can apply the following two equations, the prior and likelihood, to determine whether the review is negative or positive.

Creating decision trees to solve multiclass problems

This section will look at how to create decision trees to solve multiclass classification issues. A decision tree can be defined as a process of arriving at a solution by asking various questions. A sequence of if-then statements organized hierarchically forms a decision tree. Because of this nature, it's easy to understand and interpret.

In theory, a lot of decision trees can be developed for a particular dataset. Some of the trees are more accurate than others. There are effective algorithms for building a reasonably accurate tree in a limited time. One of these algorithms is Hunt's algorithm and CART that is based on Hunt's algorithm.

The hunt's algorithm can be defined as follows:

Provided a dataset, D, of n records and with every record featuring m attributes/features/columns and each record labeled either y_1, y_2, or y_3, the algorithm operates as follows:

- If all the records in D are found in the same class label, say y_1, then y_1 denotes the leaf node of the tree and is marked as y_1

- If D contains a record that belongs to more than one class label, a feature test condition is used to divide the records into smaller subsets.

Say, for example, during the initial run, you perform a feature test condition on all the attributes and discover a single property that can split the datasets into three smaller subsets. The attribute becomes the root node. We use the test condition on all the three subsets to determine the next level of nodes. This process is done iteratively.

Remember that once you define your classification, you need to define three class labels, y_1, y_2, and y_3. This is a multiclass problem. The Iris dataset that has been used in most examples is a three-class problem. The records are distributed across three class labels. You can generalize this into an n-class problem. Digit recognition is a great example by which you need to categorize a certain image in one of the digits between zero and nine. Most real-world problems are inherently multiclass. Certain algorithms are also capable of dealing with multiclass cases. There is no change demanded for these algorithms. The algorithm discussed in the following chapters is capable of dealing with multiclass issues. Naïve Bayes, KNN algorithms, and Decision trees can handle multiclass problems.

Now, let's see how you can make use of decision trees to deal with multiclass problems. It is also useful to have a great knowledge of decision trees.

Let's jump into our decision tree:

We shall apply the Iris dataset to demonstrate how to create decision trees. Decision trees are non-parametric supervised learning methods that can be used to complete classification and regression problems. As said before, there many benefits of using decision trees.

Some of the advantages include:
- They are easy to interpret

- They require little data preparation and data-to-feature conversion.

- They naturally support multiclass problems

Decision trees aren't without problems. Some of the problems they cause include:
- There can be more than a million trees fit a certain dataset.

- They can easily overfit. High accuracy in a training set and poor performance with test data.

- The class imbalance problem may impact decision trees heavily. The class imbalance problem emerges when the training set doesn't include an equal number of instances for both the class labels in a binary classification problem. This applies to multiclass problems too.

The most important feature of decision trees is the property test condition. Let's take time to explore the following feature test condition. In general, every instance attribute can be either understood.

Binary attribute: This is where a property can accept two possible values, for example, true or false. The property test condition should display two values in the following case.

Nominal attribute: This is the case where a property can accept more than two values, for example, n values. The property test condition should display either output n or group them into binary splits.

Ordinal attribute: This is where an implicit order in their values exists. For instance, let's consider an imaginary feature called size, which can accept the values small, medium, or large. There are three values that the property can take, and there is an order for them: small, medium, large. They are taken care of by the feature property test condition that's similar to the nominal attribute.

Continuous attributes: These are properties that can accept continuous values. They are categorized into ordinal attributes and then handled.

A property test condition is a means to split the input records into subsets depending on criteria or metric known as impunity. This impunity is computed with reference to the class label for every attribute in the instance. The property contributing to the highest impunity is selected as the data splitting attribute, or in other words, the node for that particular level in the tree.

Let's look at an example to describe it. You will employ a measure known as entropy to determine the impunity.

The entropy is defined as follows:

$$E(X) = -\sum_{i=1}^{n} P(x_i) \log_2 (P(x_i))$$

Consider the following example:
X= {2,2}

Now you can compute the entropy for the following settings using the above formula.

The entropy result for this particular formula is 0. An entropy of 0 represents homogeneity. It is easy to program entropy in Python.

For the sake of achieving the best splitting variable, you will leverage the entropy. First, you will compute the entropy depending on the class labels using the following formula:

$$Entropy(t) = -\sum_{i=0}^{c-1} p(i|t) \log_2 p(i|t)$$

Next, let's define a separate term called information gain. This is a measure to determine which attribute in the given instance is important for discrimination between the class labels.

Information gain refers to the difference between the entropy of the parent and an average entropy of the child nodes. For each level in the tree, you will utilize information gain to create the tree.

You will first begin with all attributes in a training set and compute the general entropy. Consider the following example:

Lead Actor	Oscar Winning	Box Office	Watch
Y	Y	N	Y
Y	N	Y	N
N	N	Y	Y
N	Y	Y	Y

The previous dataset represents an imaginary data gathered for a user to find out the type of movies the is interested in. There are four features: the first one is about whether the user watches a movie depending on the lead actor, the second attribute depends on whether the user makes his decision to watch the movie based on whether or not it won an Oscar, and the third one is whether the user decides to watch a movie based on whether it is a box office success.

To create a decision tree for the previous example, you will start by calculating the entropy of the entire dataset. This is a two-class problem, and hence c=2. Additionally, there are a total of four records, the entropy of the entire dataset is as follows:

$$E(D) = -\left(\frac{1}{4} * \log_2\left(\frac{1}{4}\right) + \frac{3}{4} * \log_2\left(\frac{3}{4}\right)\right)$$

The general entropy of the dataset is 0.811.

Now, let's consider the first attribute, the lead attribute. For the lead actor, Y, there is a single class label that says Y and another one that says N. For the lead actor, N, both the instance class labels are N. You will compute the average entropy as shown:

```
entropy_lead_actor_Y = 2/4.0 * -(1/2.0 * log(1/2.0,2) + 1/2.0 * log(1/2.0 ,2))
entropy_lead_actor_N = 2/4.0 * -(0 + 2/2.0 * log(2/2.0,2))
entroyp_lead_actor = entropy_lead_actor_Y + entropy_lead_actor_N
```

There are two records containing a lead actor as Y and two records with lead actors as N. Therefore, there are 2/4. 0 multiplied to the entropy value.

As the entropy is computed for this particular subset of data, you will notice that out of the two records, one of them has a class label of Y, and the other has a class label of N for the lead actor Y. Also, for the lead actor N, both records feature a class label of N. Therefore, we compute the average entropy for this particular attribute.

The average entropy value for the lead actor attribute is 0.5.

The information gain is 0.811-0.5 = 0.311

Additionally, you will calculate the information gain for all the attributes. The attributes with the maximum information gain win and become the root node of the decision tree.

The same process is repeated to determine the second level of the nodes, and so forth.

How it Operates

Let's begin with the main function. First, you will trigger get_data in the x, y, and label_names variables to retrieve the Iris dataset. You take the label names so that when you see your model accuracy, you can measure it by individual labels. As previously said, the Iris data has a three-class problem. You will need to define a classifier that can categorize any new instances in one of the three types.

Next, you need to invoke the build_model method to induce a decision tree on the training set. The DecisionTreeClassifier class has the model tree of scikit-learn implements a decision tree.

model = tree.DecisionTreeClassifier(criterion="entropy")

As you can see, the feature test condition is specified. Then, you can create the model by calling the fit function and return the model to the calling program.

Now, let's proceed to compute the model by applying the test_model function. The model accepts instances x, and class labels y, decision tree model, and the name of the class labels label_names.

The module metric in scikit-learn presents three evaluation criteria.

```
from sklearn.metrics import
accuracy_score,classification_report,confusion_matrix
```

In the previous sections, we defined accuracy.

A confusion matrix outputs the confusion matrix defined in the first section. A confusion matrix is a powerful way of computing the model performance. Our interest lies in the cell values having true positive and false positive values.

Lastly, there is the classification_report to display the recall, precision, and F1 score.

We need to compute the model on the training data first.

```
Model accuracy = 100.00%

Confusion Matrix
------------------
array([[40,  0,  0],
       [ 0, 40,  0],
       [ 0,  0, 40]])
None
[[40  0  0]
 [ 0 40  0]
 [ 0  0  0]]

Classification Report
=====================
             precision    recall  f1-score   support

     setosa       1.00      1.00      1.00        40
 versicolor       1.00      1.00      1.00        40
  virginica       1.00      1.00      1.00        40

avg / total       1.00      1.00      1.00       120
```

Now, you have done an excellent job with the training dataset. You have 100 percent accuracy. The actual test lies with the test dataset where the rubber meets the road.

Chapter 9: Predictions using Linear Regression

Linear regression analysis is the most popularly used of all statistical techniques. It refers to the study of linear, additive relations between variables. It is commonly used in industries to build models, which will support a business. For instance, when it comes to the retail industry, there are different factors that affect the sale of a product. Some of these factors could be promotions, price, or seasonal factors. A linear regression model allows one to understand the influence of each of these factors on the sales of a product as well as compute the baseline sales, which represents the number of sales of this product in case there were no external factors like promotions, and so on.

Simple Linear Regression
A simple linear regression contains a single variable, and it can be described using the following format:
Y = A + Bx
In the following case, y is the dependent variable, x is the independent variable, A is the intercept, and B is the co-efficient.
The dataset that you're going to use will feature the height (cm) and weight (kg) of a sample of men.
This code ingests the data and develops a simple scatter plot to understand the distribution of the weight versus the height:

```python
>>> import numpy as np
>>> import pandas as pd
>>> from scipy import stats
>>> import matplotlib.pyplot as plt
>>> sl_data = pd.read_csv('Data/Mens_height_weight.csv')
>>> fig, ax = plt.subplots(1, 1)
>>> ax.scatter(sl_data['Height'],sl_data['Weight'])
>>> ax.set_xlabel('Height')
>>> ax.set_ylabel('Weight')
>>> plt.show()
```

Here is the output of the above code:

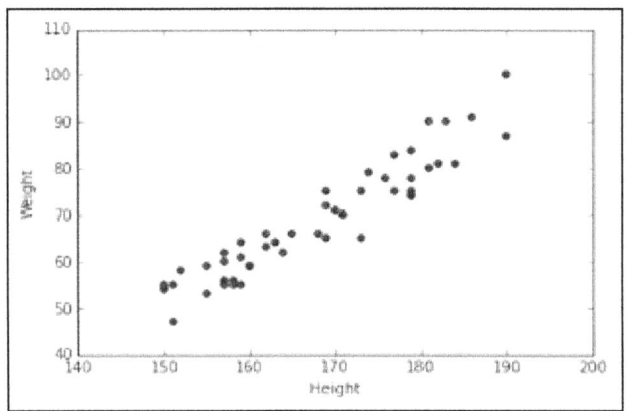

From the plot, you can learn that there is a linear relationship between the weight and height of the individual.

Let's find out how the variables are correlated to each other:

>>> **sl_data.corr()**

The above code displays the following correlation matrix:

	Height	Weight
Height	1.000000	0.942603
Weight	0.942603	1.000000

You can clearly note that the height and weight are correlated to each other depending on a Pearson correlation value coefficient of 0.94. A Pearson correlation ranges between -1 to + 1, thus when the number is more positive, the relation between the two variables is stronger if they increase or decrease together. In case the correlation value is negative, then the relation between the two variables is strong, but it's in the opposite direction.

Let's build a linear regression model using the weight as the dependent variable and x as the independent variable.

```
>>># Create linear regression object
>>> lm = linear_model.LinearRegression()
>>># Train the model using the training sets
>>> lm.fit(sl_data.Height[:,np.newaxis], sl_data.Weight)
>>> print 'Intercept is ' + str(lm.intercept_) + '\n'
Intercept is -99.2772096063
>>> print 'Coefficient value of the height is ' + str(lm.coef_) + '\n'
Coefficient value of the height is [ 1.00092142]
>>> print pd.DataFrame(zip(sl_data.columns,lm.coef_),
columns = ['features', 'estimatedCoefficients'])
```

The following is the output of the above code:

	features	estimatedCoefficients
0	Height	1.000921

In the previous code, you apply the linear_model. The linear regression () to develop a linear regression object. Next, you apply the fit () technique of lm to define the dependent and independent variable, in the following case, the weight is the dependent variable, and the height is the independent variable.

To attain the intercept value, you need to apply lm.intercept_, to acquire the coefficient, you apply the lm. coef.

The last line of the code helps define a DataFrame of the independent variable and its corresponding coefficients. This will be relevant when you explore multiple regression in detail.

Next, plot the scatter chart using the trend line to get the following output:

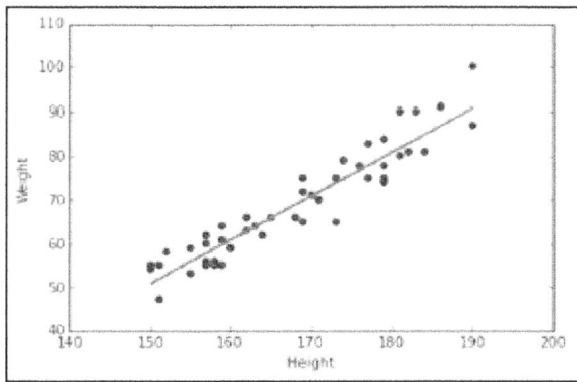

Multiple Regression

Multiple linear regression occurs when more than a single independent variable is used to forecast a dependent variable.

$$Y' = a + b_1 x_1 + b_2 x_2 + \ldots\ldots + b_n x_n$$

In the above formula, y denotes a dependent variable, a denotes an intercept, b1 and b2 represent the coefficients, and x1 and x2 represent independent variables. To create the multiple linear regression model, you will need to make use of the NBA's basketball data to forecast the average points attained per game.

Below are the data column descriptions:
- Height: Describes the height in feet.
- Weight: Describes the weight in pounds.
- Success_field_goals. Describes the rate of successful field goals.
- Success_free_throws. Describes the rate of successful free throws.
- Avg_points_scored. Describes the average points attained per game.

The code below ingests the above data, and then you apply the describe () method of the DataFrame to acquire the univariate metrics in every field.

```
>>> b_data = pd.read_csv('Data/basketball.csv')
>>> b_data.describe()
```

Below is the output of the above code:

	height	weight	success_field_goals	success_free_throws	avg_points_scored
count	54.000000	54.000000	54.000000	54.000000	54.000000
mean	6.587037	209.907407	0.449111	0.741852	11.790741
std	0.458894	30.265036	0.056551	0.100146	5.899257
min	5.700000	105.000000	0.291000	0.244000	2.800000
25%	6.225000	185.000000	0.415250	0.713000	8.150000
50%	6.650000	212.500000	0.443500	0.753500	10.750000
75%	6.900000	235.000000	0.483500	0.795250	13.800000
max	7.600000	263.000000	0.599000	0.900000	27.400000

The following observations can be derived from the above data table:

1. The mean height of a basketball player is close to 6.5 feet.
2. The shortest player is 5.7 feet.
3. The tallest player is 7.7 feet.
4. The player with the minimum weight is 105 pounds.
5. The heaviest player is 263 pounds.
6. The best field goal percentage for a player is around 60%
7. The worst field goal percentage for a player is around 29%
8. The average field goal trial for a player is 45%, but from the small standard deviation, you can see that most of the players have a field goal rate between 40% to 50%.
9. Among the free throws, there is a player who skips 3/4th of the game.
10. The best free throw player has a 90% success rate.
11. Majority of the players have a success rate for free throws of between 70-80%
12. The greatest score per game by a player is around 27.
13. The minimum score is 3
14. Averagely the players score 12 points.

Let's determine the correlation between the variables:
>>> b_data.corr()
Here is the output for the above code:

	height	weight	success_field_goals	success_free_throws	avg_points_scored
height	1.000000	0.834324	0.495546	-0.259271	-0.068906
weight	0.834324	1.000000	0.516051	-0.290159	-0.009844
success_field_goals	0.495546	0.516051	1.000000	-0.018570	0.338760
success_free_throws	-0.259271	-0.290159	-0.018570	1.000000	0.244852
avg_points_scored	-0.068906	-0.009844	0.338760	0.244852	1.000000

From the previous table, you can identify the following:
1. There is a high correlation between height and weight.
2. There exists a weak positive correlation between successful field goals in terms of weight and height.
3. The mean points attained tend to have the highest correlation with success_field_goals, but they aren't highly correlated.

Now, let's look at the distribution of each of the independent variables with reference to the dependent variable:
Below is the output:

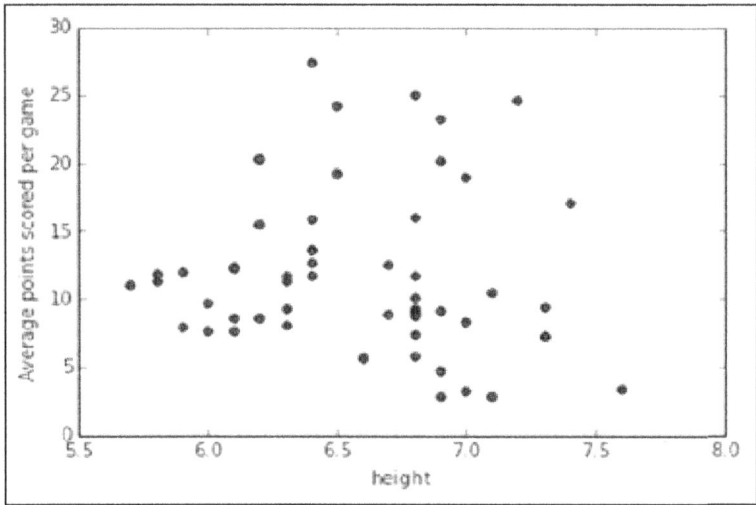

In the following scatter plot, you can see that there is no obvious pattern between the average points attained and the height. The distribution appears quite random. Let's examine the distribution between average points scored and the weight:

```
>>> fig, ax = plt.subplots(1, 1)
>>> ax.scatter(b_data.weight, b_data.avg_points_scored)
>>> ax.set_xlabel('weight')
>>> ax.set_ylabel('Average points scored per game')
>>> plt.show()
```

Here's the output:

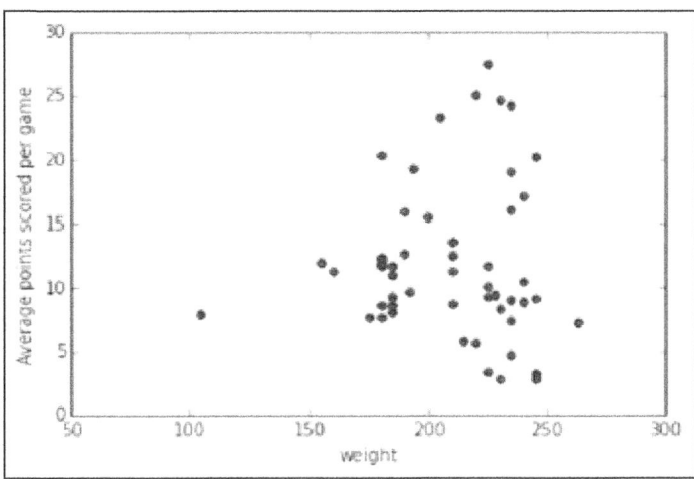

You should notice that 105 pounds appear like an outlier and also has a relatively lower average point score. You can also notice that the players who are almost 240 pounds have the highest variations with respect to score. Therefore, the hypothesis can be made taller and heavier, as well as have a greater score. On the other hand, the shorter and heavier players have a minimum score.

Now, let's explore the distribution between successful fields goals and the average points attained:

```
>>> fig, ax = plt.subplots(1, 1)
>>> ax.scatter(b_data.success_field_goals, b_data.avg_points_scored)
>>> ax.set_xlabel('success_field_goals')
>>> ax.set_ylabel('Average points scored per game')
>>> plt.show()
```

Below is the output of the previous code:

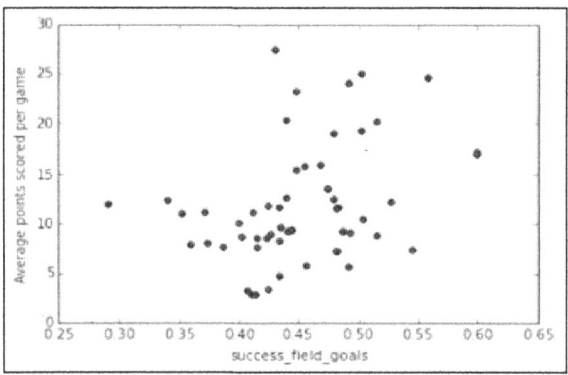

The success_field _goals variable features some linear relationship with the average points attained, but the distribution is somehow scattered.

Finally, let's determine the distribution between successful free throws and the average points scored per game:

```
>>> fig, ax = plt.subplots(1, 1)
>>> ax.scatter(b_data.success_free_throws, b_data.avg_points_scored)
>>> x.set_xlabel('success_free_throws')
>>> ax.set_ylabel('Average points scored per game')
>>> plt.show()
```

Below is the output of the preceding code:

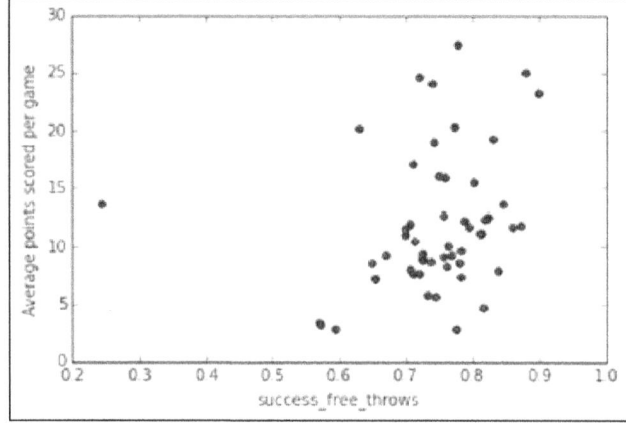

You can see that there's a player whose free throws aren't good, but the average points scored appear to be close to average compared to other players. This shows that he would be better at half field goals, or he would make more trials to score. The general distribution here is also a bit scattered.

From the previous analysts of the correlation and distribution, you should notice that there are no obvious patterns between the average points scored and the independent variables. It can be expected that the model will be built with the current data won't be that accurate.

Training and Testing a Model

In this section, you will take data and divide it into training and test sets:

```
>>> from sklearn import linear_model,cross_validation, feature_selection,preprocessing
>>> import statsmodels.formula.api as sm
>>> from statsmodels.tools.eval_measures import mse
>>> from statsmodels.tools.tools import add_constant
>>> from sklearn.metrics import mean_squared_error
>>> X = b_data.values.copy()
>>> X_train, X_valid, y_train, y_valid = cross_validation.train_test_split( X[:, :-1],
X[:, -1],
train_size=0.80)
```

First, change the data frame into an array structure using values.copy () of b_data. Next, you can apply the train_test_split function of cross_validation from SciKit to divide the data into training and test set for 80% of the data.

You will learn how to create the linear regression models using these packages:

- The statsmodels module

- The SciKit package

Still, pandas feature an Ordinary Least Square(OLS) regression, which you can test after you're done reading this chapter. The ordinary least square refers to a method used to determine unknown coefficients and intercepts for a regression equation. We shall get started with the statsmodels package. The statsmodels describes a Python module that lets users explore data, approximate statistical models, and conduct statistical tests. An extensive list of descriptive statistics, plotting functions, and result statistics are present for different data types and each estimator.

The OLS function helps in building a linear regression object using a dependent and independent variable. The fit () method is useful in fitting the model. Don't forget that there is an add_constant() function, which is used to compute the intercept while building the model. By default, the OLS () function will not compute the intercept, and it has to be explicitly described with the assistance of the add_constant function. The screenshot below is a summary of the regression model that has been trained. The screenshot displays different metrics related to the model:

OLS Regression Results

Dep. Variable:	y	R-squared:	0.265
Model:	OLS	Adj. R-squared:	0.187
Method:	Least Squares	F-statistic:	3.423
Date:	Sun, 22 Mar 2015	Prob (F-statistic):	0.0174
Time:	05:11:41	Log-Likelihood:	-130.25
No. Observations:	43	AIC:	270.5
Df Residuals:	38	BIC:	279.3
Df Model:	4		
Covariance Type:	nonrobust		

	coef	std err	t	P>|t|	[95.0% Conf. Int.]
const	15.5129	16.147	0.961	0.343	-17.175 48.200
x1	-5.9277	3.066	-1.933	0.061	-12.135 0.279
x2	0.0162	0.049	0.332	0.742	-0.082 0.115
x3	55.1647	19.044	2.897	0.006	16.612 93.717

Omnibus:	6.717	Durbin-Watson:	1.637
Prob(Omnibus):	0.035	Jarque-Bera (JB):	5.457
Skew:	0.786	Prob(JB):	0.0653
Kurtosis:	3.759	Cond. No.	5.20e+03

The above summary contains a lot of information about the model. The major parameter to consider is the r square value; this value informs you how much of the variance of the dependent variable is recorded by the model. It can range from 0 to 1, and the p-value indicates whether the model is relevant.

From the previous output, you can see that the R-square value is 0.265, which is not field. You can see that the model represents x3 as the most relevant variable, which the success_field_goals variable. In general, any p-value if a variable lower than 0.05 can be considered important.

Now, let's build the model using the successful field goals variable and identify how the model performs.

```
                            OLS Regression Results
Dep. Variable:              y                R-squared:           0.078
Model:                      OLS              Adj. R-squared:      0.056
Method:                     Least Squares    F-statistic:         3.492
Date:                       Sun, 22 Mar 2015 Prob (F-statistic):  0.0688
Time:                       05:11:44         Log-Likelihood:      -135.11
No. Observations:           43               AIC:                 274.2
Df Residuals:               41               BIC:                 277.7
Df Model:                   1
Covariance Type:            nonrobust
```

	coef	std err	t	P>|t|	[95.0% Conf. Int.]
const	-2.5735	7.546	-0.341	0.735	-17.814 12.667
x1	31.4348	16.823	1.869	0.069	-2.539 65.409

```
Omnibus:          5.440   Durbin-Watson:      1.810
Prob(Omnibus):    0.066   Jarque-Bera (JB):   4.382
Skew:             0.760   Prob(JB):           0.112
Kurtosis:         3.370   Cond. No.           23.1
```

You can see that the variable has become less important, and the r square value has become low. The previous model can be repeated multiple times using different sets of variables until the best model is found.

Now, use both models on the test data and see how the average squared error between the actual and the predicted value is. The model that displays the minimum mean squared error is the perfect model.

```
>>> ypred = result.predict(add_constant(X_valid))
>>> print mse(ypred,y_valid)
```

In this code, you include the predict function of the regression model object to predict the particular test dataset.

```
>>> ypred_alternate = result_alternate.predict(add_constant(X_valid[:, 2]))
>>> print mse(ypred_alternate,y_valid)
26.3
```

You should notice that the second model features a lower mean squared error compared to the first one.

Now, plot the predicted versus the actual plot for both models using the following code:

```
>>> fig, ax = plt.subplots(1, 1)
>>> ax.scatter(y_valid, ypred)
>>> ax.set_xlabel('Actual')
>>> ax.set_ylabel('Predicted')
>>> plt.show(
```

Below you can see the output of the previous code:

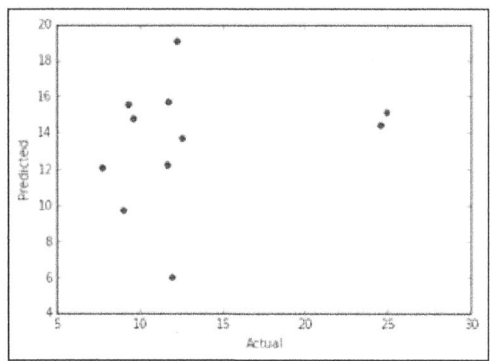

Now, let's plot the scatter for the alternate model:

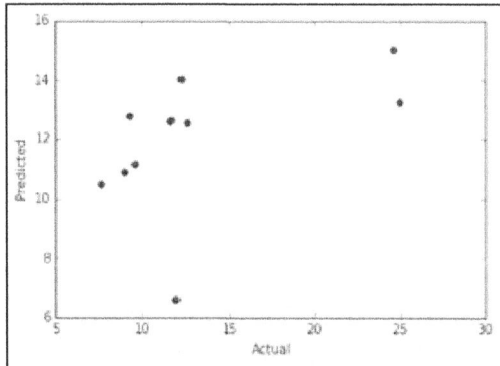

This really shows that the models aren't good enough because the predictions aren't quite random.

To create an accurate model, you need some more variables, which have an effect on the average points that are scored.

The previous model was build using the statsmodels package. Next, you will build a model using SciKit.

This code generates a Linear Regression object and then fills it with dependent and independent variables:

```python
# Create linear regression object
>>> lm = linear_model.LinearRegression()
# Train the model using the training sets
>>> lm.fit(X_train, y_train)
>>> print 'Intercept is %f' % lm.intercept_)
Intercept is 15.5129271596
>>> pd.DataFrame(zip(b_data.columns,lm.coef_), columns = ['features', 'estimatedCoefficients'])
```

Below is the output of the above code:

	features	estimatedCoefficients
0	height	-5.927749
1	weight	0.016150
2	success_field_goals	55.164717
3	success_free_throws	9.725042

The coefficient and intercepts are similar to the model that was created using the statsmodel package.

To compute the r square SciKit, the cross-validation module of the SciKit package is utilized.

```python
>>> cross_validation.cross_val_score(lm, X_train, y_train, scoring='r2')
array([-0.3043391 , -0.42402161, 0.26890649])
```

Numerous runs of the cross-validation occur, and by default, it is 3 because of which you can see three values in the previous output. The maximum value is of relevance, and you can see that it is similar to the one you created with the statsmodels.

Let's find out how the mean squared error is computed:

```
>>> ypred = lm.predict(X_valid)
>>> mean_squared_error(ypred,y_valid)
35.208
```

You should use the mean_squared_error function of the SciKit package:
Lastly, the actual versus the predicted plot will be similar to the first model plot of statsmodels:

```
>>> fig, ax = plt.subplots(1, 1)
>>> ax.scatter(y_valid, ypred)
>>> ax.set_xlabel('Actual')
>>> ax.set_ylabel('Predicted')
>>> plt.show()
```

Below is the output:

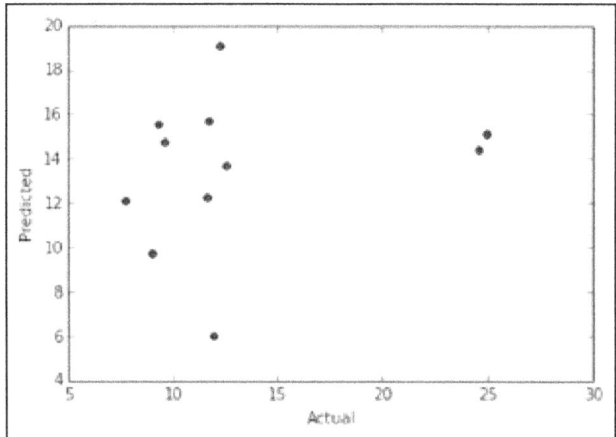

This chapter has focused on building a simple regression model as well as multiple regressions. Where there was an initial inspection analysis conducted on the data to understand it. Next, we designed the regression model with the help of statsmodels and SciKit package.

Chapter 10: Data Analysis-Deep dive

This Chapter will focus on dimensionality reduction. In the modern era, high-dimensional data is everywhere. Consider developing a product recommendation engine for a moderately-sized e-commerce website. Even with different products, the number of elements to consider are very high. Bioinformatics is another field that has high-dimensional data. The gene expression comprises of microarray datasets that feature thousands of dimensions.

If your role is either explore the data or prepare the data to be used by an algorithm, the high dimensionality, popularly known as the curse of dimensionality, is a huge obstacle. You need effective methods to deal with this. Also, the complexity of most current data mining algorithms increases exponentially with the rise in the number of dimensions. With the rise in dimensions, the algorithms become computationally infeasible and hence, inapplicable in most applications.

Dimensionality reduction approaches preserve the structure of the data as much as possible while limiting the number of dimensions. Therefore, in the restricted feature space, the implementation time of the algorithms is limited because we have a lower dimension. As the structure of the data is preserved, the results acquired can be the best approximation of the initial data space. By maintaining the structure, it means two things; first is not affecting the variations in the original dataset, and the second is preserving the distance between the data and vectors found in the new projected space.

Decomposition of a Matrix

Matrix decomposition generates different techniques for dimensionality reduction. The data is generally a matrix with the instances in rows and features organized in columns. Matrix decomposition is a technique of expressing a matrix. Say that A describes a product of two other matrices, B and C. The matrix B is supposed to feature vectors that can describe the change in the data. The matrix C is supposed to hold the magnitude of this variation. Therefore, the original matrix A is now displayed as a linear combination of B and C.

The methods that you will see in the next sections deal with matric decomposition to handle the dimensionality reduction. There are methods that emphasize that the basic vectors must be orthogonal to each other, such as the principal component analysis, and there are some that don't stress this requirement, such as dictionary learning.

Let's see some of these techniques in operation in the following chapter:

Mining the Principal Components

The first method that you will consider is the Principal Component Analysis (PCA). PCA belongs to the unsupervised method. When it comes to multivariate problems, PCA is used to decrease the dimension of the data with the minimum information loss. In other words, maintaining the maximum variation in the data. By variation, it implies the direction in which the data is dispersed to the maximum. Let's consider the following plot:

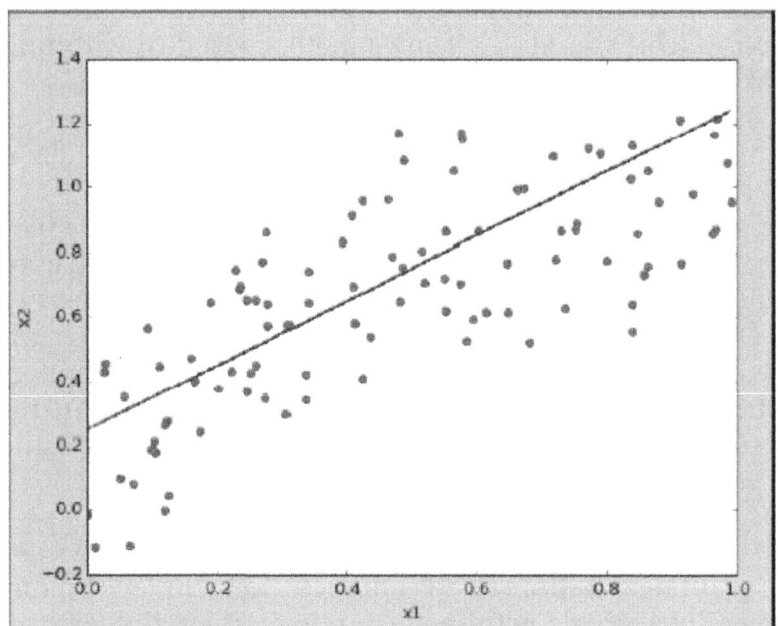

You have a scatter plot featuring two variables, x1 and x2. The diagonal line displays the maximum variation. By applying PCA, the focus is to retain this direction of the variation. Therefore, instead of applying the direction of two variables, x1 and x2, to represent this data, the aim is to look for a vector represented by the blue line and denote the data using only this vector. In general, you want to limit the dimension of the data from two to one.

You will make use of the mathematical tools Eigenvalues and Eigenvectors to determine this blue line vector. Remember, variance measures the level of dispersion in the data. However, in the case of a single dimension, it is easy to display a correlation among the variables as a matrix. When the values of the covariance matrix are normalized using the standard deviation, you receive a correlation matrix. In the following case, the covariance matrix denotes a 2 x 2 matrix of two variables, x1 and x2, and it determines how these two variables move in the same direction.

When you conduct an Eigenvalue decomposition, in other words, get the Eigenvectors and Eigenvalues of the covariance matrix, the main Eigenvector, which is the largest Eigenvalue, is in the direction with the highest variance in the previous data.

In our case, this should be the vector that is denoted by the blue line in the graph. You will then shift to project the input data inside this blue line vector to acquire the reduced dimension.

PCA can be done on both covariance and correlation matrix. Don't forget that when a dataset with unevenly scaled datasets is applied in the PCA, the outcome may not be useful.

Next, you're going to use the Iris dataset to learn how to apply PCA efficiently in shaping the dimension of the dataset. The Iris dataset features measurements for 150 iris flowers from three different species.

The three classes within the Iris dataset include:
- Iris Setosa
- Iris Versicolor
- Iris Virginica

Here are four properties within the Iris dataset:
- The sepal length in cm
- The petal width in cm
- The petal length in cm
- The sepal width in cm

Our objective is to reduce the dimension of the data. In the following example, our instances comprise of four columns. Say that you're creating a classifier to forecast the type of flower using a new instance. Can you complete this task using instances in the reduced dimension space? Is it possible to reduce the number of columns from four to two and still fulfill a nice accuracy for our classifier?

PCA is completed by following these steps:

1. Standardize the dataset to feature a zero mean value.
2. Identify the correlation matrix for the dataset and unit standard deviation value.
3. Divide the correlation matrix into its Eigenvectors and values.
4. Choose the best eigenvectors depending on the Eigenvalues in descending order.
5. Translate the input Eigenvectors matrix into the new subspace.

Now, you will proceed to standardize this data, using a zero mean and standard deviation of one, you will leverage the numpyscorr_coef function to identify the correlation matrix:

```python
x_s = scale(x,with_mean=True,with_std=True,axis=0)
x_c = np.corrcoef(x_s.T)
```

Next, you should perform the Eigenvalue decomposition and project the Iris data on the first two principal Eigenvectors. Lastly, you will plot the dataset in the reduced space. Below is the code to use:

```python
eig_val,r_eig_vec = scipy.linalg.eig(x_c)
print 'Eigen values \n%s'%(eig_val)
print '\n Eigen vectors \n%s'%(r_eig_vec)
# Select the first two eigen vectors.
w = r_eig_vec[:,0:2]
# # Project the dataset in to the dimension
# from 4 dimension to 2 using the right eignen vector
x_rd = x_s.dot(w)
# Scatter plot the new two dimensions
plt.figure(1)
plt.scatter(x_rd[:,0],x_rd[:,1],c=y)
plt.xlabel("Component 1")
plt.ylabel("Component 2")
```

Applying the function scale: The scale function can perform scaling, centering, and standardization. Centering refers to subtracting the mean value from individual values. Scaling refers to dividing every value by the variable's standard deviation, and lastly, standardization is centering, followed by scaling. Using variables having _mean and with _std function, the scale can be used to conduct all three normalization techniques.

How it Operates

The Iris dataset contains four columns. While there are no many columns, it will still meet its purpose. The intention is to reduce the dimensionality of the Iris dataset to two from four and still store all the details about the data.

You will load the Iris data to the x and y variables using the handy load_iris function from scikit-learn. The x variables represent a data matrix, and you can review its shape as follows:

```
>>>x.shape
(150, 4)
>>>
```

You will scale the data matric x to have zero mean and unit standard deviation. The rule of thumb is that if all your columns are measured with the same scale in your data and have the feature the same unit of measurement, you don't need to scale the data. This will enable PCA to capture these basic units using the highest variation.

You can move on to create a correlation matrix of our input data.

The correlation matrix containing n random variables X1... Xn is then x n matrix whosei, jentry is corr(Xi, Xj).

Next, you will apply the SciPy library to compute the Eigenvalues and Eigenvectors of the matrix. Let's consider our Eigenvalues and Eigenvectors.

```
print Eigen values \n%s%(eig_val)
print \n Eigen vectors \n%s%(r_eig_vec)
```

The output looks this way:

```
Eigen values
[ 2.91081808+0.j  0.92122093+0.j  0.14735328+0.j  0.02060771+0.j]

Eigen vectors
[[ 0.52237162 -0.37231836 -0.72101681  0.26199559]
 [-0.26335492 -0.92555649  0.24203288 -0.12413481]
 [ 0.58125401 -0.02109478  0.14089226 -0.80115427]
 [ 0.56561105 -0.06541577  0.6338014   0.52354627]]
```

In the above case, the Eigenvalues are displayed in descending order. The most prominent question is the number of components that we need to select. In the next section, you will learn different ways of determining the number of components.

You will see that you select only the first two columns of the right-hand side Eigenvectors. The discrimination potential of the retained components on the Y variable is a great test of how variation is retained in the data.

Lastly, you will plot the components in the x and y axes and color them using the target variable.

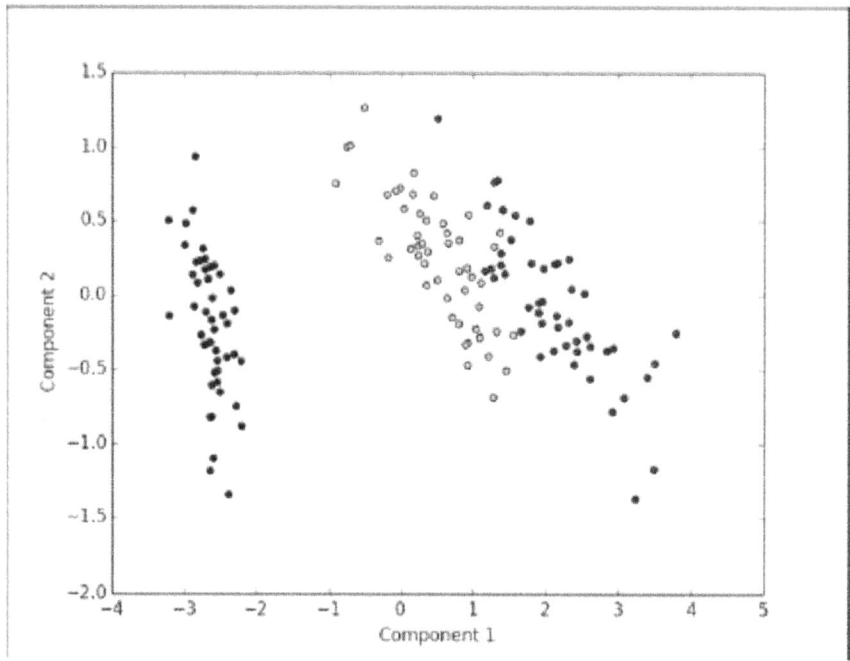

Notice that the components 1 and 2 can discriminate the three classes of the iris flowers. Hence, you'll effectively use PCA in limiting the dimension to two from four and still discriminate the instances belonging to different classes of the iris flower.

Here are additional ways to help you determine the number of components you need to include. Here is a list of methods to choose the components empirically:

1. **The Eigenvalue criterion.**

An Eigenvalue of one implies that the component would describe the variable's worth of variability.

2. The percentage of the variance explained criterion.

For every component, you print the Eigenvalue, the percentage of the variance represented by that component, and the cumulative percentage value of the variance described. For instance, component 1 contains an Eigenvalue of 2.91, 2.91/4 indicates the percentage of the variance, which is 72.80%. Now, if you add the first two components, then you can describe 95.80% of the variance within the data.

The decomposition of a correlation matrix into its Eigenvectors and values is a general method that can be applied to any matrix. In the following case, you will use it in a correlation matrix to understand the principal axes of the data distribution, that is, axes through which the highest variation in the data is observed.

PCA can be applied either as an exploratory technique or as a data preparation technique for a downstream algorithm. Document classification dataset issues typically feature advanced dimensional feature vectors. PCA can be utilized to cut down the dimension of the dataset to include only the most relevant features before directing the data to a classification algorithm.

The disadvantage of PCA that you need to know is that it is computationally expensive. Lastly, the corrcoeff function will normalize your data internally as part of its computation.

Using the Kernel PCA

PCA sets an assumption that all the principal directions of variation within the data are straight lines. This is not so in most real-world datasets.

In the following case, we shall review the kernel PCA, which will let us reduce the dimension of the dataset where the variation isn't straight lines.

In Kernel PCA, the kernel function is used in all data points. This changes the input data into kernel space. A normal PCA is conducted in the kernel space.

In the following section, you will not use the iris dataset, but you will create a dataset where the changes aren't straight lines. This way, you will not apply a simple PCA on this dataset.

How it Operates

In the first step, you will generate a dataset with the help of the scikit's data generation function. In the following case, you will use the *make_circles* function. We can create two concentric circles, the larger one holding, the smaller one. Each concentric circle belongs to a specific class. Therefore, you build a two-class problem with tow concentric circles.

First, let's examine the data generated. The make_circles function generates a dataset of size 400 using two dimensions. A plot of the previous data includes the following:

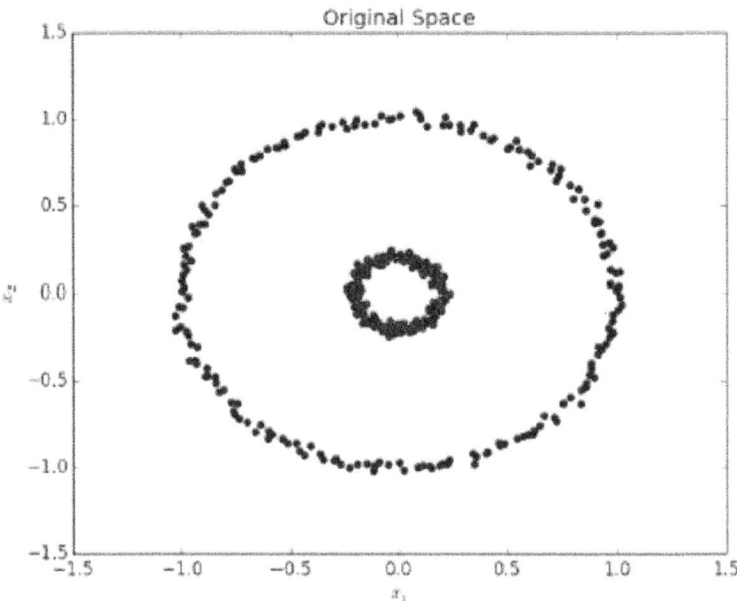

The above chart illustrates how the data has been spread. The outer circle belongs to a class one, and the inner circle belongs to class two. Is it possible to convert this data into a linear classifier? Well, you will not be able to achieve that. The changes in the data aren't straight lines. Therefore, you cannot apply normal PCA. You will resort to the kernel PCA to change the data.

Before you dive into kernel PCA, let's find out what happens if you use a normal PCA on this dataset.

Let's review the output plot of the first two components:

From the previous diagram, the members of the PCA are unable to differentiate between the two classes in a linear fashion.

Let's plot the first component and see its class differentiates ability. This graph, which you have plotted only the first component, shows how PCA is unable to differentiate the data.

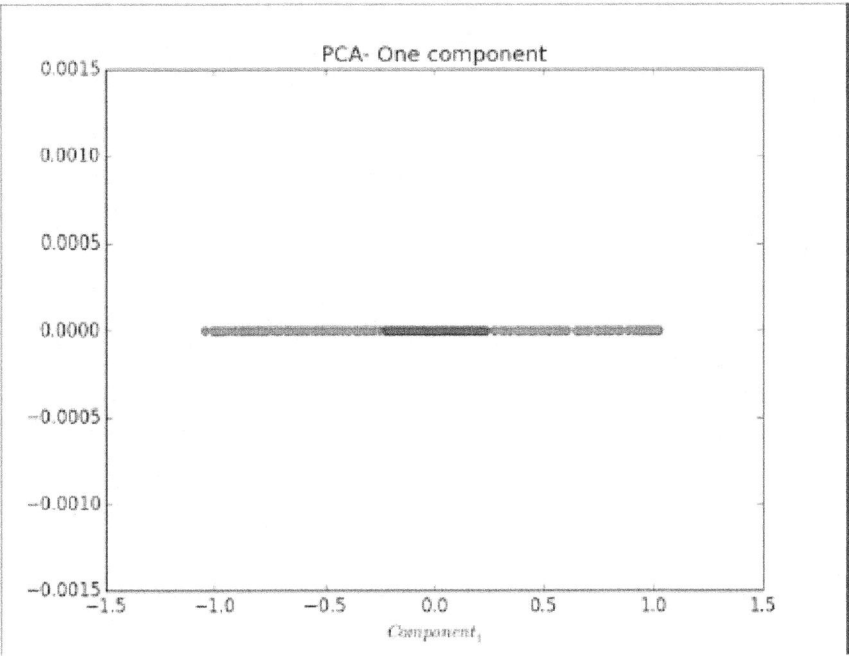

The typical PCA technique is a linear projection approach that operates well if the data is linearly separable. In cases where the data is not linearly separable, a nonlinear technique is needed for the dimensionality reduction of the dataset.

Conclusion

Python is a great choice for those who want to retrieve, process, and analyze data. With so much data available, and powerful tools that come with Python, the potential of what you want to do practically is limitless. Who knows, maybe one day, after you master data science and python, you may even win an award with the algorithm you implement in Python.

So, the future is good for data science, and Python is only a piece of the proverbial pie. Fortunately, this book should provide you with a foundation to step outside and expand your knowledge in data science. Just remember, if you dedicate yourself and commit meaningful time to master Python Data Science, you have the ability to not only acquire a new skill but also take your career to a new level.

Python Programming Language For Beginners

The First Real Guide For Beginners Towards Machine Learning And Artificial Intelligence. Learn How To Develop Your First Web App In Just 7 Days With Django!

By

Oliver R. Simpson

Code Developer Academy

Table of Contents

INTRODUCTION 286

CHAPTER 1: HISTORY OF ARTIFICIAL INTELLIGENCE 287

CHAPTER 2: INTRODUCTION TO PYTHON PROGRAMMING 292

CHAPTER 3: VARIABLES AND DATA TYPES 297

CHAPTER 4: CONDITIONAL EXECUTION 305

CHAPTER 5: PYTHON FUNCTIONS 317

CHAPTER 6: PYTHON OPERATORS 326

CHAPTER 7: FILE HANDLING 328

CHAPTER 8: DICTIONARIES 331

CHAPTER 9: OBJECT-ORIENTED PROGRAMMING 339

CHAPTER 10: INHERITANCE 343

CHAPTER 11: INTRODUCTION TO DJANGO FRAMEWORK 346

CHAPTER 12: DJANGO INSTALLATION 352

CHAPTER 13: MVC PATTERN 357

CHAPTER 14: CREATE, INSTALL, DEPLOY FIRST DJANGO APP 362

CHAPTER 15: TIPS FOR DJANGO AND PYTHON BEGINNERS 376

CONCLUSION 380

Introduction

Whether you're getting ready to build your development skills or get a new start as a software programmer, mastering Python is critical to your success.

As you know, there are many computer programming languages. You'll perhaps need more than one life to master them all. So why do we suggest you go with Python?

- It's future proof. This language isn't vanishing soon, especially with the increasing demand for Data Scientists.

- It's versatile.

- It's universal. All modern technologies can support Python code.

- It is quite easy to learn. In fact, an experienced programmer in any language can master Python quickly. It is so easy for beginners to use and learn.

The syntax of Python is clear; the language is high level and boasts of higher readability than most other languages. Plus, it's straightforward to pinpoint and correct Python errors, which means a lot to beginners.

By reading this book, you're off to a great start. This book is designed to ease your way into Python programming world. So, let's jump in.

Chapter 1: History of Artificial Intelligence

We start by exploring early efforts to define artificial intelligence.

The history of artificial intelligence may sound like a deep and impenetrable subject for individuals who are not well-acquainted in computer science and its related fields.

Regardless of how mysterious and untouchable artificial intelligence may look, when it's broken down, it becomes easy to understand than you might imagine.

So, what is artificial intelligence, otherwise referred to as "AI"?

AI is a branch of computer science that concentrates on non-human intelligence or machine-driven intelligence.

AI relies on the concept that human thought functionality can be replicated.

Early thinkers pushed the concept of artificial intelligence throughout the 1700s and beyond. During this period, it became more tangible. Philosophers imagined how the idea of human thinking could be artificially computerized and transformed by intelligent machines.

The human thinking that generated interest in AI eventually resulted in the invention of the programmable digital computer in the 1940s. This particular discovery finally pushed scientists to proceed with the concept of building an "electronic brain," or an artificially intelligent being.

Besides that, mathematician Alan Turing, had developed a test that ascertained the potential of a machine to emulate human actions to the degree that was indifferent from human actions.

From the 1950s, many theorists, logicians, programmers broadened the modern mastery of artificial intelligence as a whole.

During this period, intelligence was viewed as a product of "logical" and "symbolic" reasoning. The reasoning was executed by computers using search algorithms. The focus during this time was to replicate human intelligence by solving simple games and proving theorems. Soon, it became obvious that these algorithms could not be used to find solutions to problems such as the movement of a robot in an unknown room. Extensive knowledge of the real world would have been required to avoid a "combinatorial" explosion of the problem to solve.

Come in the 80s; it was pragmatically accepted to restrict the AI scope to specific tasks like the replication of intelligent decision making for the medical diagnosis of particular pathologies. This was the time of "expert systems", capable of successfully replicating the intelligence of a human specialist in small and well-defined industries.

Similarly, it became apparent that some intelligent actions such as recognition of written text, could not be achieved with an algorithm designed with a sequence of instructions previously set. Instead, it was possible to gather numerous examples of the objects to be identified and using algorithms that could master the essential characteristics of these objects.

It was the beginning of what we now refer to as "machine learning." The computer learning steps could be defined as a mathematical optimization problem and described with probabilistic and statistic models. Some of the learning algorithms that were used to replicate the human brain were referred to as "artificial neural networks." During the first four decades, AI has moved through moments of Euphoria, followed by times of unfulfilled expectations. In the early 2000s, the increasing emphasis on specific problems and the increase of investments resulted in the first historical accomplishments. In some functions, AI systems attained higher performances than humans.

What is an Intelligent Machine?

After the discovery of computers, the debate on the nature of the intelligence that had involved philosophers for thousands of years took the form of the title of this section. Already some years before the Dartmouth workshop, Alan Turing had asked himself this question, and while seeking a solution, he had suggested a "test", known as "Turing Test" to determine the machine intelligence. Suppose a human and a computer that claims to be intelligent are put together in one room. Another human, a "judge," can speak with them in written and spoken form, but without seeing them. The judge interrogates the two interlocutors and decides who is human and who is not. The mistake of the judge is proof of the machine's intelligence. It is proof that the machine is inseparable from an intelligent human. This definition of intelligence addresses many of the ambiguities that can be experienced in defining what intelligence is. We don't pretend that the computer acts like us, just like we did not ask that planes fly like birds. We're satisfied that the computer cannot be differentiated from a human for a sequence of tasks that demand we call for intelligence. The complexity and broadness of the tasks required to distinguish what is known as "Narrow AI" from the "General AI" of future systems that should indicate an intelligence on a human level, or higher, for a wide variety of tasks.

The Current Nature of Artificial Intelligence

First, you need to understand that the "real" AI doesn't exist at the moment. A real AI refers to AI systems that can solve all human-level tasks with the same proficiency.

So far, the current systems are referred to as "narrow"' AI. This means they can only generate useful results within a small domain. Even with that, the past few years have seen important ingredients compiling to push AI beyond early adopters to an expansive marketplace. Today, newspapers and magazines are full of articles about the current progress in AI and machine learning technologies.

Two reports predicted that in the next few decades, AI will rise to become the largest commercial opportunity for firms and nations. Progress in AI has the potential to boost global GDP to 14% between now and 2030. This is equivalent to an additional $14-15% trillion contributions to development in productivity.

As time goes, AI may become a transformative technology such as the steam engine, electricity, and the internet. Acquisition of AI in the market place will take a general S curve pattern with a slow start in the early period.

While still in the early stages, AI is already delivering significant value for those who've embraced the technology. Seventy-eight percent accept to attain significant value, while only 1% agree that they've seen none. Across business processes, the highest value was in risk management and manufacturing.

Some of the Recent Progress in AI

Text Generation

When it comes to text generation, there is the OpenAI's GPT-2 Model which can produce realistic text. While there is a lot of hype and ethical discussion around this model, but below is a list of commercial applications associated with text generation:

Fan Fiction Generation: Provide some context to a mode and let it create a whole fiction around that, or you can apply ideas and continuously guide it to establish a story you prefer within no time.

Automated News Generation: Normally, the news is created around something that takes place on social networks. For example, Elon Musk sends a tweet, and there is a good chance it will become news, and numerous articles will be written about it. You can adopt real-time social media data to create automated news generation.

Content Generation: This model can be used to collect an extensive amount of content across the internet on your blog. A single article is normally released across multiple sites, applies that context, and allows the model to rewrite the blog for you.

Personalized Articles: You read news articles every day but what if the article you read is personalized to your reading style. This has a huge problem.

Automated Storylines for Games: This may appear futuristic, but it could be possible if you train the model on a big dataset of a universe. For example, the

MCU model may release custom story-lines, and it might be applied for a separate game-ending for everyone who plays it!

Image Generation: Images showcase a large portion of the internet. From graphics designers to concepts artists, many people use images to communicate and generate their livelihood.

Face Generation: This application may already be affecting the game industry because you can use it to build realistic faces of non-existent people. You can still use it to create faces of children and the entire family trees very quickly or in real-time based on the game store-line.

Anime Face Generation: Anime is an enormous industry in Japan but it consumes a lot of time to design the face of a character. By using GANs (Generated Adversarial Networks), it is possible to generate a large number of them with a click of a button.

Photography: Recovering broken image, superzoom, noise removal, and night time realistic photos are some of the developments that are already being embedded in modern smartphones. This AI allows you to become an expert in photo editing in no time.

Audio Generation

Audio is another form of content we use online daily. Whether it's speaking or music from your beloved playlist. Here's a shortlist of advancements:

- **Music Composition & Synthesis**: If you have a music sheet, you can create music with the help of numerous instruments, but what if AI can help play those musical instruments. You can go further by letting AI compose music as long as there are certain constraints.

- **Speech Synthesis:** Realistic speech synthesis has been an issue but with recent breakthroughs, you can synthesis realistic speech. There is also research on changing the voice of one individual to another or even editing what one individual said.

Animation Generation

Video is the most popular type of content used in today's internet. YouTube is a popular platform, and many YouTubers earn online by generating great content.

- **Video Style Transfer:** You can change one type of video to a new kind of video, or if you're an artist or an animator, you create simple annotations and let AI generate some ideas.

- **Realistic Animation:** AI is also powerful at animating objects. This can be directly used in the 3D animation sector to animate complex objects without breaking a sweat. It's also relevant in-game animations.

- **3D Modelling:** GANs can be used to build a massive variety of 3d models, and it is essential to create a large number of synthetic characters and buildings.

From self-driving cars to healthcare diagnosis, stock market analysis, and small things like editing files, there's no question that artificial intelligence will play a significant role in day-to-day life as the future opens.

It may be a gradual change as the opportunities of AI grow to the challenges that humans present, but gradual, the change is coming. As that change happens, it will likely prepare a totally new era of technology and human growth in the process.

Machine Learning

In the past few years, Machine Learning (ML) has been a buzzword.

Machine Learning has a range application from automating mundane tasks to generating intelligent insights, industries in every field strive to gain from it. You might already be using a device that relies on Machine Learning. For example, a wearable fitness tracker such as Fitbit, or an intelligent home assistant. However, there are many more examples of ML in use.

Overview of the history of ML

ML is a vital element of modern business and research. It has algorithms and neural network models to help computer systems progressively changing their performance. Algorithms of ML develop a mathematical model using sample data to make training decisions without being programmed to make those decisions.

In 1952, Arthur Samuel working at IBM, built a chess program. The program could observe positions and learn an implicit model that provides better moves for the latter cases. Samuel played different games with the program and noted that the program could become better as time goes.

With that program, Samuel coined the general providence defining machines cannot extend passed the written codes and learn patterns the way human beings do. Therefore, he coined the term "machine learning," which he described as:

A field of study that provides a computer with the ability without being explicitly controlled.

Chapter 2: Introduction to Python Programming

Python programming language refers to an open-source, advanced language created by Van Rossum in the 1980s. Currently, the language is maintained by Python Software Foundation.

Python is a powerful language that you can use to build games, develop web applications, and create GUIs.

This is a high-level language. To read and write codes in the Python language is similar to reading and writing regular English statements. Since they're not written in machine-readable form, Python programs must be processed before machines can run them.

Python is a language that's interpreted. Python is an object-oriented language that lets users control data structures to build and run programs. Nearly everything in the Python language is a class. All objects, functions, classes, data types, and methods assume an equal position in the Python language.

Programming languages are built to fulfill the desires of programmers and users for an effective tool to create applications that affect lives, economy, lifestyles, and society. They make lives enjoyable by boosting productivity, improving communication, and enhancing efficiency. Languages die and become extinct when they fail to meet expectations and are replaced and replaced by more forceful language. Python is a programming language that has passed the test of time and has remained significant across industries, and businesses and among programmers. It is a thriving, and critical language that is recommended as a first programming language for those who want to jump into and experience programming.

The Ups of Using Python Language

Below are reasons why you would prefer to learn and use Python over other languages:

Readability

Programs written in Python use simple, clear, and short instructions that are easy to read even by those who have no significant programming knowledge. Therefore, Python programs are more comfortable to debug, improve and maintain.

The Least Learning Time

It's easy to learn Python. Most people find Python a great first language for mastering programming because it has shorter codes and simple syntax.

Expands Different Platforms

Python can work on Mac OS X, Windows, and other operating systems including small devices. It also can work on microcontrollers used in toys, remote controls, appliances, and other similar devices.

Installing Python

How to Install Python on Windows

To install Python on a Windows laptop, you need to first download the installation package of your preferred choice from the Python main website.

On the Python main website, you will be requested to download the latest version of Python.

Also, if you're searching for a particular release, you can scroll down the page to select download links for earlier versions.

However, it is better to download the latest version which, at the time of this writing, is Python 3.7.4. But your preference should always depend on what would be most usable for your project.

How to Install Python on Mac

If you're using Mac, you can still download the installation package from the Python main website.

How to Run the Installation File

Once you're done with the download, you can move on to installation by clicking on the downloaded .exe file. The standard installation will comprise of IDLE, documentation, and pip.

Working with Python

Python is a dynamic and flexible language that you can use in different methods. You can use it interactively when you want to test code or a statement on a line-by-line basis or when you're searching its features. You can use it in script mode or when you want to interpret a whole file of statements or application program.

Command-line Interaction

The command line is the most common way to deal with Python. It is easy to visualize how Python works because it responds to every command entered on the >>> prompt. It might not be preferred interaction with Python, but it's the easiest way to discover how Python operates.

Starting Python

There are different styles to access Python's command line depending on the type of operating system on your machine.

- If you are going to use Windows operating system, then you can navigate to the start menu and click the Python command line.

- For those working on Linux, Mac OS, and Unix, you will run the Terminal Tool.

Computer programming languages has commands to direct the computer on how to execute instructions. So, when you want to perform something in Python language, then you will need to write down several commands. After that, Python translates the commands so that it can be executed by the computer.

How to exit Python

You exit the Python language by typing the following commands:

quit ()

exit ()

Control-Z, and then press enter

Integrated Development Environment (IDLE)

This tool is found in the Python's installation package. However, if you wish you can search for complex third-party IDLEs.

The IDLE has an excellent platform to build your code and work well with Python. The IDLE is found in the same folder as the command line icon. Click the IDLE icon to take you to the Python Shell window.

The Python Shell Window

This window has several dropdown menus and a >>> prompt. Once you sign in the Python Shell window, you can begin to enter your statements for execution. However, the IDLE's editing menu allows you to go back to the previous commands. The Python Shell Window features different items on the menu like Edit, File, and Help.

The Shell and Debug menus have different functions which you would find important when creating complex programs.

The Shell menu will allow you to access the most recent reset or even restart the shell.

The Debug Menu option has relevant menu items for exploring the source file of an exception and selecting the error line. The debugger option will provide an interactive debugger window that will support the programming running. The stack viewer option describes the current Python stack through a new window.

The Option will help you to configure the IDLE to complete Python working preferences. The Help option features documentation and Python Help window.

The File Window

The items found on the File menu enables you to build a new file, create a module, create an old file, and save our session. When you click on the 'New File' option, you will be directed to a new window, a simple and normal text editor where you can type or edit your code. Initially, this file window has the name 'untitled,' but on saving your code, its name changes.

The File window's menu bar differs slightly from the Shell Window. It doesn't have the 'Shell' and 'Debug' menu located in the Shell Window, but it provides two new lists: the Run and the Format menu. When you decide to run your code on the file window, you can see the output on the Shell Window.

The Script Mode

When you work in script mode, you don't automatically see the results the way you would in an interactive mood. To see an outcome from a script, you'll have to run the script and trigger the print () function inside your code.

Python Syntax

When it comes to Python Syntax, it revolves around how human users and the system should write and interpret a Python program. If you want to write and run your application in Python, you have to familiarize yourself with the syntax.

Keywords

Keywords in Python language refers to reserved words that need to be used as variable, function name, constant, or identifiers in your code. Be keen on the following keywords if you don't want to experience errors when you implement your program:

break, def, lambda, is, not, tray, with, yield, exec, del, else, and, continue, except, from, finally, print, while, return, try, pass, global, import, assert, class

Python Identifiers

A Python identifier refers to a name assigned to a function, variable, module, or other objects that you'll be using in your Python program. Any entity you'll use in Python should be correctly named or identified as it will form part of your program.

Below are naming conventions in Python that you must know:

- An identifier can be a mix of uppercase letters, underscores, lowercase letters, and digits between (0-9). Therefore, the following are proper identifiers: my_variable, myClass, var_3, and print_hello_world.

- Unique characters like @, %, and $ are not approved within identifiers.

- An identifier should not start with a number. As a result, 2variable, is not correct, but variable2 is acceptable.

- Python is a very case-sensitive language and this should extend to identifiers.

- You cannot use Python keywords as identifiers.

- You can apply underscores to separate multiple words in your identifier.

- The class identifiers start with an uppercase letter, but the whole identifiers start in lowercase.

You should always select identifiers that are realistic even after a long gap. Therefore, although it's easy to set your variable to c = 2, you may find it more useful for future reference if you go for a longer and proper variable name such as num = 2.

Use Quotations

Python supports the use of quotation marks to display string literals. You can use triple quotes, double, single, but you need to start and end the string with the same kind. You may use the triple quotes when your chain runs across different lines.

Python Statements

Statements contain instructions that a Python interpreter can run. When you allocate value to a variable, for instance, my_variable = "dog", you'll be creating an assignment statement. An assignment statement can be as short as c = 3. There are other types of statements in Python such as while statements, if statements, and for statements.

Indentation

In most programming languages like Java, there are braces to define blocks of code. However, Python programs are different because they are formatted using indentation. Python blocks of code are indented. As a result, codes written in Python are easy to understand and read.

While you indent blocks of code, make sure that the indent space is constant. If you use IDEs to type your code, Python has a standard rule that guides on the application of indentation. In general, indentation should be around 4 spaces to the right.

Comments

When building a program, you will come to realize that it's a good practice to include some description to your code. This is the point where comments become important. A comment is a way to ensure that your code is easily understood by other programmers. Also, when you revisit your code after some few months, you will not be stranded on what exactly a given line of code was doing. Comments in Python are written by using the hash symbol. The hash symbol enables the Python interpreter to ignore the comment when executing the code.

Chapter 3: Variables and Data Types

Python programs are saved with a file extension of .py. In other words, for the hello program, the file name should be hello_world.py. This automatically shows the file contains Python programs. Your editor then executes the file using the Python interpreter, which reads through the program and determines the meaning of every word in the program. For example, when the interpreter comes across the word print, it outputs to the screen whatever is contained in the parentheses.

While you write your programs, your editor highlights different sections of your program in different ways. For example, it understands that print is the name of a function and outputs that word in blue. It realizes that "Hello, World." is not Python code and outputs that phrase in orange. This property is known as syntax highlighting and is crucial as you begin to write your programs.

Variables

A variable is like a container that holds values that you can access. It is a way of pointing a memory location that a given program uses. You use variables to help the computer save or retrieve data to and from the memory location.

Python differs from other languages when it comes to variables. Languages such as Java, C++, or C link a variable to a specific data type. In other words, it can only store a given data type. For that reason, when a variable is of type integer, you can only save integers inside that variable when executing the program.

Python is very flexible when handling variables. As a result, Python lets you change the value and data type during program execution.

Now, let us run a hello world program using a variable. First, you will need to add a new line at the start of the file and change the second line. Below is how the program will appear:

text = "Hello world!"
 print (text)

If you run the following code snippet in your Python editor, you need to see an output as: Hello world!

In this program, the variable text has been used to store the value, which is the information related to that variable. In the following example, the value is the text "Hello world!"

Adding a variable increase, the work for the Python interpreter. Once it processes the first line, it connects the text "Hello, World!" with the variable text. When it goes to the second line, it prints the value connected with a message to the screen.

Let's expand on the following program by modifying it to display a second message. Include the following lines of code:
 text = "Hello, World!"
print(text)
text= "Hello Python beginner!"
print(text)
Now when you enter the above code in your Python editor and proceed to run, you will see two lines of output:
Hello, World!
Hello Python beginner!
Still, if you want, you can modify the value of a variable in your program at any given time, and Python will always remember its current value.

How to Name and Use Variables
When you use variables in Python, you need to respect a few rules and guidelines. If you break the rules, you will encounter an error. Other instructions enable you to write a code that is simple to read and understand.
Some of these rules include:

- Variable names can only contain underscores, letters, and numbers. A variable name can start with a letter or an underscore, but not with a number. For example, it's possible to call a variable message_1.

- Spaces aren't allowed within variable names, but underscores can be used to separate words inside variable names. For example, num_year but num year will lead to errors.

- Don't use Python keywords and function names as variable names. In other words, don't use words that Python has reserved for a given pro-grammatic reason such as the word print.

- Variable names need to be short but descriptive. For instance, the name is better than n, num_year is better than n_year.

- Be keen when you use lowercase letter l and uppercase letter O because it's easy to confuse with the numbers 1 and 0.

It might take some practice to master how to build proper variable names, particularly as you become more exciting and advanced. While you write more programs and begin to read through other people's code, you'll become better at creating meaningful names.

Last but not least, computers are firm, but they don't adhere to good and bad spelling. This means you don't need to follow English and grammar rules when you try to create variable names.

Most errors in programming include single-character typos in a single line. If you spend a long time searching for one of these errors, note that you're in a good company. Most experienced and talented programmers spend countless hours searching for these types of errors.

The best way to learn new programming ideas is to try them in your programs. If you get stuck while doing an exercise, try to do something different for a while.

Strings

Python deals with different data types to support the needs of programmers and application developers for useful data. These comprise of Booleans, time, numbers, date, and time.

A string comprises of a sequence of Unicode characters that could be a combination of letters, special symbols, and numbers. To define a Python string, you can include a string in a single or double-quotes.

```
>>> stringone = 'I am enclosed in single quotes."
>>> stringtwo = "I am enclosed in double quotes."
```

A string is a Python data type.
You can define a string as a "sequence of characters".
Characters are organized in a certain position inside a String. For example:
Greeting = "hello"
In the above string, 'h' is the first character inside the string, followed by 'e' etc.
The following string has same characters but they are placed in a separate position:
Greetings = "loleh"

How to Access the Individual Characters Inside a String

Certain programming tasks will require that you access individual characters stored inside a string.

You can separate individual characters inside a string using a for loop. The featured variable inside your loop will assume every character in your string one at time. For instance: for c in "Maria":
print (c)
>> M
>> a

\>\> r
\>\> i
\>\> a

Making use of individual characters in a string for calculations
Now that you can iterate over a string it is easy to imagine how you can analyze the details of a string.
String Indexing
Indexing notation is another method to analyze a string.
Indexing refers to a means of referencing individual elements inside a string depending on their position.
You can determine an index by applying an integer value within a pair of square brackets just after the variable:

```
Word = "superman"
Print (word[0])
>> s
```

String indexes start with zero.
Iterating a String Using Indexing
You can apply a "for" loop to go over the characters in a string. For example:
word = "hello"
for c in word:
print (c)
But, if you want to go over the string by using indexing, then you will need to generate a range of numbers that correlate to the indexes you want to visit. For example:
word = "hello"
for i in range(0, 5):
print (word[i])
String Immutability
Strings are an example of immutable data type. In other words, they cannot be modified once they are created.
What really goes on behind the scene is that Python defines a different string inside the computer memory and references that string rather than the previous one.
name = 'superman'

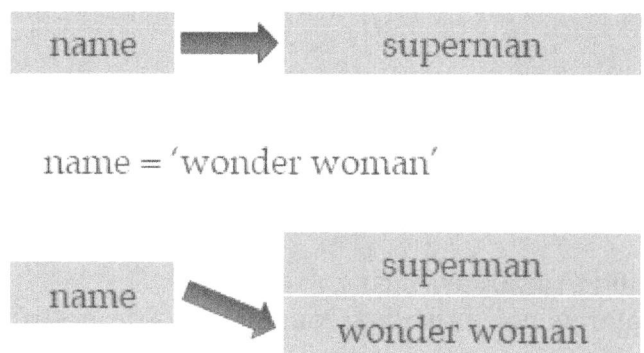

In other words, it's impossible to modify single characters within a string by applying notation. You may trigger an exception.
word = "Superman"
word[0] = "X"
# exception!

Changing a String

To make changes to a string you will require to create a new String variable.
This new variable can then store the modified version of the string.
For instance, let's take the following programming challenge:
"Write a program that replaces all vowels in a String with the underscore character."
At first, you may assume that you could simply apply String indexing to modify the characters in question. For instance:
word = "hello"
word[1] = "_"
word[4] = "_"
But since strings are immutable, this will not work!
Instead, you need to define a new string variable to store the changes and then apply a loop to check every character within a sequence to "create" the new String.
For example:
word = "hello"
newword = ""
for c in word:
if c == 'e' or c == 'o':
newword += "_"
else:

newword += c

String Functions

So far you know several functions that you can use with strings.

For instance, the len () function can count the number of characters in a string. Besides that, there are other functions that you can apply when you work with Strings to simplify things for you as a developer.

Determining the Largest and Smallest Character within a String

You can use Python built in functions to calculate the largest and smallest characters inside a string. For example:

```
a = max("python")
b = min("python")
print ("max:", a)
print ("min:", b)
>> y
>> h
```

String Slicing Notation

For Python to cut a string you must use a bracket symbol to define the index range of the characters you want.

The standard notation for the following syntax includes:

```
substring = bigstring[start:end:step]
```

You need to include at least an index value.

Substring properties comprises all the characters at the start value and continue to the ending value.

Eliminating a starting index value will trigger Python to assume that you want to begin at the start of the string or you want to proceed slicing the last section of the string. This should resemble the function range.

String Operators

Now that you know the "+" and "*" operators can be applied together with a String. The "+" operator can be applied to "concatenate" two strings together.

The "*" operator can be applied to repeat a String a specific number of times.

Testing String Using "in" and "not in"

The "in" operator represents a Boolean operator that you can apply to determine whether a substring exists within another string. For example:

When you define an expression using the "in" operator the result will compute to a Boolean.

```
word = "Jackson James John Chris Tom"
if "Chris" in word:
    print ("found him!")
else:
    print ("can't find Chris")
```

String Method
A "method" refers to a function that is member to an "object", and completes operation on that object. For example:
We haven't discussed objects much in class, but strings can be a great introduction to methods and objects.
The standard syntax includes:
stringvariable.method(arguments)

String Testing
String testing methods enable you to determine whether a specific pattern is available within a given string variable. For example:

```
word = '1234'
if word.isdigit() == True:
    print ("All chars in word are digits!")
else:
    print ("Not all chars in word are digits!")
```

In this example, the "isdigit" method is used to call "word". The following method will evaluate to True in case all characters inside a string are numeric digits, and False if not.

String Modification Methods
Keep in mind that strings are immutable and cannot be directly changed.
That said, they do have a number of "modification" methods that return a new copy of the string that reflects a given change.

```
word = "Craig"
newword = word.lower()
print (word)
>> craig
```

Searching and Replacing
Programs usually need to search and substitute functions on data, same as "find and replace" functionality that is found in your word processor.
Strings can be searched for strings and substrings with the help of find () or index () methods.
The find method returns -1 in case the substring isn't found.
The index () returns an error in case the substring isn't found.

Searching a Specific Section of a String
Both the find () and index () methods search from the start of the string, and determine the occurrence of the substring.
You can also define a start and ending index to only check a portion of the string.
How to Search Backwards Through a String
Both the rindex () and rfind() methods work the same as find() and index(), except the string is searched backwards from the end of the string.
Centering Text
s.center(w, [pad]) centers the text within a field of width w.
The optional pad character will be included to the ends of the string.
Concatenation
You can concatenate strings using the + operator.
\>>> 'welcome' + 'home'
'welcomehome'
Join Method
Strings too have a join () method.
Multiplications
Strings can even be multiplied by integers.
\>>> 'ship' * 5
Methods of Extracting Information About a String
s.count(ss)- this counts the number of times of substring ss
s.endswith(sfx)- this confirms whether a string ends with the substring sfx.

Chapter 4: Conditional Execution

There are certain conditions in life when decisions become inevitable. This is not different when it comes to programming. It is the same for every program, which has to evaluate relevant problem. There is no way to program without applying branches in the program flow.

When it comes to programming and scripting language, conditional statements are used to compute various calculations depending on whether a given condition evaluates to true or false.

The condition normally has arithmetic and comparison expressions. The expressions are computed to the Boolean Values False or True. The statements responsible for decision are referred to as conditional statements, alternatively they are also known as conditional constructs.

The if-then syntax is sometimes referred to as the if-then-else. This is common in most programming languages, but the syntax differs from language to language.

Conditional statements are found in every programming language. Conditional statements allow you to have a code that may run and at other times not run, depending on the input of the program.

Once you fully run each statement of a program, moving from top to bottom with every line executed, you aren't asking the program to execute certain conditions. By applying conditional statements, programs can tell whether a given condition is being met and then be informed what to do next.

Here are some examples where conditional statements are important:
- If a student attains over 65% on her test, print that her grade passes, if not, print that her grade fails.

- If they purchase 10 mangoes or more, determine the discount of 5%. If they purchase less, then don't.

- If he has money in his account, compute the interest, if he doesn't, charge a certain fee.

While evaluating conditions and allocating code to run regardless of whether those conditions are met or not, then you are writing conditional code.

This chapter will take you through Python conditional statements.

The if statement is one of the most popularly used conditional statements in most programming languages. It determines whether a given statement is supposed to be executed or not. When the statement checks for a given condition, and it's found to be true, then the set of code presented inside is executed.

The if condition computes a Boolean expression and executes the block of code only when the Boolean expression is TRUE.

Based on the syntax of the statement, the condition will be implemented to a Boolean expression (true or false). In case the condition is true, then the statement inside the if block is executed, and when the condition is false, program present inside the if block will not be implemented.

Below is the flow chart of the if statement:

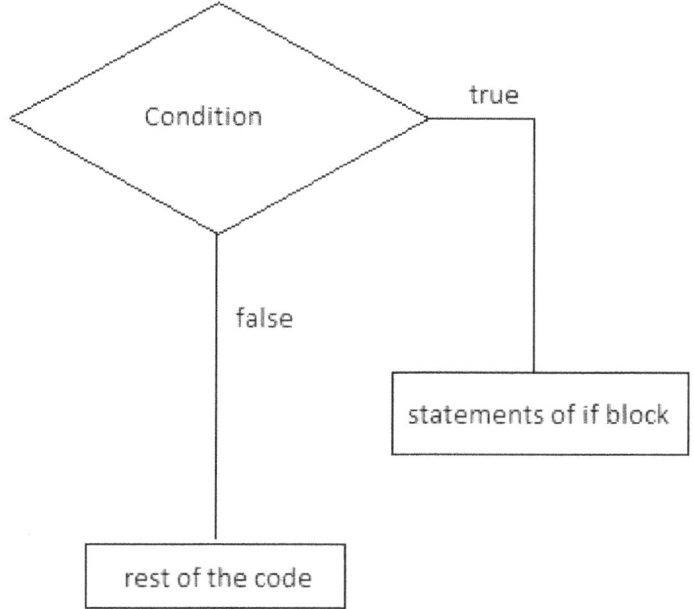

If you look at the above flow-chart, the first controller will reach an if condition and determine whether the condition is true, then the statements will be implemented; otherwise the code within the block will be executed.

If-else Statements

The statement itself indicates that if a given a condition is found to be true then execute the statements inside if block and if the condition is false, then execute the else block.

The else block will run only when the condition becomes false; this is the block where you will execute some actions when the condition is not true.

If-else statement computes the Boolean expression and implements the block of code available inside the if block if the condition is True and executes a block of code in the else block when the condition becomes false.

The syntax is:

If (Boolean expression):
Block of code
else:
Block of code

In this case, the condition will be executed to a Boolean expression. If the condition is found to be true, then the statements present inside the if block will be implemented and if the condition is false, then the statements inside the program will be implemented.

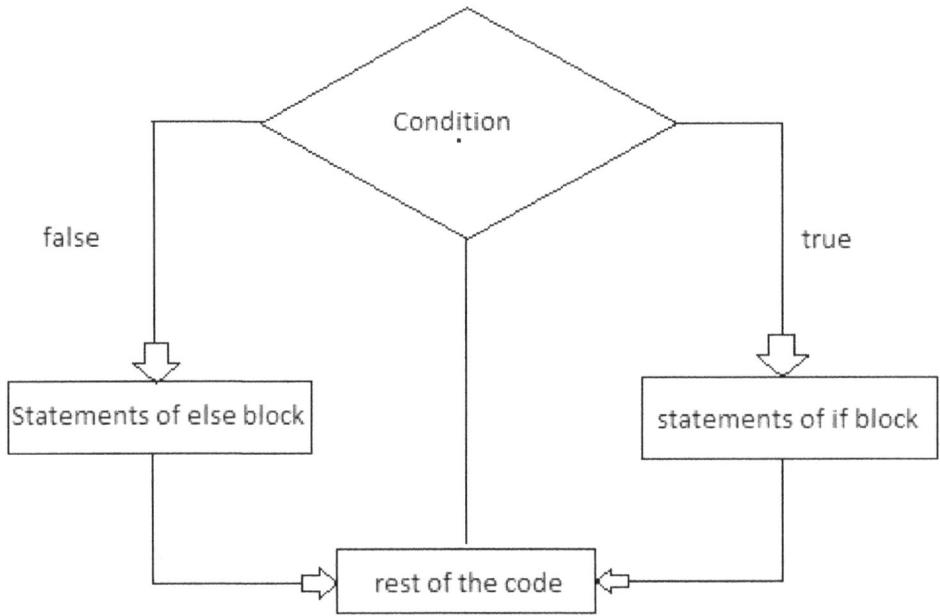

Let's explore the above flowchart

If you observe keenly, you will notice that the first controller will reach the if condition and check whether the if the condition is true, if found to be true, then the statements of the if block will be implemented otherwise, the block will be executed and later the remaining code outside the if-else block will be implemented.

The Nested if –else Statements
The nested if-else statements refer to an if statement or if-else statement available inside another if or if-else block. Python provides this property as well; this will help us to confirm multiple conditions in a given program.

An if statement available inside another if statement which is present inside another if statements and so forth.

Nested if Syntax
The syntax goes as follows:
If (condition):
#statements to run if the condition is true
If (condition):
#statements to execute if the condition is true
#end of nested if
#end of if

The above syntax clearly shows that the if block will feature another if block in it and so forth. The if block can hold 'n' number of if block within it.

Consider the following program:
Number =10
if (number >0)
   print ("this number is greater than 10")
if (number <10)
   print ("This number is less than 10")

In the above example, a variable number is declared with the value as 10.

First, it will confirm the first statement is true, then the block of code inside the first statement will be executed then it will determine whether the second if statement is true and so on.

Elif ladder
You have learned about the elif statements, but not the elif ladder. As the name implies a program that has a ladder of elif statements structured in the form of a ladder.

 if (condition):
       #Statements to execute if condition is true
elif (condition):
       #Statements to be executed when if condition is false and elif condition is true
elif (condition):
       #Set of statements to be executed when both if and first elif condition is false and second elif condition is true
elif (condition):

#Set of statements to be executed when if, first elif and second elif conditions are false and third elif statement is true
else:
#Set of statement to be executed when all if and elif conditions are false is statement is handy when you want to test multiple expressions.

Example of elif ladder

my_marks = 89

if (my_marks < 35):
    print ("Sorry!!!, You are failed in the exam")
elif(my_marks < 60): print("Passed in Second class") elif(my_marks > 60 and my_marks < 85):
    print ("Passed in First class")
else:
    print ("Passed in First class with distinction")

This program demonstrates the elif ladder. First, the control enters the if statement and determines the condition if it is true, if found to be true, then the set of statements inside the if block will be implemented else it will be skipped and the controller will come to the first elif block and compute the condition.

The same process will proceed for all the remaining elif statements and in case all if and elif conditions are found to be false then the else block will be executed.

The if-else in a Single Line

In Python, still it's possible to write if statements and elif statements in a single line without fearing the indentation.

If Statement in a Single Line

We know we can write if statements as indicated below:
If (condition):
  #set of statements to implement if condition is true
In Python, it is okay to write the above block of code in a single line.
For example:
If (condition): statement 1; statement 2; statement 3; ...statement n
In case the condition is true, then execute statement 1, statement 2, and so forth. However, if the condition is false, then none of the statements will be executed.
elif statements in a single line
syntax
if(condition):
#set of statement to implement if it's true

elif(condition1):
#set of statements to run if the condition is true
S else:
#set of statements to run if condition and condition1 is false
This block can still be written as shown below:
Syntax:
if (condition): #Set of statement to execute if condition is true
elif (condition1): #Set of statement to execute if condition1 is true
else: #Set of statement to execute if condition and condition1 is false
There can be different statements as well, you simply need to differentiate it using a semicolon (;)
Syntax:
if (condition): statement 1; statement 2; statement 3;…;statement n
elif (condition): statement 1; statement 2; statement 3;…;statement n
else: statement 1; statement 2; statement 3;…;statement n
Multiple conditions in if statements
It's not that you can just write one condition within an if statement, it is still possible to evaluate multiple conditions in if statement like below:
num_1=10
num_2 = 20
num_3 = 30
if (num_1== 10 and num_2 == 20 and num_3 == 30);
   print ("All the conditions are true")
In this example, the if statement we're evaluating multiple conditions using AND operator, this means if all the conditions are true only when the statements within an if block will be implemented.
It's also possible to specify the OR operators too.
For example:
namefruit = "Apple"
if (namefruit == "Mango" or namefruit == "Apple" or namefruit == "Grapes"):
In this example, out of the three conditions, only one condition is true, and that's the rule of OR operator. If any one condition is true, then the condition is true and the statement available inside the if block will be implemented.
Let's explore a real-time scenario to determine the number of days present in a month. You know that in a leap year the number of days will change. You will see this in a programmatic way using if, elif, and else statements.

```python
currentYear = int(input("Enter the year: "))
month = int(input("Enter the month: "))
if ((currentYear % 4) == 0 and (currentYear % 100) != 0 or (currentYear % 400) == 0):
        print ("Leap Year")
        if (month == 1 or month == 3 or month == 5 or month == 7 or month == 8 or month == 10 or month == 12):
                print ("There are 31 days in this month")
        elif (month == 4 or month == 6 or month == 9 or month == 11):
                print("There are 30 days in this month")
        elif (month == 2):
                print("There are 29 days in this month")
        else:
                print("Invalid month")
elif ((currentYear % 4) != 0 or (currentYear % 100) != 0 or (currentYear % 400) != 0):
print ("Non Leap Year")
        if (month == 1 or month == 3 or month == 5 or month == 7 or month == 8 or month == 10 or month == 12):
                print ("There are 31 days in this month")
        elif (month == 4 or month == 6 or month == 9 or month == 11):
                print("There are 30 days in this month")
        elif (month == 2):
                print("There are 28 days in this month")
        else:
                print("Invalid month")
else:
        print("Invalid Year")
```

Output:

Enter the year: 2020
Enter the month: 4
There are 30 days in this month

Output: 2

Enter the year: 2020
Enter the month: 1
There are 31 days in this month

Output: 3

Enter the year: 2019
Enter the month: 2
There are 28 days in this month

Output: 4

Enter the year: 2020
Enter the month: 2
There are 29 days in this month

Boolean Expressions

A Boolean expression may comprise one of two possible values: true or false.

The simplest Boolean expressions comprise of False and True. An expression that compares numeric expressions for equality is called Boolean expression. The simplest form of Boolean expressions contains relational operators to create a comparison of two expressions.

An expression such as 5 <10 is legal but of little significance, because it's always true. The expression is less likely to result in confusion among readers. However, because variables are dynamic, the value they hold during a program's implementation is bound to change.

Iteration

When it comes to programming, iteration means the repetition of lines of code. It's an essential property in computer programming that helps find solutions to problems. Iteration and conditional execution are the main stems of algorithm development.

Let us start with the:

While Statement

Say you want to write a program that can count to 10,000? How will you approach this problem? Will you sit down and write 10,000 printing statements? Although you can, that is going to consume a lot of your time. However, counting is frequent in computers, in fact, computers can count extraordinary values. So, there must be a way out. What you need to do is to print the value of a variable, and repeat the process until you reach 10,000. The method of executing the same code repeatedly is known as looping. Python language has two special statements, *while* and *for,* that handle iteration.

Here is an example of a program that uses a while statement.

num = 2
while num <= 5:
print (num)
num + = 1

The while statement in the above program will regularly display the variable num. The program then executes this code snippet 4 times.

print (num)
count + = 1

After each output, the program increases the num variable by one. After executing the code four times, the condition will become false, and hence the block of code is not implemented anymore.

The line while num <= 5: opens the while statement. The next expression after the while keyword is the condition that evaluates whether the block should be executed. As long as the outcome of the condition is true, the program will continue to run the block of code. But, once the condition evaluates to false, the loop terminates.

Additionally, when the condition is found to be false at the start, the program exits. The standard syntax of the while statement comprises of:

while condition:
block

The term while refers to a Python reserved word that opens the while statement. The condition indicates whether the body will be implemented or not. A colon (:) to appear after the condition.

The block consists of one or more statements that need to be executed in case the condition is true. All statements that complete the block must be indented one level deeper than the first line of the while statement. In general, the block is a member of the while statement.

The while statement looks similar to the if statements, and hence it's easy for new beginners to confuse the two. Sometimes, they can use if when they wanted to use while statement. As such, new programmers should be keen on the application of a while and if statement.

For the while statement, the running program implements the condition before it executes the while block, and then verifies the condition after the while block. Well, if the condition remains true, the program will proceed to execute the code inside the while block until it reaches a point where the condition is false. At this point, the loop terminates from execution.

Definite and indefinite loops

Let's explore the following code snippet:

```
n = 1
while n <= 10:
print(n)
 n + = 1
```

Let's find the number of iterations in the above program segment. If you carefully evaluate this code, you'll learn that there are 10 iterations. Hence, this loop is said to be definite because you can accurately determine the number of times the loop will iterate.

Now, consider the following code:

```
c = 1
terminate = int (input ()))
print (n)
n += 1
```

For this code, it is difficult to tell the number of iterations. That number depends on the input by the user. However, you can count the number of repetitions the while loop will when the user enters input before the next execution begins...

In general, the while statement is best for indefinite loops.

The for Statement

The while loop is suitable for indefinite loops. Initially, a while loop was used to execute a definite loop like:

```
n = 1
 while n <10;
print(n)
```

n += 1

In the above code snippet, the print statement will only execute 10 times. This code requires three vital sections to control the loop. That is the initialization, check and update.

Python has a handy method to display a definite loop. The for statement repeats over a series of values. One way to illustrate a series to apply a tuple. For example:

for n in 1, 2, 3, 4, 5,6, 7:
print(n)

The above code will run exactly as the while loop in the previous section. In this example, the print statement executes 7 times. The code will print first 1, then 2, and so forth. The last value printed is 7.

The for statement differs from the while statement by expecting a set of features that it will repeat over. For example, you may need a loop that runs over different numbers such as the integer values from 1 to 10. It is possible to define a counter inside a while loop to ensure this happens, but the statement is designed to handle this kind of circumstance easily and efficiently. Take for instance, a hello, world program. This program will print the string five times using a for a loop. To achieve that, you'll learn about the range function.

for x in range(5):
print("Hello, World!")

The range provides a means to access different numbers efficiently. When it's combined with a for a statement, it computes a loop that executes a fixed number of times. The program presented above will print the string "Hello, World!" five times. It achieves this by allocating the new variable x a certain value in the requested range for every iteration of the loop. If you can remember how the following indices are computed using string character positions, you'll remember that these indices begin at zero. To illustrate this, review the following code:

X for x in range (5)
    print ("The value of x is {0}.".format(x))

When you combine the for function plus the range built-in function, each loop iteration sets x to the next value in the range requested. It's like there was a counter with a while loop that you're manually requesting. The for loop takes the next value automatically, the variable x acquires a new value, and implements the inner code block.

Python Continue, Break and Pass
The control statements in Python language are used to regulate the sequence of execution of the program depending on the logic and values.
Python has 3 types of control statements
-Continue
-Break
-Pass
In summary, this chapter has looked at a conditional statement in Python as well as iteration statements. These are statements that affect the flow of execution of a program.
There are different types of conditional statements such as if, if-else, elif, nested if and many more which alter the execution of a program.
If the statement computes a Boolean expression to true or false, if the condition is true then the statement within the if block will be implemented. But if the condition is false then the statement present within the else block will be executed only if you've written the else block.
We have an additional statement known as the elif statement where the else statement is combined with an if statement, which runs depending on the previous if or elif statements.
Notes:
- Python offers conditional statements that are useful for verification and validation reasons.

- Python has two types of looping statements that help implement a specific block of code or statements repeatedly.

- You use the "while loop" when you don't know the number of times that you need to iterate and if you see the number of times you need to iterate, then 'for loop' is perfect.

- Python also has 3 control statements that allow you to control the flow of execution of a program.

Chapter 5: Python Functions

This chapter will take you through functions in Python. At the end of this chapter, you will be able to write functions in Python, call Python functions and more!

First, functions are a critical part of the Python language. Already you have come across several Python functions, including built-in features, or tasks that come with its own libraries. But, as a Data Scientist, you'll regularly need to write your own functions to solve issues that you encounter working with data.

That is why this chapter will walk you through functions in Python.

Let's dive in:

Functions in Python

You require functions in Python to help control inputs and outputs in programs. All languages of programming are built to execute data. Therefore, functions are perfect to handle and change this kind of data.

The changes typically happen to trigger results such as finding results. And, the set of instructions required to accomplish this originates from logically functional blocks of code that can be reused again.

The main code is a function. It's an essential function because every other function is connected to it, and runs from your main code. However, if the function has not yet been defined, you'll need first to define it before you proceed to use it. The definition of a function outlines the steps of its operation.

Consider this: which is better, write a code snippet 10 times, or only once and execute it 10 times.

Therefore, functions are simply tasks that a user wants to implement. However, by defining a function once using a name will allow you to reuse that functionality without making your main programs appear scary. This generally cuts down on the lines of code, and even simplifies debugging.

We'll jump into that shortly, but for now, you need to understand the reason why you need to use function is because of the property of reusability. The fact that advanced operations can be compiled into single tasks that would perform with a single call by its name is what has allowed computer codes to become more evident.

Every computer programming language nowadays allows you to create and make use of these functions to complete different tasks with just a single call. And, you can even call it any number of times without worrying about logically structuring its code into your major code every time.

Now, let's try to understand their significance to us by using a simple example:
Assume, you've got a television that can store a lot of channels, receive digital radio broadcasts, changes them into what we watch, while at the same time providing us additional options for various features.

But that doesn't imply there's an individual logically scripting the lines of codes for what you watch every time you switch on your TV. Instead, functions for every task in its working have been reasonably defined once and are often reused again and again depending on the features you attempt to use.

This happens by calling different functions as many times as possible from the main feature that is running. Therefore, even if you're increasing or decreasing the volume, its defined function is called repeatedly.

And, when you've got a system running the main code to continue calling these functions when needed has also simplified designing and innovation.

The critical aspect to remember is that whenever this function is called, it implements its tasks based on the instructions outlined.

That's how machines acquire different functions. A calculator is perhaps the most common example. It has the property of addition, multiplication, division, and other features. All these functions have been predefined into it, but it only completes those that you decide to call by pressing its respective button.

Programmers limit the time they spent to code and debug using functions, hence reducing the total development time by applying functions.

Now, let's examine what Python functions exactly are.

So, what are Python functions?

If someone was to ask you this question, what would be your response?

The functions in Python are a great example of the property of reusability. So, to server a wide range of applications from GUI and mathematical computing to web development and testing, the Python interpreter has built-in functions that are available for use. And, you may also add other libraries or modules to your program that feature pre-defined functions available for use.

All you'll need to do is to download the necessary packages based on their documentation and will freely avail of all its important functionalities by importing them over to your code.

Therefore, once it's defined, a function can be used at different times at any place in any of your codes. Now, this because Python is in line with the DRY principle of software patterns or codes featuring abstractions to avoid redundancy and make sure they can be used freely without exposing any inner parts of their implementations.

The DRY in full means Don't Repeat Yourself, and this tendency of having reusable blocks of code is significant for realizing abstraction in Python. Therefore, to use a function all that you'll need is the name, arguments, purpose and the type of results if it returns any.

It's almost like using a telephone, where you don't really need to master the working of its components to use them. Instead, they've been built to serve standard functions that you can apply directly to accomplish your goals and commit your time to implement all the innovative features of your application program. And, no one wants to understand how a function in your program works on the inside, as long as it does the work.

So, with Python, you should not be concerned about what happens inside the function unless you want to write or modify an existing function.

A function is a small program that executes data to generate output.

To use a function, first, you need to define it. Functions in Python language are defined using the def keyword before the name of the function, and include parentheses to its end, followed by a colon.

Types of Functions in Python

Python has three different categories of functions.

- Built-in functions, such as min () to determine the minimum value, print () to display an object to the Python terminal.

- User-defined functions, refer to functions that users can define to use them.

- Anonymous functions. These functions are also known as lambda functions because they're not declared using the standard def keyword.

Functions vs. Methods

A method is an example of a function that belongs to a class. You can access a method using an instance of a class. However, functions lack this limitation. It only points to a one-stop function. This means all methods are functions, but not all functions can be methods.

Take the following example. The function plus () is defined, and a class of sum () is also included.

```
# Define a function `plus()`
def plus(a,b):
  return a + b

# Create a `Summation` class
class Summation(object):
  def sum(self, a, b):
    self.contents = a + b
```

return self.contents

So, if you want to run the method sum (), first you will have to define an instance of the object class. So, let's proceed to define this object:
# Instantiate `Summation` class to call `sum()`
sumInstance = Summation()
sumInstance.sum(1,2)

Keep in mind that the above instantiation is not important when you need to call the plus () function. Still, you can execute the plus (1,2) without experiencing any problems.

Arguments vs parameters

Parameters refer to names used at the time of function definition, and into which arguments will be enclosed. This means arguments are elements included within the function.

In the preceding example, the sum () function had two arguments although the class featured three parameters, self, a, and b.

The first argument that appears in every class method points to the current class instance. In the above example is Summation.

Therefore, it's impossible to reference self because self is the parameter name for an implicitly passed argument that references to the instance method being invoked.

Defining User Functions

The four steps to follow when you want to define Python functions comprise:

1. First, write the def keyword and then write the name of the function.

2. Supply parameters to the function. The parameters need to be within the parenthesis of the function. End the line with a colon.

3. Include statements that the functions should implement.

4. Add a return statement

Example:
def hello():
 print("Hello World")
 return

Don't forget that you can define one or more function parameters for your user defined functions.

Return Statement
def hello():
 print("Hello World")

```
  return("hello")

def hello_noreturn():
  print("Hello World")
# Multiply the output of `hello()` with 2
hello() * 2
# (Try to) multiply the output of `hello_noreturn()` with 2
hello_noreturn() * 2
```

The second function returns an error because it's impossible to work on a None value. Hence, if you run this code, you will get a TypeError that will notify you that you cannot complete the multiplication operation using NoneType.

Functions immediately terminate once they come across a *return* statement.

```
def run():
  for x in range(10):
    if x == 2:
      return
 print("Run!")
run()
```

A return statement can display more than one value. Tuples allow you to return more than one statement.

Take a look at the following example to learn how you can return more than one value.

```
# Define `plus()`
def plus(a,b):
  sum = a + b
  return (sum, a)

# Call `plus()` and unpack variables
sum, a = plus(3,4)
# Print `sum()`
print(sum)
```

Calling a Function

In the previous examples, you learned how to call a function. Calling function as the name suggests means that you execute the function either directly from the Python prompt or from a different function.

 You call your hello () function by running hello ().

Adding Docstring to a Python Function

The most vital property of defining Python functions is the docstring. The docstring
Another essential feature of creating Python functions is the docstrings. Docstrings describe the tasks that your functions do such as its return values.

The descriptions work as documentation for your function so that anyone can understand the function's docstring, without the need to monitor all the code within the function definition.

The function docstrings appear instantly after the function header and are enclosed within triple quotation marks. The right Docstring for the hello () function is prints "Hello World."

```
def hello():
    """Prints "Hello World".

    Returns:
        None
    """
    print("Hello World")
    return
```

Remember that docstring can be more than the one presented here. If you would like to study docstring further, then you should check out Github repositories of Python libraries where you'll get a lot of examples.

Python Function Arguments

At the start, you read the difference between arguments and parameters. Briefly, arguments refer to things given to any function or method call, while the function or method code refers to the arguments by their parameter names. There are four categories of arguments that Python user-defined function can assume:

- Keyword arguments

- Default arguments

- Required arguments

- Variable number of arguments

Keyword Arguments
If you want to call the parameters in the correct order, you can include the keyword arguments # in your function call. Example:
```
#Define `plus()` function
def plus(a,b):
  return a + b
# Call `plus()` function with parameters
plus(2,3)
# Call `plus()` function with keyword arguments
plus(a=1, b=2)
```
By using the keyword arguments, you can also alternate around the order of the parameters and still attain the same result when you run your function.
```
# Define `plus()` function
def plus(a,b):
  return a + b
# Call `plus()` function with keyword arguments
plus(b=2, a=1)
```
Required Arguments
As the name suggests, these are arguments that have to be present. These arguments require to be passed during the function call and in exactly the correct order like in the example below:
```
# Define `plus ()` with required arguments
def plus(a,b):
  return a + b
```
Global and Local Variables
Variables defined within the body of a function have a global scope. In other words, local variables are defined inside a function block and can only be accessed within that function, while global variables can be acquired by all functions that could be in your script.
```
# Global variable `init`
init = 1
# Define `plus()` function to accept a variable number of arguments
def plus(*args):
  # Local variable `sum()`
  total = 0
  for i in args:
    total += i
  return total
# Access the global variable
```

```
print("this is the initialized value " + str(init))
# (Try to) access the local variable
print("this is the sum " + str(total))
```
You will notice that you'll get a NameError that shows the name 'total' isn't defined when you attempt to display the local variable total that was defined within the function body. On the flipside, the init variable can be displayed without any issues.

Anonymous Functions within Python

Anonymous functions also known as lambda because they use lambda. Example:
```
double = lambda x: x*2
double(5)
```
The special thing about this function is that it doesn't have a name like the previous examples you've come across in the first part of this chapter.

You use lambda functions when you want a nameless function for short term purposes. Specific contexts where this can be relevant is when you're dealing with filter (), map (), and reduce ():
```
from functools import reduce
my_list = [1,2,3,4,5,6,7,8,9,10]
# Use lambda function with `filter()`
filtered_list = list(filter(lambda x: (x*2 > 10), my_list))
# Use lambda function with `map()`
mapped_list = list(map(lambda x: x*2, my_list))
# Use lambda function with `reduce()`
reduced_list = reduce(lambda x, y: x+y, my_list)
print(filtered_list)
print(mapped_list)
print(reduced_list)
```

The Main () Function

If you've programmed with another language such as Java, you'll agree that the main function is needed to run functions. As you've seen in the previous example, this function is not a must for Python. However, if you use a main () function within your Python program, it can be handy to organize your code logically.

It's easy to define a main () function and call it the same way you've done with other functions.
```
# Define `main()` function
def main():
  hello()
  print("This is a main function")
main()
```

Currently, the code of your main () function will be called once you import it as a module. To ensure that this doesn't happen, you call the main () function when _ _ name_ _ = '_ _ main_ _'

Apart from the _ _ main_ _ function, there is also the _ _ init_ _ function that will initialize an instance of a class or an object. This acts as a constructor and is automatically called once you create a new instance of a class. With that function, the newly defined object is allocated to the parameter self.

Chapter 6: Python Operators

Python operators implement operations on values and variables. Operators can modify individual items and output results. The data items are known as operands. Operators are either represented using keywords or unique characters.

Arithmetic operators
These implement different arithmetic computations such as subtraction, division, addition, exponent, etc. There is a different method for arithmetic computation in Python like you can apply the declare variable, or call functions.
For the arithmetic operators, consider a simple example of addition where you add two-digit 2+3=5
b= 4
c= 5
print (b + c)
Still, you can use arithmetic operators such as division, subtraction, and multiplication.

Python logical operators
There are 3 logical operators in Python.
 or, and, not
Example:
 a or b
 a and b
 not a
 not b

Operator precedence

Python operators are computed based on a set of priority. Below is a table that shows the operator precedence in Python.

	Description	Operators
1	Exponentiation	**
2	Ccomplement, unary plus, and minus	~, +, -
3	Multiplication, division, modulo, and floor division	*, /, %, //
4	addition and subtraction	+ -
5	Right and left bitwise shift	>>, <<
6	Bitwise 'AND'	&
7	Regular 'OR' and Bitwise exclusive 'OR'	|, ^
8	Comparison operators	<= < > >=
9	Equality operators	== !=
10	Assignment operators	=, +=, -=, *-, /=, %= //= **=
11	Identity operators	is, is not
12	Membership operators	in, not in
13	Logical operators	or, and, not

Chapter 7: File Handling

Python provides a critical feature for reading data from the file and writing data into a file.

In most programming languages, all the values or data are kept in some volatile variables.

Since data will be stored in those variables during run-time only and will disappear once the program execution ends, therefore, it's better to save these data permanently using files.

Once you store data on a file, the next important thing is its retrieval process because it's stored as bits of 1s and 0s, and in case the retrieval does not occur well then it becomes completely useless and that data is said to be corrupted.

How Python Handles Files?

If you're working in an extensive software application where they execute a massive amount of data, then we can't expect those data to be kept in a variable because variables are volatile.

Therefore, when you want to deal with these situations, the role of files will come into the picture.

Since files are non-volatile in nature, the data will remain permanently in a secondary device such as Hard Disk and using Python to deal with these files in your applications.

Do You Consider How Python Will Handle These Files?

Let's assume how normal people will deal with these files. If you want to read the data from a file or write the data into a file, then you need to open the file or create a new file if the file doesn't exist and then conduct the normal read/write operations, save the file and close it.

Similarly, the same operations are accomplished in Python with the help of in-built applications.

Types of Files in Python

There are two kinds of files:
1. Text files

2. Binary files

A file whose contents can be examined using a text editor is known as a text file. A text file refers to a sequence of ASCII characters. Python programs are examples of text files.

A binary file stores the data in the same manner as stored in the memory. The mp3 files, word documents are some of the examples of binary files. You cannot read a binary file using a text editor.

In Python language, file processing takes the following steps.
- Open a file that returns a filehandle.
- Use the handle to read or write action.
- Close the filehandle.

Before you perform a read or write operation to a file in Python, you must open it first. And as the read/write transaction finishes, you should close it to free the resources connected with the file.

Let's now look at each step in detail.

Access_mode: This is represented with an integer e.g read, write, and append. The default setting is the read-only <r>.

Buffering: The default value for buffering is 0. A zero value shows that buffering will not happen. If the value is 1, then the line buffering will happen while accessing the file. If it's more than 1, then the buffering action will proceed based on the size.

File_name: This is a string that represents the name of the file you want to access.

File open modes in Python language
<r>
<rb+>
<rb>
<w+>
<wb+>
<r+>
<w>
<wb>

Python File Object Properties
Once you call the Python open () function, it returns an object, which is the filehandle. Additionally, you need to understand that Python files have different features. And you can take advantage of the filehandle to list the features of a file it belongs.

Close a File in Python

It is good always to close a file when you finish your work. However, Python has a garbage collector to clean up the unused objects. However, you need to do it on your own instead of leaving it for the GC.

The Close Method

Python offers the <close ()> method to close a file.

When you close a file, the system creates resources allocated to it. And it's easy to accomplish.

Closing a file releases essential system resources. If you forgot to close the file, Python will do it automatically when the program ends or the file object is no longer referenced inside the program. However, in case your program is large and you're reading or writing multiple files that can consume a massive amount of resources on the system. If you continue opening new files carelessly, you might run out of resources.

Chapter 8: Dictionaries

In this chapter, you will be learning about a new data structure—the dictionary. The dictionary (also known as a hashtable or hashmap in other languages) is one of the most powerful data structures Python has available to use. Luckily, since it's built in to the Python language, you don't have to implement it yourself. You will also be learning about tuples. What you will learn:
• How to use a Dictionary Data Structure
• How to use Tuples

Mastering the Python dictionary will help you to model different real-world objects more accurately. You will create a dictionary representing a person and store unlimited information as you would like about the individual. You can store their location, name details, profession, and other features you can describe. You'll be able to store any two kinds of information that can be compared, a list of words, and their meaning.

A dictionary in Python has key-value pairs. Each key is related to a value, and you can use a key to access the value linked to that key. The value of a key can be a string, number, or even a different dictionary. In fact, you can include any object that you can build in Python as a value in a dictionary.

Python dictionaries are surrounded using braces, plus a series of key-value pairs within the braces.

A key-value pair is a collection of values bounded to each other. When you present a key, Python will return the value linked with that key.

The simplest dictionary example has exactly a single key-value pair.
Example:
alien = {'color': 'green'}

This dictionary holds a single piece of information about alien, and that is the color. The string 'color' is a key inside this dictionary, and it's connected to the value 'green'

Getting Setup

In this section, you are going to be working in the Python Idle editor as well as the terminal. You will learn about the dictionary in the Idle editor, and then you are going to graduate to creating your own files and working with data.

How to Access the Values Inside a Dictionary?

To acquire the value linked with a key, provide the name of the dictionary and place the key within a set of square brackets as shown below:
print(alien['color'])

This returns the value related to the key 'color' from the dictionary.
It is possible to have an unlimited number of key-value pairs inside a dictionary.

Adding New Key-value Pairs

Dictionaries change every time, and you can include new pairs of key-values to a dictionary at any given time. For instance, to include a new key-value pair, you would provide the name of the dictionary followed by the new key within square brackets.

Now, we want to add two kinds of information to the alien dictionary: That is the alien's x and y coordinates. These coordinates will allow you to show the alien in a specific position on the screen. Let's position the alien on the left edge of the screen. This will be 25 pixels from the top going downwards. Since the coordinates of a screen begin at the upper-left corner of the screen, you will position the alien on the left edge of the screen using the x-coordinate to 0 and 25 pixels from the top by adjusting its y-coordinate to positive 25, as shown below:

```
alien = {'color': 'green', 'points': 5}
print(alien)
u alien['x_position'] = 0
v alien['y_position'] = 25
print(alien)
```

We begin by first defining the same dictionary that we have been using. Next, print this dictionary, and display a snapshot of its details. In the second line, you include new key-value pair to the dictionary:

```
{'color': 'green', 'points': 5}
{'color': 'green', 'points': 5, 'y_position': 25, 'x_position': 0}
```

The final dictionary version has a total of 4 key-pair values. Remember that Python doesn't consider the order of storage, it only handles the connection between every key and its value.

The Second Major Data Structure – The Dictionary

The Dictionary is a powerful data structure that has a 'key' and a 'value'. Each key is unique in the dictionary, and it has an associated value. The associated value however, does not need to be unique.

Examples of dictionaries in real life include:
o A phone book:
o Key – The phone number
o Value – The person's name

o A physical dictionary (hence where the name of this data structure comes from)
o Key – The word
o Value – The description of the word (i.e. the definition).

o A Student identification number at a university
o Key – the number
o Value – The person's name

o Your Subway Loyalty Card:
o Key – Your card number
o Value – Your points you've amassed!

The key in the dictionary can be a string or a number. In fact, it can be any data type! The takeaway though is that the key must be unique!

Here's a look at some sample tables of the above examples to again illustrate keys and values.

Key(Phone number)	Value(Persons name)
7323245	'Joe'
9822912	'Sue'
6323421	'Moe'

Note that the phone number is represented as an integer and each of the values as a string.

Key(Word)	Value(Definition)
'Cat'	'A small domesticated carnivore'
'Python'	Any of several boa constrictors in the subfamily Pythoninae'
'Byte'	Adjacent bits, usually eight, processed by a computer as a unit'

Note that the key is a string and the value also a string in this example.

Key (Student ID Number).	Value (Persons Name)
127323	'Mike'
187428	'Tomoki'
493209	'Raoul'

Key (Reward Card Number).	Value (Points)
1209482104812	47
2098520935820	434
3248098324093	434

Note that in this example, the points might change, and dictionaries allow us to modify values. Values also can be duplicated, but remember the keys cannot (the older key will be overridden if there is a duplicate!).

Note: On Learning to Program: A dictionary is one of many data structures available to us that is built into Python. In fact, there are numerous other data structures and algorithms available to us that we always have at our disposal. It may even become intimidating or overwhelming! However, what I urge you to do is to work through this exercise (and future exercises) at least once through even if you don't understand all of the details. Then revisit the details. The best way to learn is often to complete a project, and then when you revisit it you will have a better idea of what problem you are trying to solve, and what is important to learn and understand in intimate detail.

Dictionary Examples

Let's first create a dictionary to model a phonebook. The first thing we need to do is decide whether our key will be a name or a value. As you saw in the previous example, you can use a phone number. Phone numbers themselves are unique, so they are a good candidate for a key.

However, you can also use a name as a key, because it is typically easier for us to remember a person's name.

phoneBook = {'Mike': 55555555} # 'Mike' is the key

In this example, you can only have one friend named Mike. If you want more Mike's, you'd have to store them as Mike01, Mike02, Mike03, etc.

You can print out a specific entry from our phonebook using the following:

print phoneBook['Mike']

If you want to output the entire contents of the phonebook, you can simply use the print
command.

Print phoneBook
print phonebook

Over time, you will want to grow and modify your dictionary, so you can add entries like the following.

   # Add a new item
   phoneBook['Michelle'] = 43255322

```python
# Lets confirm our entry went in.
print phoneBook


# Delete Mike from our phonebook, we'll never need to call him!
del phoneBook['Mike']


# If Michelle changes her number, we can update it by accessing her
# entry with her key ('Michelle') and then simply re-assigning a new
# value.
phoneBook['Michelle'] = 3252352


# Confirm our changes have been made.
print phoneBook


# Sometimes we are not sure who is in our phonebook, so we have to
# iterate over all of # the keys. When we know what keys are available,
# we can then use those keys to quickly index into our phone book and
# retrieve the value (a phone number in this case).
# print keys
for x in phoneBook:
    print x
# Alternatively, if we just need the numbers, we can print out all of
the values.
# This might be a nice thing to do if you want to call everyone and
wish them a happy
# new year.


# This might be an evil thing to do if you want to call everyone and
try to scam them!
# Look out!
# print values
for x in phoneBook:
```

```
    print phoneBook[x]
```

ANOTHER LOOK AT THE DICTIONARY
The dictionary is what is known as an 'associative data structure'. This means that a value is associated with a key. Great, that makes perfect sense! This should be intuitive, because this is often how our brain works. We generally do not think of a number and say, oh that is Mike's number. We generally think of a name (e.g. 'Mike'), and then recall what his number is. Our brains work very well by associating one thing with the next, so it should not be a surprise we can do something similar with computers.

THE TUPLE
The Tuple is a way in Python to group information together. It is like a list, except that we cannot modify it once we have created a tuple.

Let's go ahead and create a tuple that groups together information about an individual.

Let's create a Person Tuple that will take a str, and an int as the two types of data we want to store. The first value is a string storing a name, and the second is an integer value for how many miles they ran this month.

```
Person = ('Mike',100)
>>> Person
('Mike', 100)
```

So, the tuple itself is just a collection of values held together. We can actually store tuples in a list if we want. Let's create some more tuples with names and each person's favorite number as a value in a second field.

```
>>> Mike = ('Mike',1)
>>> Willie = ('Willie',2)
>>> Tomoki = ('Tomoki', 17)
>>> Raoul = ('Raoul',14)
>>> BestFriends = [Willie,Mike,Tomoki,Raoul]
>>> BestFriends
[('Willie', 2), ('Mike', 1), ('Tomoki', 17), ('Raoul', 14)]
```

Now when the BestFriends list is output, we see that each entry (separated by a comma) is a tuple that we created. We can then access elements in our list by using their position in the list as we have previously done. Our list will now return a tuple. And if we check the type of the entry, we see that it is indeed a tuple.

```
>>> BestFriends[0]
('Willie', 2)
>>> type(BestFriends[0])
<type 'tuple'>
```

This might take some getting used to, as we're using two levels of indirection to access the
individual element we would like. With some practice however, you will be able to do this with no problem. Let's now combine what we have learned with dictionaries and tuples. Let's make the....NBA Superstar Basketball Dictionary!

CHALLENGE PROBLEM

Take in the below NBA player data, and create tuples for them. Here is the format: The first value in the tuple is the number of championships won, and the second is the number of season the player has played.

Key	Value
Bill Russel	(11,13)
Sam Jones	(10,12)
Robert Horry	(7,16)
Michael Jordan	(6,15)
Shaquille O'Neil	(4,19)
Mike Shah	(0,0)

Example:
Creating a tuple.
  samJones = (10,12)

This makes the variable 'samJones' hold the tuple (10,12).

We then want to put all of these players (or rather, their tuples) into a dictionary, and then output all of the NBA players who have won at least 1 championship. Here is an example of creating an empty dictionary, and adding our player to it.

  # Now let's create an empty dictionary
  nbaDictionary = {}

  # Add a key of 'Sam Jones' and a
  # value of samJones (which is a tuple)
  nbaDictionary['Sam Jones'] = samJones

Goals we want to achieve:
• Output all NBA players in our dictionary who have won at least one championship
• Output all of the NBA players in our dictionary who have won a championship in greater in 50% of the seasons they have played.

Hints and gotchas:

- print out your dictionary after you input your entries to visually see the data.
- Can we divide by zero in mathematics?
- Use an 'and' statement to check two conditions.

o e.g. if value > 5 and value != 0:

- When dividing two integers, we get an integer back. If we want a float (i.e. decimal number) as a result, we have to divide to floats.

o Example:

```
>>> 7/5
1
>>> float(7)/float(5)
1.4
```

Chapter 9: Object-Oriented Programming

Object-Oriented programming is an extensive concept used to create powerful applications. Data scientists are required to build applications to work on data, among other things. This chapter will explore the basics of object-oriented programming in Python.

Object-Oriented Programming abbreviated as OOP has several advantages over other design patterns. The development process is faster and cheaper, with great software maintainability. This, in turn, results in better software, which is also filled with new attributes and methods. The learning curve, is, however, complex. The idea might be complicated for newbies. In terms of computation, OOP is slower and consumes a lot of memory because more lines of code have been written.

Object-oriented programming relies on the important programming concept, which makes use of statements to change a program's state. It concentrates on illustrating how a program should operate. Examples of imperative programming languages are Java, C++, C, Ruby, and Python. This is different from declarative programming which deals with the type of computer program should achieve, without detailing how. Examples consist of database query languages such as XQuery and SQL.

OOP relies on the property of classes and objects. A class can be considered as a 'blueprint' for objects. These can feature their own characteristics and methods they execute.

Example of OOP

Take an example of a class Dog. Don't consider it as a specific dog, or your own dog. We're describing what a dog is and what it can do in general. Dogs have an age and a name. These are instance properties. Dogs can also bark; this is a method.

When you discuss a certain dog, you would have an object in programming: an object is a class instance. This is the basic state on which object-oriented programming depends.

Now let's look at OOP in Python language.

Python is a powerful programming language that allows OOP. You will use Python language to define a class with properties and methods, which you will later call. Python has extra benefits than other languages. First, the language is dynamic, and a high-level data type. This implies that development takes place faster than Java. It doesn't need the programmer to declare variable types and arguments.

This makes Python easy to learn for beginners. Its code is more intuitive and readable.

It is important to remember that a class basically provides the structure. This is a blueprint that outlines how something needs to be defined. However, it doesn't offer any real content. For example, shape () class may specify the size and name of shapes, but it will not indicate the exact name of a shape.

You can view a class as a concept of how something should be executed.

Python Objects

Although the class is the blueprint, objects or instances are members of a given class. It's not a concept anymore. It's an actual shape, like a triangle with three sides.

Put differently, a class is like a questionnaire. It will define the required information. Once you complete the form, your actual copy is an instance of the class. It has original information relevant to you.

You can complete different copies to have multiple instances, but without the form, you'll be lost, not knowing the kind of information required. Therefore, before you can create individual objects, you need to define what is required by the class.

Defining a Class in Python

Below is a simple class definition in Python:

Class Dog (object)
  Pass

When defining a class in Python, you begin with the class keyword to show that you're writing a class, then you follow it with the name of the class. In the above example, Dog is the name of the class.

The above class definition has the Python keyword pass; this is normally used as a placeholder where code will finally go. Why this keyword has been used is to avoid the code from throwing an error.

The object section enclosed in parentheses demonstrates the parent class that you're inheriting from. But this is no longer required in Python 3 because it's the implicit default.

Objects Attributes

All classes define objects, and all objects have properties known as attributes. The _init_ () method is used to specify an object's original properties by outlining their default value. This method requires at least one argument as the self-variable, which describes the object itself.

```python
class Dog:

    # Initializer / Instance Attributes
    def __init__(self, name, age):
        self.name = name
        self.age = age
```

In the following example, each dog has a unique name and age, which is critical to know especially when you begin to define different dogs. Don't forget that the class is only defining the Dog, and not creating objects of individual dogs with unique names and ages.

Similarly, the self-variable also belongs to an instance of the class. Because class instance has different values you can write Dog.name = name instead of self.name = name.

Class Attributes

While instance attributes are unique to every object, characteristics of a class are the same for all instances. In this case, all dogs.

Methods

When you have attributes that belong to a class, you can proceed to define functions that will access the class attribute. These functions are referred to as methods. When you declare methods, you will want to provide the first argument to the method using a self-keyword.

For instance, you can define a class Snake, which contains the attribute name and the method change_name. The method change name will accept an argument new_name plus the keyword self.

Now, you can instantiate this class with a variable snake and change the name using the method change_name.

```
>>> # instantiate the class
>>> snake = Snake()

>>> # print the current object name
>>> print(snake.name)
python

>>> # change the name using the change_name method
>>> snake.change_name("anaconda")
>>> print(snake.name)
anaconda
```

Instance Attributes and the init Method

You can still provide the values for the attributes at runtime. This occurs by defining the attributes within the init method. Check out the example below:

```python
class Snake:

    def __init__(self, name):
        self.name = name

    def change_name(self, new_name):
        self.name = new_name
```

Now you can proceed to directly define different attribute values for different objects.

So far you know how to define Python classes, methods, and instantiate objects, and call instance methods. These skills will be useful when you want to solve complex problems.

With object-oriented programming, your code will increase in complexity as your program expands. You'll have different classes, objects, instance methods, and subclasses. You'll want to maintain your code and ensure it remains readable. To accomplish this, you will need to adhere to design patterns. These are principles that help a person to avoid bad design. Each represents a particular program that always reoccurs in OOP, and describe the solution to that problem, which can then be repeatedly used.

Chapter 10: Inheritance

We often come across different products that have a basic model and an advanced model with added features over and above the basic model. A software modeling approach of OOP enables extending the capability of an existing class to build a new class, instead of building from scratch. In OOP terminology, this characteristic is called inheritance, the presence of a class is known as the parent or base class, while the new class is referred as the child or subclass.

Inheritance comes into the picture when a new class possesses the 'IS A' relationship with an existing class.

Dog IS an animal. Cat also IS an animal. Hence, an animal is the base class, while dog and cat are inherited classes.

A quadrilateral has four sides. A rectangle IS a quadrilateral, and so IS a square. A quadrilateral is a base class (also called parent class), while rectangle and square are the inherited classes - also called child classes.

The child class inherits data definitions and methods from the parent class. This facilitates the reuse of features already available. The child class can add a few more definitions or redefine a base class method.

This feature is extremely useful in building a hierarchy of classes for objects in a system. It is also possible to design a new class-based upon more than one existing classes. This feature is called multiple inheritances.

The general mechanism of establishing inheritance is illustrated below:

Syntax:
class parent:
    statements

class child(parent):
    statements

While defining the child's class, the name of the parent class is put in the parentheses in front of it, indicating the relation between the two. Instance attributes and methods defined in the parent class will be inherited by the object of the child class.

To demonstrate a more meaningful example, a quadrilateral class is first defined, and it is used as a base class for the rectangle class.

A quadrilateral class having four sides as instance variables and a perimeter () method is defined below:

```
class quadriLateral:
    def __init__(self, a, b, c, d):
        self.side1=a
        self.side2=b
        self.side3=c
        self.side4=d

    def perimeter(self):
        p=self.side1 + self.side2 + self.side3 + self.side4
        print("perimeter=",p)
```

The constructor (the __init__() method) receives four parameters and assigns them to four instance variables. To test the above class, declare its object and invoke the perimeter() method.

>>>q1=quadriLateral(7,5,6,4)
>>>q1.perimeter()
perimeter=22

We now design a rectangle class based upon the quadriLateral class (rectangle IS a quadrilateral!). The instance variables and the perimeter() method from the base class should be automatically available to it without redefining it.

Since opposite sides of the rectangle are the same, we need only two adjacent sides to construct its object. Hence, the other two parameters of the __init__() method are set to none. The __init__() method forwards the parameters to the constructor of its base (quadrilateral) class using the **super()** function. The object is initialized with side3 and side4 set to none. Opposite sides are made equal by the constructor of the rectangle class. Remember that it has automatically inherited the perimeter() method. Hence there is no need to redefine it.

Example: Inheritance

```
class rectangle(quadriLateral):
    def __init__(self, a, b):
        super().__init__(a, b, a, b)
```

We can now declare the object of the rectangle class and call the perimeter() method.

>>> r1=rectangle(10, 20)
>>> r1.perimeter()

perimeter=60

Overriding in Python

In the above example, we see how resources of the base class are reused while constructing the inherited class. However, the inherited class can have its own instance attributes and methods.

Methods of the parent class are available for use in the inherited class. However, if needed, we can modify the functionality of any base class method. For that purpose, the inherited class contains a new definition of a method (with the same name and the signature already present in the base class). Naturally, the object of a new class will have access to both methods, but the one from its own class will have precedence when invoked. This is called method overriding.

First, we shall define a new method named area() in the rectangle class and use it as a base for the square class. The area of the rectangle is the product of its adjacent sides.

Example:
```
class rectangle(QuadriLateral):
   def __init__(self, a,b):
      super().__init__(a, b, a, b)

   def area(self):
      a = self.side1 * self.side2
      print("area of rectangle=", a)
```

Let us define the square class which inherits the rectangle class. The area() method is overridden to implement the formula for the area of the square as the square of its sides.

Example:
```
class square(rectangle):
   def __init__(self, a):
      super().__init__(a, a)
   def area(self):
      a=pow(self.side1, 2)
      print('Area of Square: ', a)
```

```
>>>s=Square(10)
>>>s.area()
Area of Square: 100
```

Chapter 11: Introduction to Django Framework

Django is one of the most advanced Python web frameworks that allows rapid development and maintenance of websites. The Django framework handles most of the pros and cons of web development, so you can concentrate on building your app without the need to build something afresh. Django is free and open-source and has an active community and excellent documentation.

Django will help you to build software that is:

- **Complete**

Django uses the "Batteries included" principle and has about everything that developers may want to do. Since everything you require is part of the one-stop-shop, it works seamlessly together, follows a regular design principle, and has up-to-date documentation.

- **Scalable**

Django features a component-based "shared-nothing" format and can thus be substituted or changed when necessary. Having a clear distinction between the different parts implies that it can scale for increased traffic by including hardware at any level. Some of the busiest websites have successfully scaled Django to achieve their demands.

- **Versatile**

You can use Django to create any website that you want-right from content management systems to social networks and news sites. This framework can work with any client-side framework and can support content in any format.

- **Easy to maintain**

The Django framework is built according to the principles of design that support code reusability. It also allows the grouping of similar functions into reusable "applications".

- **Portability**

Django is developed in Python which runs on multiple platforms. In other words, you're not forced to use a specific server platform alone, but you can run applications on any platform of your choice.

- **It's secure**

Developers have nothing to fear that hackers will steal vital information from their websites or gain entry into their website applications. Django has an excellent security system that automatically protects the website.

Where Did Django Come From?
Django was developed between 2003-2005 by a team of web experts who were responsible for building and managing newspaper websites. After making several websites, the team started to reuse most of the standard code and design patterns. This common code resulted in a general web development framework.

Since 2005 when it was open-sourced, Django continued to expand with new releases. Each release brought new functionality and fixed several bugs.

Today, Django is driving the web development environment with thousands of users going for Django. Although it still has some properties that reflect its origin, Django has evolved into powerful framework that can build any website.

What is the Level of Popularity of Django?
There's no readily-available scale of measurement of server-side frameworks' popularity. An excellent question will be if Django is good enough to handle problems of unpopular platforms. Is it still developing? Can you get assistance if you need it? Is there a chance for you to get a job if you learn Django?

Depending on the number of high-profile websites that use Django, the number of people who contribute to the codebase, and the number of people providing free and paid help, Django is a popular framework.

Is it Opinionated?
Web frameworks are said to be "opinionated", and "unopinionated."

An opinionated framework is one that has opinions about the "correct way" to do a given task. These frameworks support rapid development in a specific domain because the proper way to do anything is well-documented and understood. Despite that, they can be less flexible at finding solutions to problems and tend to provide fewer choices for what methods they can use.

On the other hand, unopinionated frameworks have fewer limitations on the right way to integrate components to accomplish a given goal, or even what parts should be applied. They simplify everything for developers to employ the most suitable tools to finish a given task.

In one way, Django is a bit opinionated, and therefore offers the "best of both worlds". It provides a set of components to take care of web development tasks and one preferred style to use them. Despite that, Django's decoupled architecture implies that you can select and choose from different options, or include support for new ones if necessary.

Who's Using Django?

It is also good to know who is using this particular framework out there so that you can get an idea of what you can accomplish with it. Some of the most important sites using Django include Bitbucket, Mozilla, Instagram, National Geographic, Last.fm, and many more.

For more examples, you can navigate to the Django sites database; they have a list of over 5k web sites driven by Django.

8 Unique Characteristics of Django

This section will explore the unique properties of Django. The features of any technology can explain what it is best created for. Any time you learn new technology is because of a given reason. There are countless reasons as to why you should learn Django. Here is a more in-depth look at the unique characteristics of Django, and why it is such a robust framework.

1. In-depth Documentation

If there is an open-source framework with quality documentation, then Django comes first. No doubt, Django has the best documentation in the market.

Proper documentation is vital to any developer. This is like a well-documented library where you can search for anything and find whether it is a syntax or function.

The documentation for any technology is again one of the best features to rate technology. As such, it allows other developers apart from its creators to optimize the technology.

Django has been a leader at spearheading the best documentation from the start when it was made open source to the present date. In fact, the documentation has only been getting better and better with the active development of technology, and it is also available in multiple languages.

2. SEO Optimized

This is an excellent feature of Django, and makes it competitive over others. Search engine optimization is a practice of making your website highly visible to search engines. In this case, it appears in the top results when users search for Django. Search engines rely on an algorithm that sometimes may fail to be in line with the developer. However, because the website is created for humans to read and understand, and the URL from on the server too.

Django polishes the above idea by maintaining the website via URLs instead of IP addresses on the server, which increases its visibility.

3. It's a Python Web-framework

One of the primary reasons that have pushed a lot of people to learn Django is because it's a Python framework. Python is a language that solves all your problems and in any situation. It's straightforward and easy to use language. Currently, Python is the most popular language in the market. And that is because it is the most straightforward language to learn. You can use Python in almost everything, from web-development to machine-learning.

These beautiful features make Django and Python the most powerful and easy to learn the framework.

Yet you need to have some basic knowledge of Python and web-working to begin developing using Django. It provides fast development, and it accomplishes so by being logical and straightforward.

4. Highly Scalable

Most of the MNCs use Django, and it's applied without any problems. This is an excellent example of Django being scalable.

Scalability refers to the level at which the technology is implemented. For larger websites such as Instagram, there are many active users, which creates massive data. This kind of level demands application to be error-free and accurate. Of course, it's difficult for programmers and developers that have a lot of experience.

Expert programmers design Django from scratch without borrowing any Python library other than what the developers build themselves. Multiple tests and debugging and now with enough time on the market side have made Django perfect for anyone who wants to make their websites error-free.

5. Highly Versatile

Django is versatile in nature. The logical project structure and Django architecture sometimes may appear limiting. However, that is just the opposite because by presenting us the files, it is creating a solid ground that can then be transformed to whichever application we want to build.

It enables Django integration with all the technologies we use and other upcoming ones. As a result, Django is the property of web development and everyone who was initially using PHP will mainly go for Django.

6. Intensively Tested

Anytime you're learning new technology; you expect it to robust and durable enough to handle dynamic changes taking place in the industry. Well, Django accomplishes that task with significant perfectionism.

MNC across the world uses Django to build projects so it's right to say that it works well to deal with all the traffics and accomplish international standards. The framework has been in the industry for some time, and lots of bugs and errors have been fixed. So, this is the right time to start learning the Django framework. For that reason, the number of developers who use Django for web development keeps expanding every day.

7. Supports Rapid Development

While most technologies support this particular feature as the main feature, Django has many other great features.

In this case, rapid development implies that you don't need extensive backend knowledge to build a complete website. You will also not build separate server files to design the database and connect the same while also developing another file for data transfer to and from the server. Django takes care of this work and many other tasks. You don't need additional files for each task.

8. Provides Better Security

Django is a super-secure language. It's a secure language because it explores all loopholes automatically which were once left for a backend developer to handle. While it is hard to note, but experienced backend developers can understand the nature of security and work achieved by Django.

The development of Django's code is right from scratch and that accounts for its other properties as well as security. Since the framework is designed by web experts, you can expect that most of the problems faced by web developers are addressed.

Chapter 12: Django Installation

The first thing you need to do is to install a few programs on your machine so you can be able to begin using Django. The basic setup involves installing Python, Virtualenv, and Django.
Briefly:

- You first need to install Python

- Then you can proceed to install the virtual environment that will help you isolate your Python and Django projects.

- Next, you should install Django within the virtual environment. This way, you can isolate your project.

Install Python
The first thing you need to do is install the latest Python distribution. You can go to early chapters to learn how to install Python, or go to www.Python.org and scroll down until you see the download files listed.
Select the correct version based on your Windows distribution. If you're not sure which one is perfect for you, the possibilities are you want to download the Windows x86-64 executable installer version.
Navigate to your Downloads directory, right-click on the installer and select Run as administrator.
After Python installation, the next thing you need to do is search for the Command Prompt program and open it.
To check whether everything is working fine, enter the following command:
Python - -version
The output should display the Python version you've installed on your computer.
If you can see the version of Python installed on your computer, Congratulations, Python is running. Now is time to install Virtual Environments.

Installing Virtualenv
In the next step, you'll use pip, this tool will help you control and install Python packages. In order to install virtualenv, type the following command in the Command Prompt.
pip install virtualenv
Until this point, the installation that have occurred consists of system-wide. Moving on, everything you install, including Django itself, will be installed inside a Virtual Environment.

Now that you have your virtual environment installed, everything that you're going to install from now will go right into a Virtual Environment.

Consider this: for every Django project you start, you will first build a virtual environment for it. This is like creating a sandbox for every Django project. So you can play around with it, without damaging anything.

After you create your virtual environment, you need to activate it before you use it.

Type the following commands to activate it:

venv\Scripts\activate

You'll know that it worked if you see (venv) in front of the command line. For example:

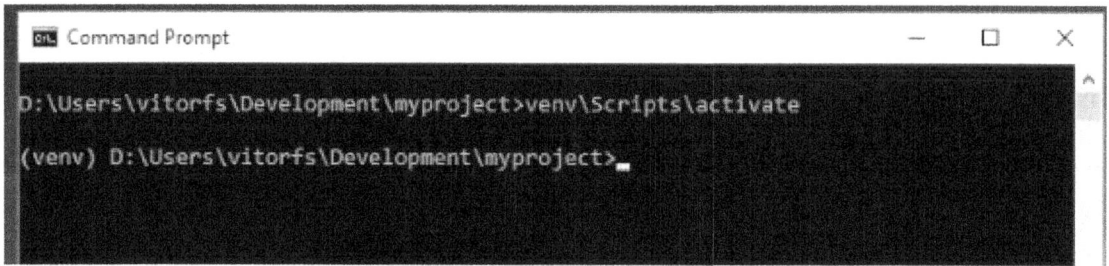

Another critical thing is that pip program is already running, and when you use it to install a Python package such as Django, it will be installed within the Venv environment.

Next, in case you want to deactivate the venv, you should execute the following command:

venv\Scripts\deactivate.bat

Well, but let's have it activated for the next steps.

Django Installation

The installation of Django is a straightforward step. Now that you have the venv active, you can type the command below in the Command Prompt.

Pip install Django

That's it. You are now set up. The next step is to start the Django project. Now is time to build something.

Starting a New Project

To start a new Django project, type the command below:

django-admin startproject myproject

After you execute the above command, it will generate the base folder structure for a Django project.

So far, your myproject directory is composed of the following:

```
myproject/                      <-- higher level folder
  |-- myproject/                <-- django project folder
  |     |-- myproject/
  |     |     |-- __init__.py
  |     |     |-- settings.py
  |     |     |-- urls.py
  |     |     |-- wsgi.py
  |     +-- manage.py
  +-- venv/                     <-- virtual environment folder
```

Django Apps

The Django philosophy has two major features:
- App: this is a web application that performs something. An app is made up of a set of models, templates, test, and views.

- Project: this is a collection of configurations and apps. A single project is made up of multiple apps, or a single app.

It's important to understand that you can run a Django app without the presence of a project. A simple website such as a blog can be powered inside a single app, which can be named weblog.
Django embraces the concept of an app.
This is a way to arrange the source code. At the start, it's not trivial to determine what's an app or what is not. How you can organize the code, and so forth. However, don't worry about that right now! Let's first familiarize ourselves with Django's API and the fundamentals.
Well, so to demonstrate, let's build a simple Web Forum Board. To develop the first app, navigate to the directory where the manage.py file is and run the command below:
Django-admin startapp boards
Notice that startapp command is used this round.
This will present us with the following directory structure:

```
myproject/
 |-- myproject/
 |    |-- boards/              <-- our new django app!
 |    |    |-- migrations/
 |    |    |    +-- __init__.py
 |    |    |-- __init__.py
 |    |    |-- admin.py
 |    |    |-- apps.py
 |    |    |-- models.py
 |    |    |-- tests.py
 |    |    +-- views.py
 |    |-- myproject/
 |    |    |-- __init__.py
 |    |    |-- settings.py
 |    |    |-- urls.py
 |    |    |-- wsgi.py
 |    +-- manage.py
 +-- venv/
```

Now, that you have created the first app, let's configure the project to use it.
To accomplish that, open the settings.py and try to search for Installed_apps variable:

Settings.py

Django already has 6 built-in apps installed. These apps provide common functionalities that many Web applications require, such as sessions, css, static files management, etc.
You will learn more about these apps in the later chaps. But for now, let them be and only add your boards app to the list of INSTALLED_APPS:
Hello, World!
Let's create the first view. You will learn more about in the next chapter. But for now, let's check out how it feels like building a new page using Django.
First, open the views.py file within the boards app, and include the following code:

```
from django.http import HttpResponse

def home(request):
    return HttpResponse('Hello, World!')
```

Views are Python functions that accept an HttpRequest object and displays an HttpResponse object. Accept a request as a parameter and return a response as a result. That's the flow you need to remember.

So, here is a simple view definition known as home which returns a message Hello, World

Next, you have to instruct Django when to serve this view. It happens within the urls.py file:

Urls.py

```
from django.conf.urls import url
from django.contrib import admin

from boards import views

urlpatterns = [
    url(r'^$', views.home, name='home'),
    url(r'^admin/', admin.site.urls),
]
```

Chapter 13: MVC Pattern

The previous section dealt with the installation of everything you need. Hopeful, you're all set up with Python and Django. We already created the project you're going to use.

The MVC Pattern
This section will review the MVC pattern. You will understand more about the MVC pattern. Django MVC architecture solves many problems that were available in the traditional approach for web development.

For every website on the internet, it has three main components; Input Logic, UI logic, and Business Logic.

These sections of code perform different roles, the input logic within the dataset, and how the data organizes in the database.

It merely accepts input and directs it to the database in the right format. Business logic is the primary controller that takes care of the output from the server within the HTML. The UI logic as the name goes, refers to the HTML, CSS, and JavaScript pages.

When the traditional technique was used for running all this code was implemented in a single file. This was not a huge problem back in the time, the web pages were highly static, and websites didn't feature multimedia and extensive coding. Additionally, this architecture presents challenges for developers during testing and project maintenance.

Now, the times are different, and the websites are getting larger and larger every day while supporting applications such as online artificial intelligence, cloud computing, and online development environment, these projects are all built within the MVC architecture.

Well, what is MVC? This is a short form for Model View Controller. Don't be scared, and you'll learn every feature of the MVC pattern and associate it to Django.

The MVC pattern is one of the Product Development Architecture. It computes the traditional approach' challenges of code in a single file. There are three major parts of the MVC. That includes the Model, View, and Controller.

The difference between these parts allows the developer to concentrate on one major feature of the web-app and thus, robust code for one function with significant testing, scalability and debugging.

Let's look at the components:

1. **Model**

The Model represents the section of web-app, which works as a mediator between the website interface and the database. In technical terms, the object executes the logic for the application's data domain. There are moments when the application may only consume data in a given dataset, and directly send it to the view without requiring any database then the dataset seen as a model.

While nowadays, if you want any website you need to have some type of database because its extra user input even if you're building a simple blog site. The Model refers to the component which carries the Business Logic within the Django architecture.

For example:

Once you sign up on any website, you'll be sending information to the controller, which later transfers it to the models which have business logic and stores in the database.

2. **View**

The View section contains the UI of the Django framework. The View is made up of HTML, CSS and other technologies. Overall, the UI develops from the Model components.

3. **Controller**

The controller is the engine part. In other words, the controller takes care of the user interaction and clicks a view based on the model.

The main function of the controller is to choose a view component depending on the user interaction and apply the model component.

This architecture has numerous benefits, and that's why Django is built on this architecture. It takes the same model to a complex level.

For example:

When you combine the previous standards, you can clearly understand that the component which is choosing different views and transferring the data to the model's parts is the controller.

MTV Pattern

MTV stands for the Model-Template-View framework. It carriers the Templates terminology for Views and Views for Controller.

Templates are connected to the View within the MVC pattern because it describes the presentation layer that handles the presentation logic in the framework and controls the content to display and how to present it for the user.

Advantages of Using the Django Architecture

The Django framework is developed on the above architecture, and it communicates between all these three parts without the need to create complex code. That's the reason why Django is becoming popular.

There are various advantages that Django architecture comes with:

1. Rapid Development

This Django architecture divides into different components that simplifies it for numerous developers to work on separate features of the same application simultaneously. That is one of the properties of Django.

2. Loosely Coupled

The Django architecture has different parts that depend on each other to varying stages of the application at every point that enhances the security of the general website.

3. Easy to Make Changes

This is a great feature of development because there are different sections in the Django architecture. If there is a change in section parts, you don't need to change it in other parts.

This is one of the key features of Django because it provides more adaptability to the website than other frameworks.

This section has explored the MVC pattern of the Django framework and described the parts in detail. You have also learned some benefits of the Django framework.

Django Project Layout and Different Files Contained in Root Directory

When you build a Django project, the Django framework develops a root directory of the project using the project name. This root directory contains files and folder, which deliver the basic functionality to your site and on that robust ground you'll be creating your complete website.

Files That Make Up the Django Project Root Directory

The root directory refers to the root that carriers the manage.py file. Additional files such as db.sqlite, are database files that may be available when you migrate the project.

The Django root directory has the default app which Django provides to you. It features the files which will be relevant in the entire project.

The files within the root directory contain specific functions, and once you understand them Django will appear more logical to you. All these files are meant for completing special functions and are in a very reasonable order.

Let's start with the manage.py file:

1. Manage.py

This is the file that holds details of the command line for the project and you will use this file to run, debug, and test the project.

The files stores code for running the server, migrating the server and controlling the project using the command-line.

The above file provides all the functions just like Django-admin and it also delivers certain project functionalities.

While building your project, you will make use of the following commands often:

Runserver: You will use this command to run the test server in the Django framework. This is also one of the advantages of Django over other frameworks.

Makemigrations: This command is useful for combining the project files you have added in it. This command will basically review for any new additions within your project and add that to the same.

Migrate: The last command is to include those migrations you have engineered in the last command with the entire project. The difference between this command and the previous one is that the initial command is used to save the changes within the file, and the later one applies that change to the entire project.

2. My_project

This is a Python package for the project. It contains the files for configuring the project settings.

_init_py

This particular file is empty, and it's available in the project for the main reason of letting the Python interpreter understand that the above directory is a package. That's one of the standard guidelines for Python packages.

Settings.py

The settings.py is the primary file where you will be adding all applications and middleware applications. As the name goes, this is the main settings file of the Django project. This file has installed applications and middleware information which are installed on this Django project.

Any time you install a new application, you will be adding that in this file.

Notice that there are certain pre-installed applications. By default, these applications provide all the basic functionality you will ever want for your website such as the Django admin app.

Urls.py

This file features the project level URL details. The URL is the general resource locator and it presents you with the address of the resource plus other components for your website.

The major function of this file is to link the web-apps with the project. This urls.py file will execute anything that you'll be typing inside the URL bar. Then, it will relate your request to the particular app you connected it to.

```
from django.contrib import admin
from django.urls import path

urlpatterns = [
    path('admin/', admin.site.urls),
]
```

In the above example, by default, the file adds one URL to the admin app. The path () accepts two arguments.

First, the url to be looked inside the URL bar on the local server, and secondly, the file you want to run when that URL request is matched. The admin is the pre-made application and the file is URL's file of that app. This file acts as a map of your Django project.

Wsgi.py

Remember that Django is developed using Python, which relies on the WSGI server for web development. This file handles that and you won't be using this file a lot.

Wsgi is still significant though if you want to run the applications on Apache servers, or a different server because Django is backend, you will require its support with various servers. However, you should not worry because, for each server, you will get a Django middleware which will solve all the connectivity and integration challenges. You only need to have an important that relevant middleware for your server. It's that simple.

This last section has explored more about the Django project layout and the way all files in the Django architecture align, and what's their purpose.

These files are fundamental and will be available in any Django application you build individually. Their primary function is to make available all the backend support and resolve connectivity problems. It takes place while you handle the database creation. It also handles frontend and the uniqueness of your website or web-application.

Chapter 14: Create, Install, Deploy First Django App

In this chapter, you will learn how to create, install, and run your first Django app. Furthermore, you'll learn how to add the app in urls.py file and build views.py file for the Django project.
Let's dive in.

1. Creating a Django App

The main reason web applications are used is to make use of the Django code's reusability property. This will allow you to not only migrate the pre-built apps within the project but also personalize web applications.
All the commands are available in the root directory or within the directory where there is the manage.py file.
Additionally, before you build Django application, run this command on your system within the project directory.

```
python manage.py makemigrations
```

Once this command is finished executing, run the following command:

```
python manage.py migrate
```

Building a Django project is simple because you only need to write some commands that will be implemented on your system.
In the case below, both terminal and PowerShell users share the same commands:

```
$ django-admin startapp application name
```

Now, running these commands will create the application. If you look at the root directory, you will see files that the new application will require, and you will be editing them to accomplish set goals.
Here are some tips that might help you:
- Name your applications based on different tasks that they're going to execute.

- Build applications if the task can be accomplished using a separate application.

If you adhere to the above tips, you will create modularity within your project. This habit will not only help you in general practice, but anytime you will be building future projects you can be specific as to what kinds of apps to include in your current project. Hence, boosting your development speed and reducing the workload without losing any quality in your work.

Below are files that will come pre-installed when your application is developed and the formats for every application file doesn't change.

2. Install Django App

Once you have defined your application, the next step is to install the application. So, you need to open the settings.py file and change it.

Keep in mind that you will be changing the main settings.py file of your Django project, not the one within the app directory.

You will only need to type your app-name in the INSTALLED_APPS list once you add the application in the list of Installed Apps.

Once you complete that, congratulations, you have installed custom Django application.

Now, you will need to include the app to your urls.py file so that anyone who searches the URL of the app within the browser will open the above app.

3. Adding App in urls.py file

To include the app in the urls.py, you will need to write some code. First, you need to define a new Python file in the demo directory and paste the following code in that file.

```python
from django.urls import path

from . import views

urlpatterns = [
    path('', views.index, name='index'),
]
```

In the above code, you are passing a message to the Django project that you've to trigger this function in the views.py file.

Don't be scared; you'll be changing that file too.

In the above code, you've imported the django.urls package and path function from there.

The path () function is new functionality in Django 2.0. If you have any previous versions, then it's better to upgrade.

This code passes two arguments, first, there is the URL which was searched and relayed to the URL bar from the browser. The other argument is to run the file or function, which is an index function.

Now, you'll be changing the urls.py file in the main Django project.

There is only a single item on the list and you'll need to add the new data.

```
from django.contrib import admin
from django.urls import include, path

urlpatterns = [
    path('admin/', admin.site.urls),
]
```

After including the apps urls.

```
urlpatterns = [
    path('demo/', include('demo.urls')),
    path('admin/', admin.site.urls),
]
```

By completing the following step, you'll be making the system direct your server to search the URL for the demo keyword. Then next, direct the URL to the urls.py file within the demo application directory.

4. Building the views.py file

Lastly, you'll create the views file of the Django project. This file will create a view on the browser.
Just use this code snippet, it's already in the demo directory and views.py file.

```
from django.http import HttpResponse
def index(request):
    return HttpResponse("DataFlair Django Tutorial<html><body><h1> Hello World DataFlair Dango tutorials</body></html>")
```

Going by its name, this is the file where you'll create views that the browser will render.
As you can see, you will be importing a function of HttpResponse and also create a function called index, which has been used in the urls.py file.
That function accepts the request the same manner a server would interact with the server. You'll be returning HttpResponse() and within that, anything that you include in the argument of this function will be deployed by the browser.
There are no extra responses besides the HttpResponse and you will be using that in the future.
If you have followed everything until this point, then you've just created your first Django App and webpage.
If you like, you can proceed to open the admin app, but that will be covered in the next section.
If your app doesn't start, then you will need to run the following command in the URL:

ⓘ localhost:8000/demo/

This section has taught you more about Django file structure, and how to create your first app. Don't worry if the app failed to start there could be some errors. Just go through this section again.
Django Admin Interface
Django Admin interface is the most prominent feature of Django Framework and the convenience it delivers to the site maintainers is powerful. Additionally, it is a vital part of the Django Framework and will benefit you in many different ways. First, let's explore the Admin Interface of the website.

The Admin interface as the name suggests is the engine of your project. This is used by site administrators to add, delete, and modify the content on the site. Besides, it's used to maintain other functionalities created by developers.

Well, there is a tricky part, admin interface is the main controller, it's required to be coded by the developer individually. You need to handle everything right from database connection to enhancing security of the admin interface because anyone who uses it is a controller, and any loophole left will be devastating for your website.

Interacting with Django Admin Interface

Django Admin is the kind of interface designed to meet all the needs of the developers. Its language is a bit generalized.

The Django Admin has a complete interface and you won't need to worry to write an Admin interface for your project now. To start with, it is better to master the process of setting up Django Admin site because you will need it in your future projects.

Getting Ready Django Admin Site

Here are steps you should follow to set the Django Admin Site and run user models
1. Start the Django server, then search in the URL bar:

   localhost:8000/admin/
   You should see an image appear, and the site should ask for the username and password. Now, you can proceed to create one.
2. Open the PowerShell or terminal and break the server by pressing CTRL +C.

   Next, type the following command:

   ```
   python manage.py createsuperuser
   ```

3. After you run the above command, it will ask you to enter a username, which should be your preferred choice. Then it will request you for the email id, and password. So, you should be able to complete the details without any problems.

   There are certain inbuilt security features such as if your password is numeric it will generate a complex password, and many such security problems have been fixed up for users.

Superuser

A superuser refers to the details of the admin for your website, which can complete any data manipulation and content manipulation connected to your website.

Additionally, you should never reveal or share the superuser details with anyone because it is the key driver of your website. When the website is active, it is crucial for managing and controlling your website.

After you successfully build the superuser, you will log into that admin page to start your Django server once more.

1. Login in admin using the details you've created.

You will see the options and a beautiful looking interface:

Since the custom applications aren't registered with the Django admin interface, it will not show any of them. There are only two fields here, and you have two options with each of them.

   3. Now select the users' field, and you should see something like this.

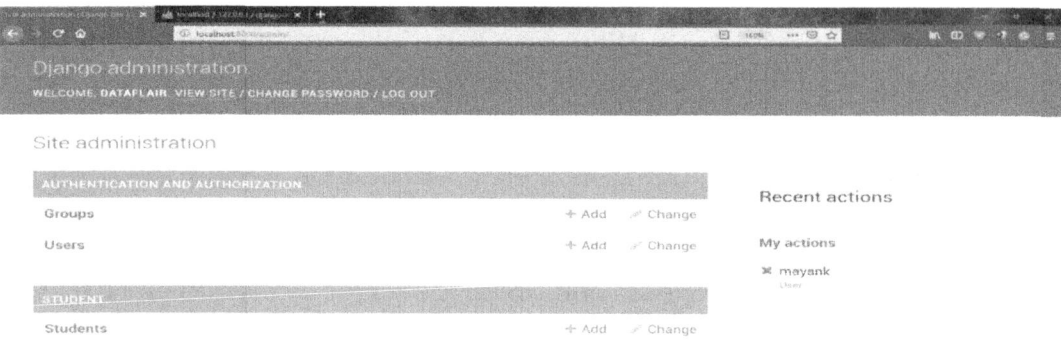

Here, you should see only one user and the details which you inserted inside. Though you wouldn't be able to see the password. That is an advantage from the Django's side, all passwords are encrypted using a unique key in the settings.py file.

3. Confirm whether the user you created was saved.

4. Now open phpmyadmin and open the Django's project database which you developed. Next, if you open auth_users table, you will see the details as it is except for the password.

You will also see that there are additional tables that you didn't create but are inside the database. Well, don't be worried, these are all Django.contrib package's imported models tables. The Django.contrib refers to a package for Django which is similar to the relation of standard library using Python. Almost all the functionality required is on the Django.contrib package.

5. Navigate to home in the Django Project.

6. Next, open the file admin.py of your app. The structure of the directory should look this way:

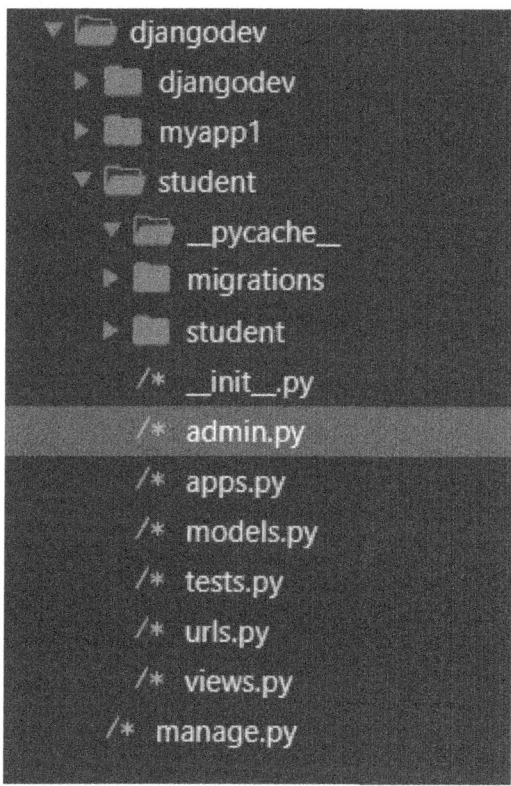

7. Open the admin.py file and enter the following two lines:

```
from .models import Student

admin.site.register(Student)
```

The first statement is used to import class Student or the custom model created. The second line passes the model or registers the model to the Django Admin interface.

8. Now, open admin again, and it won't request for a password.

You have the student model in admin and now open that student field.

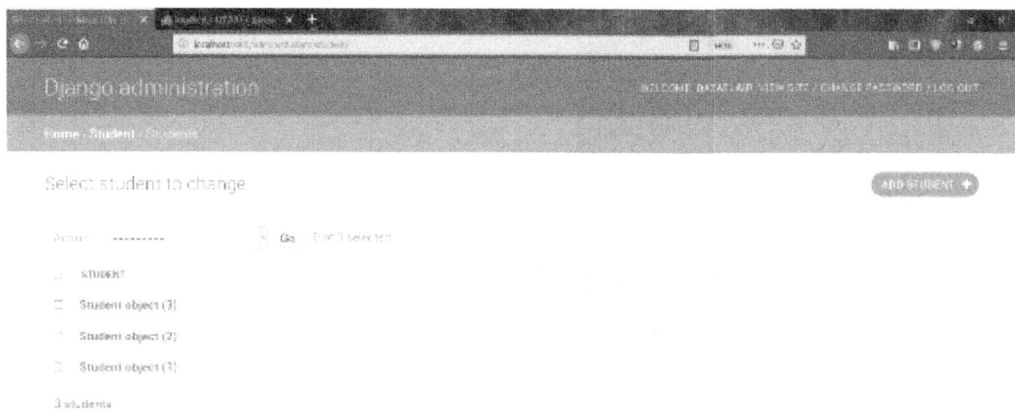

You'll see a list of students you have, and you can view a vital option there such as add a new student.

Adding a new student will create a new record in your database; all of it is the role of the Django Admin interface that combines with Django ORM.

9. Next, click on any student-object

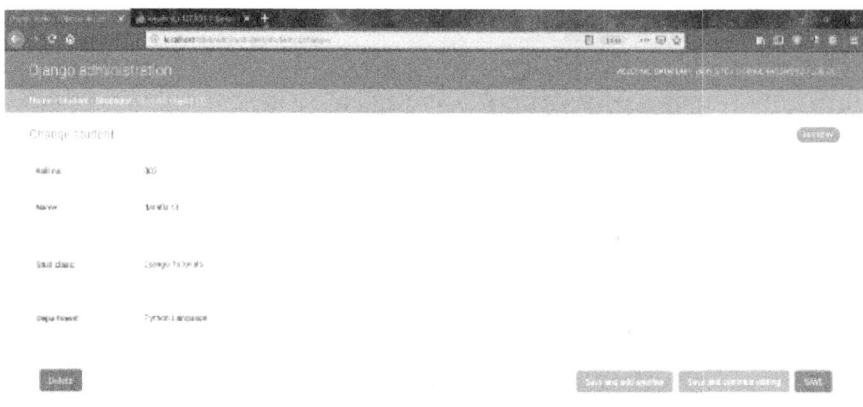

Here, you can directly access and modify the information without even heading into the database.

Also, you should see various options such as save and delete.

See the power it grants you without creating the Django Admin interface itself. In other words, it's easy to use plus it's more secure than anything you've done for the same.

If you have many developers working on the same task, then more interface functionality will be necessary. You can decide which developers get what privileges without typing anything, you only select.

In summary, the Django Admin Interface is a great tool but it is also true that certain websites may not require an admin interface because of their nature. However, that will not be too scalable or won't be for commercial purposes. If you want quick content management without the option of reinventing the wheel, then Django is the best framework to select, and the best admin you can get with many features as a developer.

This chapter has taken you through the steps of building a superuser and how you can integrate your project with the Admin interface. You should try to deploy various models with admin and then you'll become familiar with it.

Django Database

This section will look into how to connect databases with Django project.

Anytime you're building a web project or any type of project, you will need some form of input by the end-users or consumers. Now, all that data entered by the consumers take care of by databases. In the modern era, it's impossible to develop a website without building a database. Even if it's a blog site, you will still need a database.

To accomplish that you will require to have software. The function of this software is to store that data efficiently and also some middleware that can allow you to communicate with the database.

Connecting Your Database with Django Project

By default, when you created the first app and started the server, you probably saw a new file in your project directory. This file is called 'db.sqlite3'. The file is a database file where all the data that you will generate will be kept.

- myblog
- write
- db.sqlite3
- manage

This file is automatically generated because Django has a default setting of the database set to the SQLite. While it is useful for testing and provides many properties, if you need a scalable website, you should change it to an efficient database.

In this case, you will be using MySQL, and this section will teach you how to integrate your project with MYSQL.

Databases Dictionary Indexes

First, open the settings.py file in your web-application/project, and you will see the following part:

```
# Database
# https://docs.djangoproject.com/en/2.1/ref/settings/#databases

DATABASES = {
    'default': {
        'ENGINE': 'django.db.backends.sqlite3',
        'NAME': os.path.join(BASE_DIR, 'db.sqlite3'),
    }
}
```

A database is a pre-defined dictionary in Django Framework having the 'default' as the index value for the significant database where all data is kept.

You can have multiple databases because you need data backups, but a default database is only one, although you will not be adding numerous databases now.

The default contains a dictionary where there are 2 indexes:

Engine

It describes the library to be used once connected to a particular website. The value should hold "Django.db.backends.sqlite3". This is a Python library for sqlite3 database and will transform your Python code to the database language.

Therefore, you don't need to master any new database language, and you can find every code in Python.

Name

In this part, you've got the name of the database you're using and the path of the database. This parameter shifts based on the kind of database you're using. Here you can test the database file.

You will also pass the name of the database file or if the file is not available, this will define the db.sqlite3 file. In case you change the name to db1.sqlite3 or anything of your choice, it will generate that file in your root directory every time you run the server.

As you can see, there is no big struggle when it comes to database creation using Django framework. Remember, every database has features that become the default dictionary indexes that you can create based on the database you are connecting to.

2. mysql and Django

MYSQL is a robust database that comes with multiple features and provides flexibility. Here's how you can integrate it into your project.

1. First, install Xampp

Xampp is a free opensource tool which comes with the Apache server and PhpMyAdmin which is the right source for beginner programmers to work with MySQL.

To download XAMPP, click the following url https://www.apachefriends.org/download.html

2. Open the Xampp control panel

After installation, you will need to open the Xampp Control Panel and start 2 services there: Apache and MySQL.

First, run the apache server, and then the MySQL server.

Simply click on the start button, and you'll see the following image:

Modules Service	Module	PID(s)	Port(s)	Actions			
	Apache	16256 16024	80, 443	Stop	Admin	Config	Logs
	MySQL	9660	3306	Stop	Admin	Config	Logs
	FileZilla			Start	Admin	Config	Logs
	Mercury			Start	Admin	Config	Logs
	Tomcat			Start	Admin	Config	Logs

Next, click on the Admin of the MySQL Service, that should display a web page.

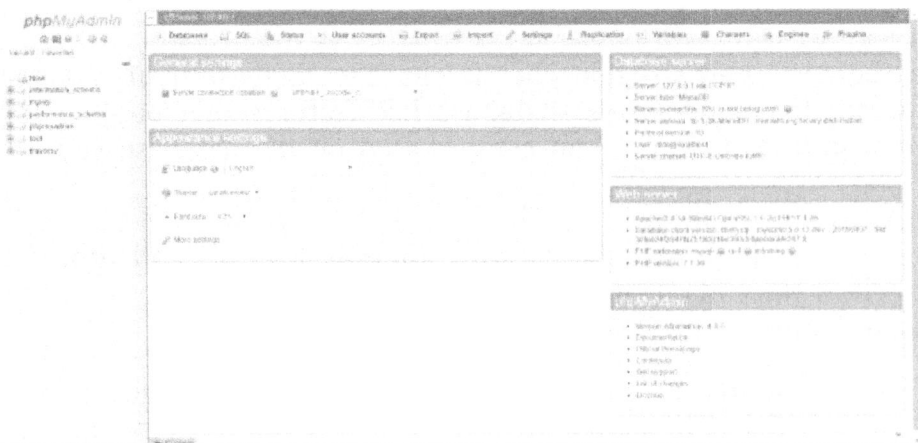

This is the main page where you will be monitoring your database.
The advantage of Xampp is that it has a powerful interactive environment, and the time of deploying your model, that too will take place here.
So, you'll get an efficient database for your project. That's quite easy.
Simply click on the new button as shown below. Then, fill the desired name of your database and click on the create button.

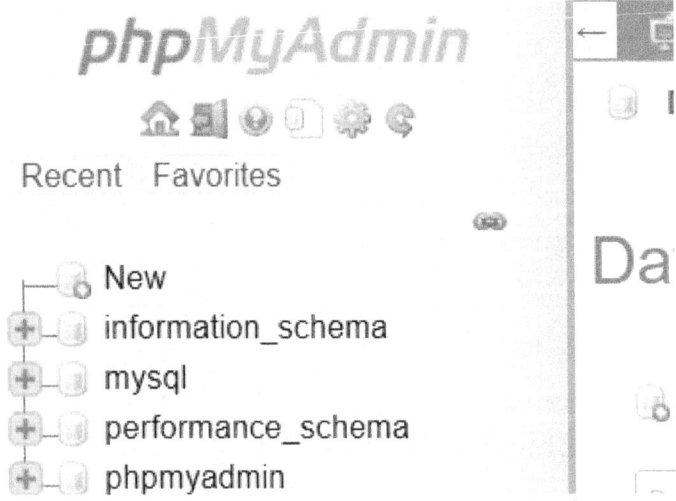

Once you're done with that, it will add your database in the list.
That's it, now you don't need to do anything here. You will only be working with Python and the models component of Django will prepare everything.
3. Changing settings.py

In the following last step, you will be changing the dictionary of the database in the main project settings.py.
First, you should install the following file by typing the following command in the command line:

Entering this command will install the Django code for connecting the MySql Database.
Next, exchange this code with the DATABASE dictionary in settings.py.

```python
DATABASES = {
    'default': {
        'ENGINE': 'django.db.backends.mysql',
        'NAME': 'dataflair',
        'USER': 'root',
        'PASSWORD': '',
        'HOST': '',
        'PORT': '',
        'OPTIONS': {
            'init_command': "SET sql_mode='STRICT_TRANS_TABLES'"
        }
    }
}
```

In this case, the attributes are higher in number as Mysql provides additional features from the sqlite3. The engine, in this case, is "Django.db.backends.mysql" which has the same name as the Python library for MYSQL.
It's good to leave the password empty so that to avoid any errors.
In the above example, the HOST is the host server, but when left blank it takes the localhost as the default.
OPTIONS is an interesting feature. Here, you're merely passing the SQL as a string via Python, which later the SQL server parses itself.
Here you need to write:

```
SET sql_mode = 'STRICT_TRANS_TABLES'
```

Basically, this is SQL being passed on as a string.
For the final steps, execute the following commands:

```
python manage.py migrate
python manage.py runserver
```

Next, refresh the phpMyAdmin page, and you will see some tables show up.

You're done! Now you have all the things ready for your website. The components and parts setup is finally over.

Chapter 15: Tips for Django and Python Beginners

So, you've made up your mind to learn Python or Django. Or maybe you're already learning the language and the framework. Here are tips that will help you speed up your learning.

1.   **Master the Rubrics**

You must get your primary down. And thanks to the syntax of Python, you can use Django without being an expert in Python because it is amicable for new programmers. Python code resembles the English language.

Despite its simple syntax, you cannot ignore the basics. Mastering the basics, it the path to fully understanding Django. So, ensure that you learn the basics as your first step to becoming a Django pro.

2.   **Begin to Solve Problems**

You've mastered the basics. You have the foundation of the Python language. Now is the time to start working out small issues.

Come up with a function that can compute taxes. Define a loop that asks the user to enter his or her age until the user stops the loop and computes the average of all ages

There are certain websites where you can take on small tasks. Then you earn points depending on the answer, and you start to graduate. One such website is the CodeWars.

3.   **Create small, simple projects**

If you can complete small problems, why not start building fun projects?

If you have learned how to use Python to solve more significant problems, this is the time to give yourself a tougher challenge.

The idea is to build small projects in Python, and slowly increase the level of difficulty. However, don't try to create a Youtube kind of project on your own.

Just start to build something simple, something you can enjoy to work on. A game of tic-tac-toe or a guess the number game.

Once you're done, proceed to build another one. Or start adding new features on the one you've built.

I know it's going to take your time, you will need to spend a lot of time Googling, but that's how the best developers start.

Start with a Flask
If you have never learned any programming language or web development, and you want to learn Django, a great idea is to begin with a flask.

Flask is great option for Django. It's more straightforward and easier to understand.

Flask is good for the introduction, as it has more functionalities, but they need to be implemented by you.

With flask, what you see is what you get. Nothing else. And it's pretty damn easy.

Dive into Web Development with Django
Once you master the basics of Python language, and you completed your first small programs. Now, you're ready to learn Django.

Master New Django Concepts
You have learned how to create a project in Django. You understand how the Model View Template works. Well, but there is a lot more to learn. So much more. The secret is to learn new concepts such as Signals, Logging, Testing, and so on.

Remember, this is not a race. Spend time to read the documentation. Try it. Don't even attempt to memorize. But learn how it works. What elements are moving, why should you apply that concept, and when should you use it.

And next....

Start Applying Those New Concepts
Immediately you learn something new, use it. There is no perfect way to internalize something than applying it right away.

Develop a small pet project where you can use it, or better, add it to the current one.

Read Code from Experts
If you want to become an expert Django developer, then you need to read code from professionals.

The internet is an excellent resource for information. Why don't you get Django Github projects to study?

You can still download the project and improve it. And to accomplish this, you need to read, read, read, and master the code.

Surround Yourself with People Learning
When you surround yourself with people who are learning the same language as you, it provides you with a sense of camaraderie. In other words, you're all moving

towards the same goal, and each one can depend on each other. It could be that your problem was solved a few days ago by one of your friends. Why not find out from him how he arrived at the answer.

Surround Yourself with Experts
You need both your peers and experts to become the best. Your friends, workmates, and mentors that have been using Django or Python can solve complex problems that beginner developers can't.
A professional can solve your problems and provide you with a bigger picture.
A beginner may describe to you how to do something, but only an expert can tell if your current solution is optimal or not.

Read Lots of Django Books
Sometimes it can be hard to surround yourself with experts, or you may not find time to interact with them because of the nature of jobs they handle.
Thankfully, that is not the end. There are lots of books written by these professionals.
What is interesting about books is that you can learn something in hours, something that took many years for professionals to learn.
While these books may not turn you into a Django pro, it will set you a great path to becoming a good developer.

Write Code Every Day
You should code daily. How much, that depends on yourself.
Single mothers may have a harder time setting aside time compared to teenagers. People who spend most of the day outside working have little time to code. Those working as programmers also need to time outside the job to code.
Whatever time you can create, code every day even if it's only for 20 minutes.
Creating a routine of coding every day will help you become a better programmer.

Take Some Breaks
After a long period of studying, you need to take breaks.
Taking breaks allows your brain, not only to rest but to organize what you've learned.
It's easy to lose your focus of the bigger picture, and lock yourself into a piece of code. It's easy to get disappointed because a certain concept isn't sinking into your brain when you've been studying for 2 hours non-stop.
So, you should take a break, come with your mind clear, and well-rested.

Ask Other People
When you're learning, you'll not know a lot of things. Or maybe you don't see how they work. You will have a lot of questions related to coding. And the best way to solve something is to ask.
There's a lot to learn from just asking people. Go to coding forums and post your question. Ask your workmates. And don't be afraid to ask. Remember, it's better to ask a dumb question than don't ask and put yourself in risk.
Ask, and you'll learn.

Teach Your Friends
Teaching is an excellent way to master something.
When you learn something, you understand how to use it. However, when you're teaching others, you need to know how to use it, and how it works operates internally. What it does in the backend, what happens if you do this, what happens if you skip this, why the developers made it work this way, and no other way.
There is so much to explore and going deep into the subject when you teach other people.
These are the tips you need to follow to become a good programmer in Python. Now it is up to you to follow them.

Conclusion

Now that you're done reading this book, we hope that it's been amazing, and you've learned plenty of Python concepts and its Django framework. If you prefer to learn more interactively, you can check out some online tutorials. Remember that Django is a popular framework, but there are other frameworks for web development, and depending on the kind of project, you may consider using different frameworks.

However, if you feel you've attained a solid foundation of Python and Django fundamentals, you can take a new challenge by expanding your knowledge reading intermediate to advanced books.

Made in the USA
Monee, IL
23 April 2021